The World of the Newborn

The World
of the Newborn

DAPHNE MAURER
CHARLES MAURER

Basic Books, Inc., Publishers   New York

Library of Congress Cataloging-in-Publication Data

Maurer, Daphne, 1946–
   The world of the newborn.

   Bibliographical notes: p.244.
   Includes index.
   1. Infants (Newborn)—Psychology.   2. Infants (Newborn)   I. Maurer, Charles, 1946–   .   II. Title.   [DNLM:
1. Infant, Newborn. WS 420 M453w]
BF719.M38 1988   155.4'22   87–47519
ISBN   0–465–09230–6

Contents

Acknowledgments

We could never have begun this book without facilities provided by Cambridge University, and by Munich's *Max Planck Institut für Psychiatrie*: for these we thank Janet Atkinson, Oliver Braddick, and Wolf Singer. We would also like to thank Terri Lewis for taking over many of Daphne's responsibilities; Jo Ann Miller for extraordinary patience and excellent guidance; Frances McDonnell and Melba Barnes for helping to proofread; Edith Maurer for all manner of support; and Harold Guite for teaching us just how perspicuous and precise the English language can be.

The World of the Newborn

1

Perspectives

A YOUNG MOTHER appears at our laboratory door. She holds in her arms her newborn baby wrapped in the pale-blue towels provided by Maternity down the hall.

"Hi," she says. "I'm Georgina Byer. One of your assistants asked me if I'd come here this morning while the baby's awake. He's awake now. Are you ready for him?"

We are studying the development of vision during infancy. Mrs. Byer is doing us a favor by letting us test her child, so of course we invite her in immediately. We take the baby from her arms, set him in an infant seat, then begin to show him a series of pictures that allow us to gauge how well he sees. Almost immediately he begins to cry.

"Maybe he's hungry," Mrs. Byer says. "Is it okay if I nurse him here?"

"Certainly," we say; and we settle her comfortably into a chair.

While she nurses her baby, Mrs. Byer chats with us. She is thirty-four years old, and Peter is her third child. She is excited about giving birth again, thrilled to see her new son and feel him in her arms. We can see that she feels comfortable with him and handles him easily, naturally.

"This time I'm not at all anxious about myself as a mother," she tells us. "But I am curious about the baby himself." She can see from the research reports tacked to the walls that we have studied thousands of babies like hers, so she takes this opportunity to ask us some questions: Why does Peter sleep so much? Why does he sleep so irregularly—six hours between feedings one time, one hour the next? Why doesn't he lie still while he sleeps? Why does he cry while his diaper is being changed? How much does he see and hear?

Mrs. Byer is surprised at our answers. Many parents are; for nearly twenty years of studying babies have taught us that much "common knowledge" about babies is wrong. This holds among not just laymen but also developmental psychologists, pediatricians, and other child-care professionals. In many ways a newborn is far more competent than he is usually given credit for, while in other ways he is far less competent. He recognizes his mother's voice, for instance, when he is only hours out of the womb, yet he does not realize that he has a mother until he is six to eight months old.

Babies frustrate psychologists, for their behavior often defies explanation. A newborn baby will often learn better while he is asleep than while he is awake, for example. This just does not make sense—at least, not if we look at the baby from our adult point of view.

We have found babies to be more intelligible—and more interesting—when we look at them from their own point of view, shedding all that we can of our adult knowledge and perceptions. We have found it fruitful to examine scientific studies not just from the perspective of the scientist looking down at the baby, but from the perspective of the baby looking up at the scientist: To try to determine what it was like to live in the womb, then to be delivered from it into the world. To learn how that world looks and sounds, tastes and smells. To learn what it feels like, during the first year or two, to be alive.

This is what we shall do in this book, by examining from several new directions the scientific literature on infancy. Our plan is first to see what the baby sensed while he was still a fetus in the womb, then while he was being born. After birth, since the baby sleeps most of the day, we shall look at his sleep to see whether he is as dead to the world as an adult would be or whether he learns in the midst of it. We shall find that he is actually conscious all the while he is asleep. Next we shall explore what the newborn sees, hears, smells, tastes, and feels. With this information we can deduce what he perceives about the things he senses—that is, what he is actually conscious of. We shall discover that his world is a looking-glass world, a world in which things that we perceive to be stationary he perceives to move, and things that we perceive to move he perceives as stationary. Finally, we shall read the baby's mind as he grows up and leaves this looking-glass world, as he develops into a toddler with the beginnings of adult thought and emotion.

We began to work on this book seven years ago. At that time Daphne had been teaching developmental psychology for a decade and had published a respectable number of research papers on how infants see and learn; and Charles had read extensively on the topic, both out of interest and to help deal with some of the technical aspects of Daphne's laboratories. We knew a fair amount about babies, but only from the adult's point of view. We had vague expectations about what we might learn about the baby's point of view, but we held them tenuously, for we were entering new territory. Everyone who had ever tried to do what we were doing to any extent had taken a more or less psychoanalytical approach, making inferences from adults' memories and dreams. No one had ever based such a study on science—at least, not to any significant depth, across any significant breadth.

Soon after we began, we found that most of our preconceptions (as well as most of the psychoanalytical notions dealing with the legacy of the womb) did not square with empirical facts. Then came the question of what conceptions to replace them with. We uncovered paradox after paradox, feeling like the sorcerer's apprentice trying to halt his master's broom: every time we resolved one paradox, two more reared up to take its place. However, ultimately we were able to piece together what we found into a complete picture. What emerged is bizarre and often startling, but it fits all the data we have been able to uncover.* And it makes sense.

*The thoroughness of our research depended on the age of the children being studied and the language we had to contend with. In English we read every scientific study of newborns that we could find, plus every medical study of newborns that sounded even remotely germane. Information on older babies has been synthesized better, so it demanded less effort. In French and German we read less assiduously than we read in English, but we tried not to slight the literature, and we traveled extensively in Western Europe visiting labs and talking to researchers to find out what we should keep an eye out for. For the very little work published exclusively in the other European languages, we had to depend on interna-

In describing this picture, we shall avoid psychological jargon. We have found that using psychological jargon guides our thought along conventional psychological paths, paths that we are trying to escape. Ordinary English is more neutral and hence, in this task, more helpful. When we do need to use technical terms—usually from fields other than psychology—we shall always explain them.

For the sake of clarity, we shall follow several conventions with pronouns. We shall not distinguish between the two authors of this book, regardless of whether we have one or both in mind. Neither shall we distinguish in the text or footnotes (although we shall in the endnotes) between the "we" that means us and the "we" that means Daphne plus another colleague or colleagues. Finally, since the parent we are discussing is usually the mother, we shall always refer to the representative parent as "she" and to her child, by contrast, as "he" (unless, of course, we are making an explicit distinction between mothers and fathers, or boys and girls).

If you have specialized knowledge of some area that we cover, you may be surprised by some of our interpretations and wonder at the absence of certain conventional explanations backed by well-known studies. We tried to anticipate these questions and to address them in notes at the back of the book. These notes also supply representative references. The footnotes are of more general interest: they contain information that did not quite fit into the topic at hand but was too interesting to leave out. They are the equivalent of sidebars or boxes in a magazine article. You may want to glance at them even if you have no interest in the academic notes.

Although the world of the newborn baby is a sensible place, it does lie on the far side of a looking glass. It is remarkably akin to Wonderland, and hence is difficult for an adult to understand. We need to accustom ourselves to it gradually. Accordingly, let us begin with its most ordinary aspect. Incredible as it sounds, this is the life the baby led during the month or so before he was born, while he was yet a fetus lying on his head, curled up within the womb.

---

tional conferences, personal contacts, and the odd informal translation. Research published exclusively in Japanese or Russian we could find only when the title was indexed in English.

2

The View
from the Womb

ALL OF US would like to withdraw into the womb at some time or another—or, at least, so we say when we are feeling tired and annoyed. Perhaps this would not equal ascending into heaven, yet according to conventional wisdom it ought to be the next best thing: silent, stable and warm, exquisitely comfortable and secure.

However, the womb is actually quite the opposite. It can be boomy, bumpy, unsettling, and foul tasting. To an adult, withdrawing into the womb would resemble flying cramped inside a light airplane, through turbulent weather, with the taste of air-sickness in your mouth.

But this would be to an adult, not the fetus. Although the fetus senses the noise, the taste, and the movement, he does not sense them strongly, for few of his sensory systems are fully developed. Nor does he find the environment particularly unpleasant, for he has very weak notions of comfort and discomfort. Primarily he finds the environment varied; for it changes from minute to minute as his mother walks, talks, eats, drinks, smokes, and becomes worried or merry. This variety is not much by adult standards, but it is substantial by his.

Tossing and Turning

Far from living stably in an unchanging environment, the fetus tumbles and is tumbled about like a jumping bean inside a rattle.

Investigations using ultrasonography* show that by the end of the first trimester of pregnancy, the fetus is moving. The mother cannot feel his movements that early because the uterus has no sense of touch: she can feel his movements only toward the middle of pregnancy, when he has grown large enough that his movements can be sensed beyond the uterus by the abdominal wall.[1] At first the fetus's movements look like spasms of his entire body, and he is as likely to be found with his head up as with it down; but by the middle of gestation his movements look more controlled, and he is more likely to be found with his head down than up.[2] This may be simply because his head is heavier than his feet. But since his organs of balance are fully mature and of adult size by six months (these are the only organs in the body that become adult during gestation),[3] we think the fetus maintains his position at least partially of his own accord.† This he does without any understanding of up and down: we shall see in chapter 8 that he has none. He does it because, when his head is upward, a reduction in the flow of blood to his brain renders him uncomfortable, much as adults who are short of breath feel less comfortable upright than lying down.

The fetus probably feels changes in position constantly, for during most of gestation he welters about in sufficient amniotic fluid to turn somersaults, and he is thrown into somersaults when his mother moves. But his somersaults, like all his movements, are damped into slow motion by the amniotic fluid. "His movements

*Ultrasonography creates images of the inside of the body from sonic waves which are too high to hear: a machine beams these waves into the body, then uses their reflections to form pictures on a television screen.

†School-aged children who were not born in the normal, head-downward position seem to have an abnormally weak sense of balance. We suspect that a weak sense of balance in utero contributed to their abnormal presentation.[4]

look like the movements of astronauts on the moon" is the description of H. Holländer, a Dutch physician who did early investigations with ultrasonography.[5]

Toward the end of gestation, the fetus no longer has enough
room to move his whole body at once. No longer will he kick the
soap off his mother's abdomen while she is lying in the bath. Instead
he fidgets with his arms and legs, plays with his fingers and sucks
his thumb, shifting his position several times a minute while his
mother is lying still and being shifted in position as she moves and
breathes.[6] Continually he bumps into the umbilical cord; constantly
he touches the wall of the uterus and himself. All of this he feels,
for like his sense of balance, his sense of touch appears to be excellent. Davenport Hooker, an anatomist at the University of Pitts-
burgh, found that a fetus aborted during the third month of gestation (but not yet dead) will respond reflexively to the touch of a hair
around his mouth; and he found that a baby born three months
prematurely will respond reflexively to the touch of a hair anywhere
on his body.[7]

Taste

The most immediate portion of the fetus's world is the amniotic
fluid that surrounds him. During the first half of pregnancy, the
amniotic fluid is essentially enriched saltwater, like blood plasma.
Since the young fetus's skin is only a few cells thick, some of the
amniotic fluid may actually be blood plasma that has diffused out
of the fetus. By the second half of pregnancy the fetus's skin has
become watertight. Then his major contribution to the amniotic
fluid is urinating into it.[8]

Besides water, the bulk of amniotic fluid is comprised of the
fetus's urine plus salt, sugars, fatty acids, and cholesterol. If an adult
lived in this environment, he would be able to savor a mixture of
all four tastes (sweetness, sourness, saltiness, and bitterness), with
different tastes predominating at different times. So should the
fetus, for the fetus has a multitude of taste buds,[9] and as we shall
see in chapter 8, a baby appears to be able to taste sweetness,

sourness, bitterness, and perhaps saltiness, when he is only hours out of the womb. If a baby can taste these when he is just born, he can taste them toward at least the end of his gestation as well.

Indeed, the fetus has a sweet tooth. At the University of Frankfurt in the 1930s, as an experimental therapy tried toward the end of pregnancy, a physician named DeSnoo injected saccharin into the amniotic fluid of women who were bloated with excess amniotic fluid.[10] He injected enough to make the fluid sweeter than anyone normally takes coffee, hoping that the sweetness would induce the fetus to drink the excess. To see whether it did, DeSnoo injected a dye along with the saccharin, a dye that shows up in the mother's urine when the fetus swallows it: the dye passes from the fetus's stomach into his blood, from his blood through the placenta into his mother's blood, then from his mother's blood through her kidneys into her urine. When DeSnoo injected dye but no saccharin, a little came out in the mother's urine, which was to be expected since the fetus normally drinks some amniotic fluid.[11] Then, when he injected saccharin along with dye, much more came out, showing that the fetuses were indeed drinking additional amniotic fluid. The mothers' girth shrank in turn—except for one mother. Upon delivery, her baby's esophagus proved to be blocked, so as a fetus he would have been unable to drink anything at all. This was unexpected, circumstantial evidence that the other fetuses had drunk the amniotic fluid. Injecting saccharin ultimately proved to be impractical as a therapy, but one of the reasons for this is interesting: the fetuses seemed to become sated with the extreme sweetness, just as adults would.

Sound in the Womb

Freud wrote that the womb is "free from stimuli"; but as a physician trained to listen to a patient's chest he should have expected instead that the womb would make a racket. For alongside the womb are several loud organs—anatomical pumps that rumble and belch continuously: the heart, intestines, and lungs. In engineering terms, these are a pulsating water pump with flap valves, a twenty-five-

foot-long peristaltic sludge pump, and a double bellows, hardly the
stuff of peace and quiet. Moreover, every time a woman speaks, her
voice travels downward into her lungs and body as forcefully as it
travels outward into the world. No matter how soft-spoken an
expectant mother is, every word she utters, she yells into her fetus's
ear.

To find out how noisy the womb is, several teams of researchers
have inserted microphones into the uterus. The two most careful
studies turn out to be highly complementary, although they were
done a decade apart on opposite sides of the world. One comes from
three French physicians named Querleu, Renard, and Crépin; the
other comes from three Australians named Walker, Grimwade, and
Wood.[12] These studies found that the sonic pressures within the
uterus average eighty-five decibels and reach ninety-five decibels
with every heartbeat. This is a high amount of sonic pressure. Under
some circumstances, it can sound (to an adult) as loud as a motorcy-
cle. Moreover, these sonic pressures were measured inside mothers
who were resting quietly, not talking or engaging in any bone-
jarring activities like walking or climbing stairs.

However, the sonic pressure that a microphone detects is not
sound. Sound is not a physical phenomenon; it is a perceptual
phenomenon, a psychological response to a physical stimulus. A
guitarist plucks a string, making it vibrate; the vibrating string
strikes molecules of air, making the air vibrate; the vibrating air
strikes the ear, making parts of the ear vibrate; cells within the ear
convert these vibrations into electrochemical impulses; then the
brain converts these electrochemical impulses into the sound of the
guitar. Only after the brain has received and converted those impulses does the sound exist. The microphone does not measure this.
It measures only the energy reaching the ear in the form of vibrating
molecules of (usually) air.

This distinction is important, for although eighty-five to
ninety-five decibels of sonic pressure can sound loud, it can also
sound quiet or even inaudible. This is because loudness is determined not by sonic pressure alone, but by sonic pressure in conjunc-
tion with the rate, or frequency, with which the molecules of air
vibrate against the ear. To account for the influence of frequency—
to convert decibels of sonic pressure into decibels of loudness—
researchers feed the output of a microphone into an electronic de-

vice that discriminates among different frequencies, and discounts those an adult's ear is not sensitive to. The measuring stick that results, the "A-scale," provides a coarse approximation of what adults hear. Measured by this A-scale, the womb averages sixty to seventy-five decibels, depending on whether the mother is talking.[13] This is comparable to the range of noises heard in a typical home when people are talking quietly and the stereo is not switched on. But this is when the mother is lying still. When she is walking, the pounding of her heels against the floor causes considerable skeletal vibration. Her footsteps should augment significantly those sixty to seventy-five decibels within the womb, raising the noise level from moderate to loud.

On the other hand, neither her voice nor her footsteps are heard in the womb as she hears them herself. The body's tissues transmit low-pitched tones but absorb nearly all tones pitched higher than a man's voice, including most of the high "overtones" that impart to a sound its timbre.[14] To hear the result of this absorption on a woman's voice, put your ear to a woman's abdomen while she talks; to hear what happens to footsteps, try walking with your fingers stopping your ears. The microphone tells us that not only would the mother's voice and footsteps boom like that within the womb, but so would loud noises emanating from the outside world, like automobile horns, jet planes, and rock bands. Moreover, the body's own internal noises turn out to be mostly low-pitched as well—growls and deep murmurings. In an apartment building, when someone above plays the stereo, you may hear the bass boom through the floor while the treble is virtually inaudible. If you could put your ear inside the womb, this is how the whole world would sound to you.

What the Fetus Hears

Again, that is what *you,* an adult, would hear. Until recently it was by no means clear that a fetus might hear it similarly, for it was by no means clear that a fetus can hear anything at all. Many women conclude that the baby they are carrying can hear during the last three months of pregnancy, because after the women hear a loud noise they often feel a kick. This kicking can be so forceful and frequent that some mothers find they can no longer enjoy a concert. But a loud noise also causes physiological reactions within the mother, like a release of adrenaline. In this circumstance it is not clear which causes the kicking, the noise or the mother's reaction to the noise.

To tell whether the fetus can hear, a sound must be presented to the fetus alone; his mother must not hear it. Japanese otologists Tanaka and Arayama[15] tried this during the second half of pregnancy: they generated tones directly against the mother's abdomen while presenting to the mother through earphones a continuous noise that masked the experimental tones. The tones were pitched within and slightly above the range of a woman's voice and are likely to have been about as intense inside the body as the body's own sounds. Before the last three months of pregnancy, Tanaka and Arayama found no evidence that the fetus can hear; but during the last three months, in 119 of 123 fetuses, the presentation of a tone led immediately to a quickening of the fetus's pulse. Apparently, during the last three months, but not before, the fetus can hear.

This is also what anatomists would predict from the physical development of the fetus.[16] From the fetus's anatomy and from our knowledge of the newborn's hearing (see chapter 7), we think that the sounds of his mother's body are clearly if quietly audible to an older fetus, as are some of the louder, lower-pitched sounds coming from outside her body. His world is a world of rumblings and groanings punctuated by his mother's utterances. And constantly, through everything, he hears the thumping of his mother's heart.

Mother's Heartbeat

The mother's heartbeat is so pronounced that many people believe the heartbeat makes a permanent impression, an impression that is imprinted forever on the mind of fetus, baby, and then adult. According to this theory, first postulated by a psychologist in New York named Lee Salk, this "imprinting" of the heartbeat is in some vague way responsible for a universe of phenomena from the way mothers hold babies (on the left—"near the heart") all the way to music, dance, and poetic metaphor ("I love you from the bottom of my heart").[17] This theory has found its way into numerous articles in both the scientific and the popular press, yet it is unfounded.

Salk based the theory on his own observation that newborns in a hospital's nursery cried less and gained more weight when they heard a very intense (eighty-five-decibel) heartbeat played around the clock through a loudspeaker. Yet when James Tulloch and his associates at the University of Rochester tried to replicate and expand Salk's work, they found that the eighty-five-decibel heartbeat was of such "terrific intensity" that the nurses would not put up with it.[18] (Although this was probably comparable in intensity to the heartbeat within the womb, the fetus and newborn are protected from its full force by a creamy substance called vernix that fills the outer ear, and by the immaturity of their auditory system.) They then learned that Salk had conducted his study in a hospital near the main approach to New York's busy LaGuardia airport, and had set the noise of the heartbeat to approximate or drown out the sound of incoming planes. Because the babies most likely would have heard the noise of planes roaring into the airport as a fairly loud, unexpected, and hence mildly unsettling noise, a continuous noise that masked it might have proved calming no matter what its nature. Moreover, Salk timed the babies' crying from tape recordings made not by individual microphones placed near individual babies, but by one microphone placed far enough away from them all to record nine babies in the room simultaneously. In this situation, since the *LUB-DUB-LUB-DUB* was loud enough to mask some of the sound of the airplanes overhead, it would have been loud enough to mask some of the cries of the newborns as well. It is not surprising that Salk heard the babies cry less.

Other researchers have tried to replicate Salk's findings, but all have failed.[19] It is true that, under some circumstances, the sound of a heart will affect the baby (we shall discuss this in chapter 4). But contrary to Salk's theory, under those circumstances, so will lullabies, conversation, and other sounds quite unlike the heart.[20] Also contrary to his theory, rhythmic sounds that calm the baby will calm him no matter whether they are much faster or much slower than the mother's heartbeat.[21] In short, as attractive as Salk's theory may be, it is wrong.

It is more likely that a fetus rarely notices the heartbeat at all: he probably habituates to it, just as adults habituate to background music in stores and restaurants. Habituating to a stimulus requires only rudimentary parts of the nervous system[22] and is well within the capability of the older fetus. Indeed, many researchers have presented a noise to a fetus, noted a twitch or a racing pulse in response, and then found that repeating the noise soon stops causing the response.[23] This is one reason a pregnant woman feels her baby kick when she first turns on the radio but soon feels him no longer, until the volume suddenly rises for an ad: both she *and* her baby are habituating to the sound. The constant sound of the beating heart is unlikely to obtrude upon the fetus's attention.

Mother's Voice

The fetus is much more likely to be aware of sporadic sounds. And he definitely notices the most frequent, loud, sporadic sound that he hears: his mother's voice.

When his mother speaks, her vocal cords vibrate like guitar strings, inducing waves of vibration in the air in every direction, both outward through her mouth and inward through her trachea into her lungs. After the vibration reaches her lungs, most of its energy is absorbed by tissue, but much of the energy responsible for lower-pitched tones does pass through into her uterus.[24] Her voice becomes indistinct, but deep and resonant.

A woman's voice heard from within her body would be so different from her normal voice that there is no reason to expect a newly born baby to recognize his mother's voice as the same voice he had heard as a fetus in the womb. He would be even less likely to recognize individual words. Yet something about her speech—probably its rhythms—does make an impression. Anthony De-Casper and Melanie Spence of the University of North Carolina at Greensboro showed this by asking sixteen women to read a story aloud twice daily during the last five to six weeks of pregnancy.[25] Three days after birth, the babies were enabled to choose between hearing that story or another story read through a loudspeaker: the babies chose by varying how they sucked on a pacifier. Thirteen of the sixteen babies chose the story that their mothers had read aloud during pregnancy, the story they had heard repeatedly in the womb.

The fetus hears his mother's voice so often, it becomes familiar to him. It sounds radically different after he is born, of course; yet its patterns and rhythms remain the same. Thus after he is born, a baby comes to recognize his mother's voice long before he recognizes his father's.[26]

Stress and the Fetus

MOTHER'S EMOTIONS

Many people believe, with Freud, that the womb insulates the fetus from the kinds of physical and emotional stress that occur later in life. Others believe that if an expectant mother is under physical or emotional stress, then this stress can easily strain the fetus: anxiety alone, if it is strong enough, is supposed to be able to stunt fetal growth, cause birth defects, or even induce miscarriage. These beliefs are clearly contradictory. Enormous amounts of research have gone into sorting them out, and professional and popular publications alike are flooded with accounts of the effect or noneffect on the fetus's well-being of coffee, smoking, alcohol, job pressures—you name it. Yet when we sifted carefully through several hundred studies, we found only a few that were scientifically sound. From these we learned that physical and emotional stresses do indeed affect the fetus, and if the stresses are severe or prolonged, they can affect him permanently. But usually they affect him only momentarily. Stress can create a nasty climate, but normally it creates only momentary winds and rains that are the equivalent in the womb of bad weather.

Let us begin with one of the best studies of emotional stress. To see if a mother's emotional stress affects a baby's birth weight,

Jon Shaw, Peggy Wheeler, and Donald Morgan tested 150 pregnant wives of servicemen at Walter Reed Hospital in Washington.[27] All of the women were bearing their first child. Each woman took a written test of anxiety halfway through her pregnancy. Higher scores on this test predicted lower birth weights a little more often than chance would have allowed. Overall, the mother's anxiety proved a rough predictor of her baby's weight at birth 6 percent of the time.[28]

Now, tests of anxiety, including the one Shaw, Wheeler, and Morgan employed, are not very sensitive. They are like old-fashioned crystal radios: if you can hear any music at all through one of these, the station must be fairly strong. If only one measurement taken with such a test can predict birth weight 6 percent of the time, then an expectant mother's psychological stress might seem to be a potent force indeed. But this is by no means necessarily the case, for *the more anxious people are, the more they tend to smoke and drink;* and as we shall show, *smoking and drinking in themselves appear to cause reduced birth weight.* These researchers paid no attention to the mothers' smoking and drinking, so we cannot know that anxiety per se had anything to do with the outcome.

Although more than forty studies purport to find or not to find a relationship between an expectant mother's anxiety and the condition of her baby at birth, nearly every study ignored smoking and drinking, and the few that did consider them used questionnaires or interviews after birth to "measure" what the mother's anxiety had been months earlier—a procedure that is almost certain to produce inaccurate results.* In short, we could find no sound, direct evidence that an expectant mother's emotional stress affects the baby she is carrying.[29]

However, we have been able to piece together a story from

---

*Try to recall some details about your recent past—How many colds did you catch last winter? When did you catch them? How long did they last?—and you can see that questioning about the past is bound to elicit uncertain and often erroneous answers even when the questioning is trying to define something as concrete as a cold, not something as subtle as anxiety. Moreover, the inaccuracy is likely not to be random but to be biased: a hypochondriac is likely to exaggerate coughs and sniffles that a person who prides himself on his health would ignore. Similarly, a woman questioned after she has given birth to a healthy infant would be caught up in the pride and joy of motherhood, and so would tend to forget or ignore many cares of the past, whereas a woman questioned after she has just borne a sickly baby would likely be racking her brains like Job for possible explanations. Any study comparing two groups of women like this is almost certain to find a difference in their answers, whether a difference exists in reality or not.

indirect evidence—from a combination of studies, each of which is related only partially to the topic. The first is an experiment on rhesus monkeys by Ronald Myers at the (U.S.) National Institutes of Health. Myers anesthetized fifteen pregnant monkeys, then inserted catheters in each mother and fetus.[30] The catheters enabled him to monitor a number of vital signs, including the amount of oxygen dissolved in the blood. He found that as the anesthetic wore off, the fetuses suffered a shortage of oxygen—"hypoxia." Eight of the fifteen fetuses became so hypoxic that they seemed about to die, so Myers reanesthetized the mothers. This put things back nearly to normal—and also demonstrated that neither the surgery nor the anesthetic per se had caused the reaction: pain and/or terror must have done it. The monkeys' vital signs indicated that the mothers were reacting according to the common "fight-or-flight" pattern wherein the body prepares to fight or flee by sending more blood to the heart, brain, and voluntary muscles (those that we have control over—those in the arms, legs, neck, and so on) at the expense of most of the visceral organs, including the placenta. Since the placenta's supply of blood is the fetus's supply of oxygen, restricting the one restricts the other.

Seven of the monkeys came out of anesthesia without reacting strongly enough to endanger their offspring. Each of these Myers tied to a chair and kept in the dark, except when, occasionally and without warning, he turned on the lights, "suddenly appeared in front of the mother," and, without hurting her, "threatened her by patting her on the head, grasping her on the shoulders, shouting at her, etc." Each time this set the fetus's oxygen levels plummeting. Since Myers was not hurting the mothers, additional fear rather than additional pain was the cause of this reaction. Since human beings evince a comparable fight-or-flight reaction, human mothers' severe emotional stress is likely to induce hypoxia in human fetuses as well.

A human fetus can become hypoxic for other reasons too. The mother can smoke, drink, or live at high altitudes, or the umbilical cord can become kinked during the baby's passage through the birth canal. When any one of these things happens, the baby is unusually likely to be fussy and irritable.[31] Unfortunately, each one of the studies showing this demonstrates only that hypoxia is *related* to irritability; none demonstrates that hypoxia *causes* irritability. However, in animals as well as in human beings, in a wide variety of circumstances assessed by a wide variety of means, wherever there is evidence of fetal hypoxia, the newborn infants seem to be unusually irritable. As weak and circumstantial as each individual piece of evidence is, the evidence is so consistent and comes from so many directions that error, coincidence, and hidden factors seem unlikely to explain it all. Hypoxia looks to be not merely a correlate of irritability, but a cause.

Now consider what often happens with fussy and irritable babies. The baby cries for no apparent reason. His parents check his diaper, cuddle him, and offer him a bottle, all to no avail. They become so fed up with his crying that they put him in his crib and close the door to his room. As we shall see in chapter 4, this reaction usually proves to be effective in this circumstance: usually the baby will go to sleep. But if the baby cries frequently for no apparent reason, the parents may come to act like the shepherds when the boy cried wolf: they may stop attending appropriately when he has a real want. Then the baby will cry even more. Thus a vicious circle can develop, a pattern of interaction in which the baby acts irritable, the parents act irritable in reaction, and the baby acts more irritable in turn. This vicious circle has a chance of continuing throughout childhood into adulthood and expanding throughout the child's relationship with society. Antisocial behavior as an adult might sometimes be the result.

This we can see in data gathered by two Finnish psychiatrists, Matti Huttunen and Pekka Niskanen,[32] who searched through official records of births and deaths until they found the names of 167 children whose fathers had died before they were born. Their mothers, they assumed, would have suffered unusually severe emotional stress during pregnancy. At the same time they found the names of 168 children whose fathers had died during the children's first year of life. Next they followed all 335 of these children through thirty-five years of medical records. Most of the fathers had died during the Second World War, when cigarettes and alcohol were rationed severely when they were obtainable at all, so smoking and drinking would not have affected most of the pregnancies. In both groups, the parents were of comparable age and came from comparable social classes; and all the children grew up fatherless. In sum, there seemed to be no difference between the two groups of children other than the timing of the mothers' anguish, yet the percentage of children who later "evinced psychiatric and behavior disorders" (alcoholism or criminality) proved to be significantly higher among those who had still been in the womb at the time of the bereavement: 14 percent instead of 6.5 percent.*

Apparently the fetus is not perfectly insulated from his mother's emotional stress—nor may the world be perfectly insulated from the fetus's reaction to her stress. If the world stresses his mother *severely* and for a prolonged time, then there is a small possibility that the child will add to the stress of the world in his turn.

MOTHER'S DRINKING

If a fetus can be affected by his mother's emotional stress, then other stresses should be able to affect him too. Since many stresses occur in life, and since it is rarely possible to experiment with them in a controlled fashion in the laboratory, it is difficult to isolate individual stresses and identify their individual effects. Of all the stresses that occur commonly in western society, only two have been studied extensively and carefully enough to let us draw conclusions about how they feel to the fetus: alcohol and cigarette smoke.

Minutes after the mother takes a drink, alcohol begins to enter her bloodstream. Almost immediately it crosses the placenta and enters the fetus's bloodstream.† About half an hour after the concentration of alcohol in the mother's blood reaches its peak, the concentration in the fetus's blood reaches a similar peak.[34] Roughly half of the mother's blood flows to her brain, so half of the alcohol in her blood flows there too; in the fetus, the proportion is even higher. Alcohol depresses activity in the mother's central nervous system (brain and spinal cord). Even minute amounts of it slow her reflexes, and larger amounts can dull her senses enough to permit

---

*It is also possible that, when a mother lost her husband in the months before birth, her anxiety distorted her relationship with the baby during the first months of life in some way that exacerbated the vicious circle. (We will deal with such distortions in chapter 11.) It is even conceivable that this distortion began the circle; but in light of the other evidence that we mentioned in the text, we doubt it.

†When the mother drinks, some alcohol also passes into the amniotic fluid, which the baby drinks. Alcohol reaches the amniotic fluid after it reaches the blood, but remains there longer.[33]

its use as a surgical analgesic. (In fact, our information on alcohol's passage into the fetus comes from blood samples taken in the delivery room while mothers were made high on vodka administered intravenously—"an ethanol infusion"—to dull their pain.) Needless to say, larger amounts can also make the mother appear lethargic and content.

Now consider a fetus after his mother has drunk one jigger of vodka. Normally during the last weeks of gestation a fetus spends one-third to one-half of his time "breathing": going through the motions of inhaling and exhaling, thereby developing the muscles of his breathing apparatus so that they will be able to function continuously after birth.[35] Peter Lewis and Peter Boylan of London's Hammersmith Hospital used ultrasonography to observe the breathing of six fetuses. They observed that before and after the mother drank a glass of orange juice, the fetus "breathed" an average of 46 percent of the time—but after the mother drank a glass of orange juice laced with a jigger of vodka, the fetus "breathed" only 14 percent of the time.[36] Since fetal "breathing" is a reflex of the central nervous system, it looks as though alcohol depresses the fetus's central nervous system much as it depresses his mother's.

Next consider a medical report of fetuses who were nurtured outside the womb on vodka and water—"premature infants receiving an intravenous, alcohol-containing 'hyperalimentation' solution."[37] Physicians were injecting this solution into premature babies, apparently because of a recommendation of the Neonatal Intensive Care Center of the University of Oregon's Medical School. (This recommendation had been published two years before, in 1971, in an article by S. Gorham Babson in the *Journal of Pediatrics.* [38] Babson did not explain why alcohol was included in the solution, but he did sound authoritative.) Nurses noticed that some of the babies they were caring for seemed unusually lethargic and contented. One of those babies turned out to have almost enough alcohol in his blood to be jailed for drunken driving, and another baby had twice that much. Those two babies were especially lethargic. When the physicians abruptly stopped giving alcohol to one baby, "she had symptoms resembling delerium tremens." This is not proof that the babies were drunk, but babies borne by mothers who are administered alcohol shortly before giving birth also show "muscular hypotonia" (flaccidity); babies borne by alcoholic moth-

ers not uncommonly show signs of delerium tremens;[39] and we have
heard more than one expectant mother say at a party, "Gee, he
seems quiet tonight." It certainly looks as though when an expectant mother gets drunk, the baby she is carrying gets drunk too. (A
fetus can become addicted to heroin and methadone as well as
alcohol.[40] We suspect he can become addicted to whatever his
mother can, including diazepam [Valium].)

This sounds portentous; and indeed, many dozens of studies
purport to find long-term, durable effects of an expectant mother's
drinking on her baby. However, most of these studies have grave
methodological flaws, like failing to account for the mothers' smoking or age, or questioning the mothers after birth about how much
they had drunk months before.* What is more, their flaws are
largely similar, so the studies probably err similarly. This leaves
most of them uninterpretable, either singly or as a group. Let us look
at two of the best, one by Ruth Little at the University of Washington and another by her colleagues Ann Streissguth, Helen Barr,
Donald Martin, and Cynthia Herman.[42]

Little questioned mothers during pregnancy about how much
they were drinking and smoking. All of the mothers belonged to a
prepaid medical plan, so all were provided with comprehensive
health care; and the mothers were predominantly well educated and
middle class—for the most part healthy, well fed, and not living
arduous lives. It took a while for Little to find a significant number
of women who drank even a moderate amount of alcohol, because
alcohol makes most pregnant women nauseous, but eventually she
identified seventy-three women who did admit to taking an average
of two drinks daily. Little questioned these women again toward the
end of pregnancy, then compared their babies to 198 babies of
light-drinking women and abstainers. All three groups—the moderate drinkers, the light drinkers, and the abstainers—included the
same proportion of women who smoked. After Little accounted for
age and childbearing experience, she found that the women who
drank moderately during the last three months of pregnancy bore
babies weighing six ounces less (on average) than the others.[43]
Moreover, Little's colleagues (Streissguth and associates) found

---

*Like her memory of anxiety, a mother's memory of her drinking will change with time
and with the birth of her baby. One study which interviewed mothers both during pregnancy
and after delivery found a threefold difference in the number who admitted drinking heavily.[41]

that, on average, the more a woman had drunk during her pregnancy, the harder it was to arouse her baby the morning after he was born, the less likely he was to habituate to repeated sights or sounds, and, eight months later, the lower he scored on a test of motor and mental development.[44]*

This looks like clear evidence that alcohol retards fetal development—until we consider the difficulty Little had in finding pregnant women who drank. This is a common experience of researchers, even in countries like France and Germany where drinking has no social stigma.[46]† Apparently one of the normal physiological changes during pregnancy is to render alcohol nauseating—so if women are able to drink moderately during pregnancy, they seem not to be perfectly normal physiologically. Rather than alcohol itself, this other, more basic physiological abnormality may be retarding their babies' development.

To rule this out, one might study only women who drink, but compare women who drink different amounts: if alcohol stunts fetal growth, then more alcohol ought to stunt fetal growth more; so if all else were equal, babies borne by heavy drinkers ought to weigh less than babies borne by moderate drinkers. However, all else is not equal: heavy drinkers tend to smoke more than moderate drinkers, eat less well, be in poorer health, take more psychoactive drugs, and live more arduous lives in less salubrious surroundings.[48] Consider how these might interact with each other and with alcohol. A pregnant woman walks back from the store—she cannot afford a car—dragging a cartful of groceries. She lugs these up two flights of steps to her third-floor walk-up. Since she is in poor health as well as pregnant, she is flushed and panting when she reaches her door. This indicates that her circulatory system is favoring her limbs and heart at the expense of most of her visceral organs, including the placenta; so her body is restricting the amount of oxygen available to the fetus. To refresh herself, she lights a cigarette—thereby inhal-

---

*At four and seven years of age, those children whose mothers had drunk heavily during pregnancy had more difficulty sitting still and paying attention. In another good study of predominantly middle-class women, thirteen-month-olds whose mothers had drunk moderately had lower scores on tests of motor and language development.[45] Of course, all of these long-term effects could result from differences in the way the children were treated after birth.

†Even monkeys that have learned to enjoy screwdrivers, and have seen nothing on television about the undesirable effects of alcohol on the fetus, take less alcohol while they are pregnant, then resume drinking after the baby is born.[47]

ing carbon monoxide, and hence providing carbon monoxide to the
fetus instead of oxygen. Finally she goes inside and takes a drink.
Now the alcohol begins to restrict the amount of oxygen available
to the fetus in the same way her exertion has been restricting it: by
inducing her circulatory system to send extra blood to the periphery
of her body at the expense of most of the viscera.[49] (This extra blood
coursing through your skin is what makes you feel warm shortly
after you drink.) The woman's overexertion might not have restricted the oxygen enough to cause hypoxic damage to the fetus,
nor might the cigarette alone, nor the alcohol alone; but combined
they increase the risk considerably.

We have found only one study of heavy drinkers that comes
even close to sorting out alcohol from these other factors, a study by
the Boston City Hospital's Prenatal Clinic.[50] Women coming to this
clinic were interviewed about their living habits. Those who said that
they were drinking heavily were advised to stop (or at least to reduce
their drinking until they delivered), and they were offered counsel-
ing to help do this. By the last third of pregnancy, fifteen of sixty-
nine heavy drinkers claimed to have stopped drinking, and another
ten claimed to have reduced their drinking materially. (Actually,
more women than this claimed to have reduced their drinking, but
the researchers sometimes chose to believe instead clinical signs to
the contrary.) Both groups of women—the heavy drinkers who had
cut back and the heavy drinkers who had not cut back—measured on
average similarly low on several socioeconomic indicators and reported similarly poor diets, similar use of marijuana, similarly heavy
smoking habits, and similar drinking habits at first: imbibing the
equivalent of nearly a pint of whiskey per day. Of the mothers who
continued to drink, 45 percent delivered babies so puny that they
were among the lightest one-tenth of all babies born in the United
States. In contrast, of the twenty-five mothers who had reduced their
drinking, only two delivered babies this lightweight.[51] Once again
alcohol seems to be the culprit—until we remember that the mothers
who had not cut down were probably less likely to take care of
themselves in other ways as well: less likely to follow dietary advice,
to take dietary supplements, to get adequate sleep, and so on. And
nonalcoholic factors like these simply must be considered: they
caused fully 35 percent of even the nondrinkers in this inner-city
study to bear babies that were abnormal in some way. The most we

can conclude is that *when other deleterious factors are present,* then a lot of alcohol can have some kind of durable, detrimental effect.

However, even in the best of pregnancies, any drink the mother takes will affect the fetus temporarily at least as much as it affects her. As she gets high, the fetus will feel lower and lower.

FETAL ALCOHOL SYNDROME

Readers who have heard about fetal alcohol syndrome may be surprised at such a cautious statement, since it has recently been claimed that alcohol causes this affliction in as many as half of all babies borne by alcoholics.[52] However, this claim is fallacious, the result of archetypical errors in epidemiology.

In the early 1970s physicians at the University of Washington noticed that eleven babies of alcoholic mothers were born with similar sets of defects involving mental retardation, stunted growth, and facial abnormalities. Because the babies had alcoholic mothers, the physicians concluded that alcohol was at fault. Because the babies had similar defects, the physicians concluded that these particular defects occur together in a syndrome, a specific combination of signs and symptoms that indicates a specific underlying problem. The result was a paper announcing the discovery of "fetal alcohol syndrome."[53] The name is catchy, and the subject attracts attention, so other physicians have looked for it—and in a very small proportion of the babies borne by alcoholic mothers, they have found it, and written up their findings, thereby perpetuating the error.

But an error it is; or rather, two errors. First, babies borne by alcoholic mothers do indeed have more than their share of these defects; but as we have seen, many other factors are likely to be involved. There is no way to pin the cause on alcohol alone. Second, babies borne by alcoholics are likely to have many other defects as well as the few forming the "syndrome." Those defects appear in many combinations. They come together in the "syndrome" no more often than you would expect them to come together by chance. Their simultaneous appearance is not a special phenomenon reflecting a specific ill; it is a coincidence.[54]

Unfortunately, because "fetal alcohol syndrome" sounds so dramatic, people tend to focus their attention on it instead of on the real problem, which is much broader. This "syndrome" is not a special trouble visited upon some babies of the relatively few mothers who are alcoholics; it is a general tendency of some very common (albeit ill-defined) unhealthful habits and circumstances to induce birth defects.

MOTHER'S SMOKING

Of other habits and circumstances that affect the fetus, the one most thoroughly studied is smoking. When a woman puffs on a cigarette, she inhales as much carbon monoxide as she would if she were puffing on the exhaust pipe of a car. By the time she finishes that cigarette, she will have inhaled about one-tenth of the lethal dose of nicotine, a substantial amount of cyanide, plus greater and lesser amounts of more than two thousand other chemicals, most of them irritating if not toxic.[55] Against these stresses the body instantly rebels: as soon as someone draws on her first cigarette, she coughs and gags, feels nauseous and dizzy. If she persists in smoking, her body will try to adapt, and it will succeed well enough to quash the unpleasant sensations and to prevent itself from being overcome. But the result is equivalent to a car being driven with the choke half on and the spark advanced as "compensation": the carbon monoxide from smoking even half a pack a day chokes off—throughout the day, not just during a cigarette—one-third to one-half of the oxygen that is normally available to the body's cells, while the nicotine provides preternatural sparks of nervous stimulation.

The adult body is strong enough and stable enough to withstand to some extent this physiological maladjustment. Its physical endurance will be lessened, and it will become sick more often and more seriously, but it will usually function for decades before it begins to show serious, premature wear. However, the fetal body is still developing. An amount of nicotine that stimulates the adult's nervous system may overwhelm the fetus's, thereby not increasing but decreasing its activity. And in the fetus, a shortage of oxygen may not merely reduce the efficiency with which tissues function, it may reduce the efficiency with which they *develop*. Thus it should not be surprising that the instant his mother lights up, the fetus begins to "breathe" less, as though his central nervous system is being depressed.[56] Nor should it be surprising that a mother's smoking seems to stunt the fetus's growth. Ruth Little's study of drinking shows this clearly:[57] taking into account alcohol as well as all the other factors we have mentioned so far, Little found that on average, smoking appears to reduce birth weight by 10.7 grams per cigarette smoked per day, or roughly half a pound per pack smoked per day.

Note that we said "on average." Any one mother who does not smoke may bear a smaller baby than her neighbor who does, and Cousin Joan who puffs her way through two packs a day may bear a ten-pound giant. Nonetheless, the evidence that *on average* an expectant mother's smoking stunts her fetus's growth is substantial. For example, one excellent study shows that with drinking, socio-economic status, use of marijuana, age, number of previous pregnancies, and six other less obvious factors like diet and the mother's increase in weight during pregnancy all held constant, when pregnant women smoke, their babies tend to weigh less at birth.[58] Moreover, every study purporting to show that something other than smoking might be the cause has been inadequate.[59] At this time a more sensible question to address is not whether a pregnant woman's smoking can stunt her fetus's growth, but whether her husband's smoking can also stunt it. Sidney Bottoms and his colleagues at Case Western Reserve Medical School recently measured the amount of thiocyanate found in fetal blood remaining in the umbilical cord after birth.[60] The body produces thiocyanate after it is dosed with cyanide, and the largest source of cyanide is usually cigarette smoke. Thus in this study thiocyanate was much more plentiful in the fetal blood when mothers had smoked than when they had not smoked, and the more they had smoked, the more plentiful it was. However, when the mothers had not smoked but the fathers had, the thiocyanate was still significantly more plentiful than when neither had smoked.

If smoking depresses fetal "breathing" and stunts fetal growth, it might conceivably have more serious consequences. Any monkey wrench thrown into the body's physiological works will tend to affect the development of tissues that are developing rapidly more than it will tend to affect the development of tissues that are relatively stable; and at any given time during gestation, some tissues are developing more rapidly than others. So if, like cigarette smoke, the monkey wrench retards development, it could retard development unevenly: the fetus could be not merely stunted but also distorted. Congenital defects might result—perhaps gross malfor-

hypoxia →

mations like pinheadedness; or perhaps physiological imbalances inducing miscarriage or stillbirth; or perhaps flaws within the cellular structure of the brain which would be visible only under a microscope but which could cause mental or sensory deficiencies. Significant increases in defects like these have in fact been found in more than twenty studies.[61] However, we could find no creditable study reporting such differences that has taken into account the mothers' drinking habits. Moreover, all of the creditable studies that account for maternal drinking have not found differences at birth in anything but weight.[62] This does not prove that such differences do not exist, but it does indicate that they would be small and infrequent. Smoking definitely depresses the fetus's "breathing" and stunts its growth, but it may have no other significant consequences—by itself.

HYPOXIA

We can learn little else about the fetal effects of anxiety, drinking, and smoking from studies that have investigated these directly. However, it is clear that all of these stresses restrict the amount of oxygen that is available to the fetus;* so studies of other restrictions of oxygen let us infer more. They let us see how these stresses add to one another from the fetus's point of view.

Oxygen is restricted naturally at high altitudes, for there the air is thin. When unacclimated adults climb or even drive to the top of a high mountain, they are likely to suffer hypoxia—acute mountain sickness. They will develop a headache, feel weak and irritable, and find it difficult to pay attention to things or to sleep.[67] Pregnant women dwelling at extremely high altitudes produce unusually large placentas, which compensate for the limited oxygen; so although there is less oxygen available to be transferred from the mother's blood to the fetus's, at least it is transferred more effi-

---

*We saw earlier that this occurs when the mother is anxious or takes a drink. It also happens when she lights up a cigarette, for the carbon monoxide from the smoke replaces oxygen in the blood. This both reduces the oxygen-carrying capacity of the blood, and makes it more difficult for whatever oxygen is there to be transferred to tissues.[63] Also, nicotine causes hormones to be released that cause peripheral blood vessels like those in the uterus to constrict and hence send less oxygen to the fetus.[64] This is probably the reason that the placentas of smokers often look diseased, as if they had been inadequately supplied with blood.[65] Studies of monkeys confirm this by showing that the fetus becomes hypoxic shortly after the mother's head is placed in a helmet filled with tobacco smoke.[66]

ciently.[68] However, this compensation is not complete. Consider a comparison by Carmen Saco-Pollitt of Peruvian babies born at four-teen thousand feet in the Andes to babies born near sea level in Lima.[69] After taking into account parents' education, father's occu-pation, ethnic background, and much else, she found that the babies born in the Andes weighed less, as we would expect—and she found that they were more flaccid, moved less often and more jerkily, were less attentive, and were less wont to stop crying. In short, they acted like hypoxic adults.

Oxygen can also be restricted by premature birth, for the pre-mature baby's lungs may not work adequately at first. Any shortage of oxygen this causes can be measured in the blood—and it can be seen in the baby's behavior, for a baby who is short of oxygen does not sleep normally.[70] A premature baby and the fetus share certain immature neurological patterns while they sleep;[71] so since hypoxia disturbs the premature baby's sleep, it doubtless disturbs the fetus's sleep too, just as it disturbs the adult's.

Finally, we have circumstantial evidence that hypoxic fetuses, like hypoxic adults, suffer headaches. Several postmortem studies have found that when medical signs indicate a fetus had endured hypoxia within a few weeks of his birth, then no matter why he died as a newborn, he probably sustained damage to those parts of the brain that are most likely to be responsible for the headaches of hypoxic adults.[72] We shall see in the next chapter that the new-born feels little pain; so the fetus's headaches should hurt him little if at all. Still, a headachy feeling is uncomfortable even when it is not accompanied by pain. A hypoxic newborn is likely to feel an unpleasant pressure and pounding in his head.

We cannot know to what extent a mother's anxiety, drinking, and smoking are comparable to her living at Andean altitudes, giv-ing birth prematurely, and so forth; so we cannot say that a mother's anxiety, drinking, and smoking have the same effect on her baby that those other circumstances have. However, even though nearly all studies of these factors confound them thoroughly, we have seen that, in whatever (unknown) admixtures they occur, anxiety, drink-ing, and smoking do seem to induce mothers to bear babies who sleep abnormally and are flaccid, tremulous, irritable, and inatten-tive—like hypoxic babies. Although we cannot apportion the causes of this among the different forms of stress, it seems likely that through the common mechanism of hypoxia, all of these stresses contribute to one extent or another. From the fetus's perspective, it matters little just what stresses his mother undergoes: if they are intense enough or prolonged enough, he will feel headachy, crabby, and tired.

The Value of Stress

If life in the womb is a paradise, then it is a paradise that can be noisy, bitter-tasting and bumpy—at times downright unpleasant. The noises, tastes, bumps, and grinds are different from those outside the womb, but they provide a wide range of sensory stimulation, from barely noticeable to barely tolerable.

This should not be surprising; for generally after birth, muscular and mental capabilities increase only with stimulation, and without stimulation they atrophy. There is no reason to think that stimulation would suddenly become necessary after birth yet not be necessary before.

Thus we arrive at a paradox. Any stimulation applied intensely enough becomes a stress; the intensity at which it becomes a stress depends not on the stimulation itself, but on the tissue or organ that is stimulated; and different tissues and organs can accept differing amounts of any given stimulation without incurring strain—so the same stimulation that is beneficial to one part of the body may be stressful to another. This is a paradox adults experience as well. Joggers strengthen their hearts by damaging their knees.

Even with an adult it is difficult to tell when stimulation like jogging becomes more harmful than good overall. With a baby in the womb, comparable judgments are not just difficult; for the most part they are impossible.

Moreover, once a baby leaves the womb, the variety of stimulation he receives becomes so great that the effect of any one prenatal influence becomes virtually impossible to isolate. Pregnant women who smoke, for instance, bear lighter babies. They also usually continue to smoke after they give birth, thereby polluting the air in their home with significant amounts of carbon monoxide, cyanide, and other poisonous gases. By puberty, if the children of these women are shorter than their peers, is this because they began life stunted—or because the polluted air they have grown up in has left them more susceptible to respiratory illnesses, so that they have spent more time sick and less time growing? If they are also a few months behind in school, is this because the development of their brains suffered from fetal hypoxia—or because they have missed more school from being sick more often and longer?*

Although we have placed much emphasis on the stimulation and stress that life in the womb provides, we do not mean to imply that the womb is unprotective. Obviously it is protective. The young fetus has skin only a few cells thick: the womb must be protective if he is to survive. But the womb is protective, not insulating. It is like a good mother: it shields the fetus only from extremes of stress, not from those lesser levels he will have to learn to handle every day.

In addition, the fetus is protected by his very immaturity. He is protected physically, for the younger an organism is, the more easily it is hurt, but also the more easily it heals. And he is protected mentally and emotionally. No infant, no child, no adolescent, no adult—nobody at any age is able to learn anything that requires greater physical maturity than he has reached at that moment. The maturational limitation on all but muscular endeavors lies within the cortex of the brain, the "gray matter" responsible for all but the most rudimentary of animal behaviors. As we shall see in later chapters, the fetus's gray matter is barely beginning to develop. Without it, nothing that happens within the womb is likely to make more than a shallow and temporary impression on his mind or character. A prenatal impression may possibly be maintained or deepened by a child's experiences after birth, but it is far more likely to be pressed out. Whatever a baby's prenatal experiences happen to be, their influence is unlikely to be indelible.

*During the week of March 3, 1953, in the United Kingdom, seventeen thousand babies were born. Studies following these children found that those whose mothers had smoked during pregnancy grew up to be slightly shorter, slightly less capable intellectually, and slightly less skilled at reading and mathematics than those whose mothers had not smoked during pregnancy. Although these studies take into account such factors as the mother's height, age and childbearing experience, and the family's size and socioeconomic status, they gathered information about the pregnancy after the baby was born, and they did not take into account the effects of drinking, or of postnatal exposure to coal smoke, which seriously polluted the air of much of the country at that time.[73]

3

Being Born

SINCE LIFE in the womb does not feel like life in paradise, obviously birth does not feel, as many writers have assumed, like a fall from paradise. Yet birth changes the fetus's existence radically. In this chapter we shall see that the fetus/baby certainly feels this change, but not in the traumatic way that people commonly assume.

Pain

Let us begin our discussion by considering the baby's passage through the birth canal. This can be excruciating for an undrugged mother; and because the baby is being squeezed by her contractions, you might think it would be excruciating for the baby too. However, the mother's body is being stretched while the baby is being squeezed. In adults, stretching the body hurts much more than squeezing it. Women have withstood corsets tight enough to deform and even to kill them, yet a pea-sized kidney stone passing through the urethra will cause a three-hundred-pound linebacker to double over in pain.

Indeed, although her exertions feel mighty to a mother, electronic sensors taped to fetuses during labor and delivery show that the actual pressures on the fetus are comparable merely to the pressures on an adult's body while he lies in bed. The average uterine contraction exerts pressures on the baby reaching no more than about one pound per square inch, and even where the force is most concentrated—at the back of the baby's head while the cervix is partially dilated—the pressure is usually only two to five pounds per square inch.[1] This, of course, is as it ought to be: pressures much higher would bruise the baby's skin, as forceps do.

The fetus is likely to feel these contractions, for as we saw in the last chapter, his sense of touch appears to be excellent. However, he is even less likely than an adult to find such modest pressures painful. For one thing, if he is born in the West, he will probably be dosed with painkillers—analgesics given to the mother which pass immediately into his bloodstream. We shall discuss these at length later in this chapter. But medication notwithstanding, a baby's sense of pain is almost certainly duller than an adult's.

To understand this, we need to look at the adult's sensation of pain.[2] Pain does not involve any special anatomical system: there are no sensory "pain receptors," nor is there a specialized neural network transmitting "pain impulses." Neither is pain tied directly to the sense of touch: intense lights and sounds induce pain as palpable as that induced by a punch in the nose. Nor is pain caused by an excess of force or stimulation: an artillery shell applying sufficiently excessive force to remove an arm or a leg commonly will not cause the body to hurt for several hours. (There are innumerable anecdotal reports of this following industrial accidents and battlefield injuries. Careful studies show this to be not the exception but the rule.[3])

Pain seems not to be a primary sensation at all. It seems to be a secondary sensation based partially on learning. Among others, Henry Beecher of Harvard demonstrated this by questioning soldiers wounded in battle and civilians wounded on the operating table.[4] Beecher talked to the soldiers on average ten hours after they had been wounded and had been trucked away from the battlefield of Anzio Beach. These soldiers were as sore as they were likely ever to become. They were neither in shock nor doped by painkillers, and they were perfectly capable of feeling pain. "They complain as vigorously as normal men at an inept venipuncture [hypodermic needle]," Beecher noted. Yet of 150 men who had been wounded seriously, only 48 answered yes when asked whether they would like a painkiller. In contrast, 125 of 150 civilian men answered yes when queried four hours after suffering less extensive wounds from surgery. Apparently the situations these men found themselves in played a major role in their perception of pain. But of course, the situations per se could have been only a distal cause in this perception. The proximal cause had to be within the men: it had to be the perceptions and/or expectations that they associated with their circumstances. And associations of this sort are learned.

Such associations are not learned consciously, nor even learned unconsciously in the psychoanalytic sense; they are learned at the most basic neuronal levels. Within your body, as you do and perceive things akin to what you have done and perceived before, neurons tend to fire in characteristic patterns, and various parts of the brain become familiar with these patterns. Pain seems to be the conscious registration of untoward variations of these patterns. Your brain tells your legs to walk. Shortly afterward, throughout your legs, innumerable nerve endings signal to your brain what each part of the leg is doing. Simultaneously they report "Right knee extended against moderate pressure, right thigh swinging backward under moderate pressure, left knee extended with pull against it, left thigh swinging backward. . . ." At the same time your face reports a barely perceptible cooling, and your eyes report that objects toward the periphery of your vision appear to be moving backward. All these reports and more reach the brain simultaneously. From experience, your brain puts them all together and concludes that this is a normal pattern of sensory stimulation for stepping forward with the right foot; so it deems all to be well. This particular pattern of neuronal reports happens often, so your brain deals with the reports routinely at unconscious levels—until you tread upon a tack. Then, superimposed on the routine reports, comes another: "Severe pressure on a small spot under the instep of the left foot." This untoward variation from normal sets alarms ringing inside the brain. These alarms are the feeling of pain. You hurt.

On the other hand, if instead of treading upon a tack, you should tread upon a land mine, then there would occur no mere variation of neuronal activity but rather a wholesale change—a wholesale change that is also novel and unexpected. This the brain would not deal with routinely, unconsciously: you would feel consciously the shredding of skin and the splintering of bone. But the change in neuronal activity would be so significant in extent, so novel, and so surprising that the brain would need several hours to recover from its surprise, to marshal all of its experience, and then, eventually, to sort out what the new neuronal activity means. Only as it finishes this process would it begin to sound the alarm of pain.*

Compared to adults, babies have had the chance to learn few neuronal patterns, so fewer stimuli seem abnormal to them. Therefore, they are less likely than adults to feel pain. An indication of how much less comes from the pediatric ophthalmological clinic where we have one of our laboratories. We routinely study babies just one month old when they are first being fitted with a hard contact lens to replace the eye's natural lens after surgical removal of a congenital cataract. When a skilled technician inserts the lens (which takes less than a second), the babies seem to take no notice at all, nor do they later seem in the least bothered by it. Yet to an adult, a mote in the eye feels painful, and it takes days of inurance before a hard contact lens stops feeling like an implanted chisel.

Newborns have had even less time to learn neuronal patterns, so they are even less likely than one-month-olds to feel pain. Moreover, to the fetus, birth is as novel, great, and unexpected a change as stepping on a land mine. Surely he does not feel his birth as hurt.

What Babies Feel

On the other hand, like a soldier feeling his wound without pain, a baby does feel his birth. He feels the gentle but firm pressure of uterine contractions, of being squeezed through the birth canal, of

---

*This kind of response appears to be common in other species besides man. Most animals will fight if need be almost to death without appearing to feel wounds, then will lie quietly and irritably until they recover. As psychologist Peter Wall points out, this delayed action of pain is lifesaving. If severe pain normally occurred at the same time as a serious injury, the animal—or person—would be too debilitated to fight or escape. On the other hand, if pain did not occur shortly afterward, the animal would do itself further harm by not permitting itself time to convalesce.[5]

the physician's or midwife's hands. He feels the sharper pressure of forceps, if they are used. And most important, he feels a side effect of being squeezed through the birth canal. Gentle as that pressure is, it often squeezes the umbilical cord against the baby tightly enough to reduce the supply of blood flowing through it, inducing a shortage of oxygen—hypoxia.[6] During labor, the fetus stops making the breathing movements that he made earlier: this may be because the hypoxia makes him feel weak.[7] Even in normal deliveries, hypoxia can be severe enough to cause the electrical activity of the baby's brain to stop momentarily, an indication that the baby has passed out for a moment.[8] We cannot tell how often this occurs—too few babies have been studied to admit an estimate—but it seems likely to happen in a substantial minority of births, and to be especially likely when the mothers receive any of the drugs commonly given during delivery. Moreover, hypoxia also seems to cause strain that is less extreme than passing out; for the longer a baby is exposed to contractions, the longer and more quietly he will sleep for the next few days.[9] Indeed, a mother who has just endured a particularly long and difficult labor may find herself with a baby who will not wake up even to be fed. We shall see in the next chapter that such sleep indicates the baby cannot cope with all the stimulation he is receiving. The sights, sounds, and smells of the world are overwhelming him.

We saw in the last chapter that a pounding head is the likely result of this hypoxia—a pounding head plus a light-headed, "spaced-out" feeling. In addition, the dazzling light, the novel sounds and smells, being jolted about, becoming cold—these stimulate and overwhelm the newborn much as a western tourist is overwhelmed by his first visit to an Oriental bazaar. To an adult, sensory hyperstimulation like this provides a neurochemical kick to the central nervous system, inducing a natural high. If the adult's central nervous system is simultaneously starved of oxygen—if it is depressed by hypoxia—then the result is a combination of low and high. You can feel such a combination if you run long and hard enough to induce hypoxia alongside a busy, brilliantly lighted street. It is a weird mixture of feeling supremely alert yet dissociated from reality, a kind of alert mental haze—followed by a "crash" into fatigue. This, overlain by a pounding head, is likely to be what a newborn feels too—if his mother was not medicated during delivery. Certainly he is more alert (and more enjoyable to interact with) for a few hours after he is born than he will be for weeks afterward; and then he falls into periods of sleep longer than he ever will fall into again.[10]

Painkillers

This headachy feeling may be delayed and/or exacerbated, and the high may be increased or turned into a dopey low, by drugs given the mother during delivery: painkillers ("analgesics"), tranquilizers, sedatives, and general and local anesthetics. These drugs have a profound effect on the baby, not just as he is being born but for days afterward. They are the single most potent influence on how the baby feels his birth. For this reason we want to consider them at length. The drugs we need to consider fall into three broad classes, two of which are similar. Let us deal with those two first.

Sedatives, "minor" tranquilizers, and general anesthetics form one class. All of these depress the central nervous system. They include phenobarbital, diazepam (Valium), chloral hydrate (the knockout drops of spy stories), meprobromate (Equanil and Miltown), nitrous oxide, ether, and innumerable others, including alcohol. Most people think these differ greatly from one another, and obviously they do differ in detail—in how they are administered, how quickly they act, how soon (and how) the body disposes of them, and side effects. Nevertheless, in their overall functioning they are all very similar and form a closely knit family. At certain doses, the effects of any one become indistinguishable from the effects of any other, by either the person taking them or a physician examining him; and any one of them appears to be able to replace any other one to satisfy, at least partially, a physical addiction.[11] In some poor areas, when whiskey has been made prohibitively expensive, people have switched wholesale to ether: the drunk is just the same.

Members of this family can also substitute to a limited extent for the members of another family of depressants, the opioid ("opiumlike") analgesics. The natural archetypes of this class are opium,

morphine, heroin, codeine, and the other fruits of the opium poppy;
but nowadays synthetic equivalents are more fashionable, especially one drug called either meperidine or pethidine (Demerol).*
Like the first group of depressants, the opioids differ from one
another in how fast they act, how fast they are eliminated, and so
on, but the similarities among them are marked. In adults, there is
little difference among them in the ability to relieve pain or in side
effects, and virtually any one of them seems able to satisfy an
addict's demand for virtually any other. The opioids do differ from
the other depressants in many significant ways, but both groups are
rightfully, if not legally, called narcotics.†

These two families of narcotic form the vast bulk of drugs
administered during childbirth, and recent surveys show that the
vast majority of western women receive at least one of them.[12]‡
Whenever a mother receives one of these drugs, the fetus does too.
Just as alcohol begins to cross the placenta immediately, so do the
other narcotics. Just as alcohol quickly reaches concentrations in the
fetus's blood nearly as high as in the mother's, so do the other
narcotics.[14] And just as alcohol lingers longer in the newborn than

---

*If the nomenclature of drugs seems confusing, that is because it *is* confusing. Most
drugs have at least three names: a long chemical name that is too cumbersome for everyday
use, a shorter name given it by a standards-making body, and a catchy trade name given it
by the manufacturer. That is simple enough, but international standards are not always
adhered to, and different manufacturers use different trade names, often in markets where
advertisements and other literature overlap. Thus meperidine/pethidine/Demerol has at least
thirty-five names. The chemical name is 1-methyl-4-phenylpiperidine-4-carboxylic acid
ethyl ester hydrochloride. Pethidine is the international standard, but in the United States
it is called either meperidine or meperidine hydrochloride. And to confuse the nomenclature
further, manufacturers advertise it in various countries as Algil, Alodan, Alodan Gerot,
Centralgin, Demer-Idine, Demerol, Dispadol, Dolantin, Dolantine, Dolcontrol, Dolenal,
Dolestin, Dolestine, Doloneurin, Doloneurine, Dolopethin, Dolosal, Dolvanol, Endolat,
Lidol, Lydol, Mefedina, Mepadin, Pantalgine, Pethadol, Pethoid, Pro-Meperdan, Sauteralgyl,
Spasmedal, Spasmodolin, and Synlaudine.

†For at least five hundred years, a "narcotic" has meant in English "a substance which
when swallowed, inhaled or injected into the system induces drowsiness, sleep, stupefaction,
or insensibility, according to its strength and the amount taken." The *Oxford English Dictionary*
records this and no other usage. With this history, the modern legal meaning is absurd: it
excludes a drug like alcohol, which is obviously a narcotic, yet it includes marijuana, which
cannot induce a condition even remotely resembling narcosis; and it includes amphetamines,
which are stimulants of the central nervous system, the antithesis of narcotic.

‡Many people are incredulous at this statement. They have heard so much about
natural childbirth in recent years that they believe physicians are interfering less with childbirth than they used to. Yet the evidence indicates that, if anything, physicians are interfering
more: in many hospitals now, they are delivering one baby out of five surgically.[13] In any
case, our statement is based on surveys from the late 1970s and early 1980s. In routine matters
of this sort, medical practice changes very slowly. We would be very surprised if the situation
has changed much since then.

in the mother, so do the other narcotics, and for the same reason: the newborn lacks sufficient enzymes to break them down.[15]

Because of all this, if the mother receives narcotics during childbirth, her newly born baby is likely to act drugged. If she receives even a low dose, then during the first few hours after birth, the baby is likely to be depressed—to have weaker muscle tone and reflexes, to be less alert, to sleep more, and to be less able to habituate to his new surroundings. This depression will linger for several days. The more narcotics the mother receives, the longer her baby's depression is likely to last (although an antidote can mitigate it to some extent, if it is administered either to the mother just before the baby is born or to the baby just after his birth).[16] Apparently, narcotics commonly given the mother during delivery transform the high that a baby would naturally experience during birth into a dazed, groggy, dopey low.

This low may be even lower in the newborn than it would be in an adult. In an adult, narcotics depress most behaviors, yet at some doses they stimulate other behaviors simultaneously. A banal example is the cocktail which stimulates conversation while it slows reactions. A more serious example is the general anesthetic which causes a woman who is insensible to flail about on the delivery table in delirium, or even to try to climb off and walk away. This kind of paradoxical behavior is easy to identify in adults, yet there is little evidence of it in newborns whose mothers received narcotics during childbirth, unless the mothers also received stimulants. We think that these effects are not seen at least partly because narcotics depress the newborn more deeply and/or more broadly than they depress adults. Alcohol reduces the flow of maternal blood to the placenta, thereby causing fetal hypoxia. Other narcotics do the same. Thus narcotics are likely to exacerbate the natural hypoxia caused by constriction of the umbilical cord. This would intensify the headachy feeling that any newborn is likely to endure and add to the depression of his central nervous system. As groggy and woozy as a medicated mother is, her baby is likely groggier and woozier still, and will remain so long after she perks up.

If the mother is heavily drugged by narcotics, the baby can even be born partially anesthetized—in the first stage of anesthesia, awake but numb. We have found indications of this in several studies, all using similar methods to study babies delivered "normally" during the first half of this century, when "normal" usually meant deliveries under a general anesthetic and/or other narcotics. Typical is a report from 1924 by Mandel and Irene Sherman of Northwestern University. The Shermans pricked newborns' legs and faces with a needle and counted how many pricks it took to make the babies flail their arms, pull away, and cry.[17] A baby delivered without medication will object to even one pinprick, especially around the face; but these babies did not object until they were pricked six or seven times on the face, or eleven times on the leg. They were born partially numb. This numbness took several days to dissipate, and followed exactly the time course of the general depression that the mother feels after delivering with narcotics.

Needless to say, babies who are born partially anesthetized would feel little of their passage through the birth canal. Nor would they feel headachy immediately after birth. But as the anesthesia wears off, the baby would still be deeply depressed, more deeply depressed than babies who had never been brought down near the threshold of anesthesia. Thus, after the anesthesia wears off, the baby's headachy feeling would be worse than it would have been if he had never been anesthetized; he would feel more deeply depressed; and his depression would linger even longer.

Local Anesthesia

Many physicians try to avoid narcotic effects by employing local anesthetics instead of narcotics.[18] Their assumption is that local anesthetics work mainly on the mother's peripheral nerves, so they should have little or no effect on the rest of her body or on the fetus. However, local anesthetics find their way into the fetus's blood in surprisingly high concentrations, even from minimal doses given for an episiotomy just minutes before delivery. And like the narcotics, once they are in the baby's blood, they remain there for several days.[19]

This is not auspicious, for every injectable, local anesthetic is a close chemical relation of the stimulant cocaine. It is commonly

assumed that cocaine's cousins—lidocaine (Xylocaine), bupivacaine, procaine (Novocain), and other -aines—share cocaine's
chemical structure and anesthetic properties without sharing its
stimulating effect. Yet experiments with animals contradict this,
and experienced cocaine users cannot distinguish cocaine from lidocaine when the two are administered in comparably anesthetic
doses through the nose.[20] Moreover, there is evidence that several
local anesthetics often used in childbirth can stimulate the newborn.
Two studies have compared babies delivered with local anesthetics
alone (administered as epidural blocks) to babies delivered without
drugs. One of these studies, by Patricia Linn and Betty Kuhnert at
Case Western Reserve, compared babies delivered with a low dose
of lidocaine or 2-chloroprocaine to babies delivered without
drugs.[21] They found that babies delivered with lidocaine had more
abnormal reflexes; and three days after birth, babies delivered with
2-chloroprocaine were more labile in their moods: these babies cried
more readily, were less consolable, slept more in fits and starts, and
were less willing to cuddle in someone's arms. In the other study,
by Ann Murray and associates at The Women's Hospital in Sydney,
Australia, babies delivered with bupivacaine cried more than babies
delivered without drugs, and slept more lightly from the beginning
of the study through its end, five days after birth.[22]

In these babies, the natural high of birth seems to have been
exaggerated and prolonged. However, these studies represent only
a few usages of local anesthetics. Where and when the anesthetic
is injected, how concentrated it is, whether narcotics precede or
follow it—all of these vary from one clinical situation to another,
and all of them influence how a local anesthetic affects the baby.
These other factors often influence the local's effect paradoxically,
by adding to its stimulation one or another form of depression. For
example, if some regions of the body are anesthetized, labor is
slowed and prolonged, which increases fetal hypoxia, deepening
hypoxic depression. And, predictably, narcotics accompanying lo-
cals during deliveries appear to induce a narcotic depression: sometimes this depression seems to compensate partially for the local's
stimulation, but other times the depression seems to overcompen-
sate, and often some behaviors seem to be depressed while others
seem to be stimulated. Moreover, in adults, after a stimulant wears
off, a "crash" results, a crash that can deepen other depressions. The

permutations of all this are innumerable and unpredictable, but one thing is clear: if a mother in childbirth receives *any* of the drugs commonly given, then her baby is likely to be born in some kind of drug-induced state and to remain in such a state for days thereafter. These effects do eventually dissipate, but until they do, the baby will not act entirely normal. When he feels high, he will be jumpy and irritable and will cry a lot. When he feels low, he will feel floppy and may be hard to wake up even to feed.

Consequences

At present, there is no sound information on whether obstetrical medications affect the baby beyond the first few days of life. In 1978 psychologists Yvonne Brackbill and Sarah Broman announced to the press that analgesia and anesthesia given to mothers during labor and delivery adversely affect the development of their children through at least age seven. Brackbill later stated on television that a child loses an average of four IQ points because of these drugs. Their statements have since been booted about so often that many people believe them to be the established truth. However, Brackbill and Broman have published no study reporting these findings in the scientific literature, so we have no way to judge their validity.[23]

The only published study of comparably long-term effects failed to find any once children reached the age of four. But this study is actually uninterpretable, for mothers classified as having received local anesthesia often received narcotic analgesics as well, and mothers classified as having received no drug often received local anesthetics.[24] On the other hand, two well-designed studies in which a number of tests were administered at one or three months of age found no effects from a variety of drugs.[25]

The medical community assumes that the drugs they commonly use do not have any long-term effect; and from what we know about the plasticity of the child, we suspect that this is normally true. However, we do think the medical community should be more circumspect in their use of drugs and other interventions, for nowadays childbirth is rarely a medical problem.

Indeed, it has never needed to be a medical problem among people who are reasonably well fed. The great danger of childbirth used to be "childbed fever." This horror decimated women giving birth—literally decimated them, in many times and places killing mothers after one pregnancy in ten. But in 1847 Ignaz Semmelweis proved that mere cleanliness could prevent it: childbed fever was an infection carried by the *accoucheur* who probed the vagina with unsterilized hands.[26] In the hundred years after Semmelweis, antiseptics, anesthetics, and eventually antibiotics removed nearly all of what little danger remained, by making it practical to remove a baby from his mother's body surgically in the occasional instance that she could not squeeze him out naturally. This has left death during delivery a minuscule problem. Primarily discomfort remains.

Medical intervention is supposed to alleviate this, and often it does—but probably at least as often it makes it worse. Compare the aftereffects of having the flu for a day with the aftereffects of abdominal surgery: this is similar to the difference between delivering a baby vaginally, without drugs, and having him removed by cesarian section. And consider normal vaginal deliveries: medical practice keeps the woman lying on her back while nature and gravity call for her to squat.[27]

If a woman today wants to deliver her baby at home instead of in a hospital, with a well-washed midwife or husband catching him instead of a physician pulling him out, she may find the experience more pleasant. Nor is she or her baby in any more danger, unless she is one of the relatively few women with certain specific and identifiable conditions, such as a fetus presenting the wrong way around. She may even be safer (see the appendix for a discussion of modern obstetrical care). Yet to be prudent, she ought to have a physician on call to deal with a medical problem in the off chance that one occurs; and to arrange this can involve a struggle against the medical establishment and medico-legal authorities that is difficult at best and can be impossible to win in some jurisdictions.

Even if a woman feels strongly about delivering her child naturally, without drugs, there is a good chance that she will find herself taking them, both because of pressures from people around her and because delivery rooms are rarely set up to minimize the mother's discomfort. This causes women a lot of guilt and anguish—senseless guilt, for as we said before, a newborn baby is so plastic that these drugs are unlikely to cause any lasting problems. Moreover, if they did, the guilt should lie not with the mother, who is being pushed while she is too weak to resist, but with those who are applying the pressure.

The First Moments

As soon as the baby emerges from the birth canal, his universe changes to something radically different from anything he has known. In many ways his senses are bombarded with stimulation. But not always, nor in all ways. As we have seen, a baby delivered with narcotics may be born partially anesthetized: he then feels less during birth and immediately afterward than he had felt for weeks before. Even a baby delivered without medication may feel less against his skin than he felt before; for the squeezing and massaging his body receives while passing through the birth canal may numb him somewhat, as a massage numbs an adult.

Yet on the whole, if the baby is not anesthetized, birth rakes his senses like chainshot and canister. No longer is he curled inside a sack that is gently supporting the entire surface of his body: he is poked, prodded, and pushed, and his joints are stretched. For the first time he feels rapid motion: he is picked up, set down, and otherwise jolted about far more quickly than he was in the womb, with the movements of his head undamped by amniotic fluid. High-pitched noises sear his ears—treble tones and overtones that are omnipresent in the world but are nearly absent in the womb. And as we shall see in chapter 6, the newborn hears innumerable echoes, echoes that we do not hear.

However, the total amount of sound does not increase immediately. Remember that within the womb, the mother's bodily noises and voice seem about as loud as the background noises and conversation in a home or hospital. These noises intensify during labor, for while the fetus passes through the birth canal, the uterine muscles contract directly against his ears. You can imitate this by holding your palms against your ears and squeezing repeatedly: it makes a rumbling racket. To an adult, emerging from hours of this out into the world would seem a relief—a relief accompanied by a shrill surprise, like switching off an air conditioner at the end of the day and noticing anew the sounds from the street outside.

Still more novel than any sound, and more burdensome, is light. While the baby was in the womb, some very dim, vague glow might occasionally have seeped into his eyes through his mother's body, but this would have been of negligible import.* The baby's first contact with the full force of light comes as he is being born, as his head leaves the birth canal. Even premature babies can see as soon as they are born—they follow moving objects in front of them with their eyes[29]—so to some extent the newborn's visual system is prepared for the onslaught. Yet, as we shall see later, the newborn's visual system is immature. Some of this immaturity cushions the newborn's eyes from light. His pupils will not widen as much as even a two-month-old's, for example.[30] But these cushionings are unable to compensate for the newborn's inability to endure more than the most modest amounts of light. Even low levels of light make him squint.

We see this daily in our own laboratory. If we place newborns near a lamp brighter than fifteen or twenty-five watts, they do not just squint: they close their eyes. At various universities with various coworkers, Marshall Haith, Philip Salapatek, and we ourselves have used invisible, infrared light to photograph the eyes of one- to five-day-olds.[31] We have found that in complete darkness, newborns open their eyes widely and scan the blackness before them smoothly with small, controlled eye movements; but when presented with a dim, featureless surface—something comparable to a snow-covered pasture in moonlight—newborns narrow their eyes and alternate between sweeping their eyes over the surface broadly and slowly on the one hand and making tremorous eye movements, called nystagmus, on the other. If a figure is then presented—a face,

*An intense light can shine through the abdomen of a pregnant woman and be visible on the other side of her body; so the fetus inside her body may sometimes be exposed to light. Eliahu Sadovsky and Wolfe Polishuk reported that the fetus often moves when a 250-watt lamp is switched on next to the mother's abdomen. However, it appears from their paper that the mothers reported both when the fetus moved and when they saw the light, so it is not clear whether the investigation recorded the fetuses' reactions or the mothers' expectations. In any case, normally the fetus is not exposed to marked changes in illumination.[28]

a square, a squiggle—then immediately the baby's eyes find a corner of the figure and stare at that one corner intently and fixedly, making only the tiniest of eye movements around it. In other words, in the dark the newborn moves his eyes peacefully, but in dim light he glances about frenetically until he happens upon something to see. This he fixes upon with extraordinary concentration, as though he has finally found his tenuous way and is intent on not losing it. He may stare at your hair for minutes at a time.

Fear and Anxiety

This looks for all the world like a reaction of fear and anxiety, but it is not. For fear, like all emotions, incorporates knowledge and experience. Emotions require three elements: (1) sensory perceptions, either real or imagined; (2) a low-level, reflexive response of the nervous system to these perceptions, a response causing physiological reactions, like the release of adrenaline; and (3) a high-level evaluation of the original perceptions, an evaluation recalling experience of similar perceptions from the past and considering possible consequences. This evaluation, superimposed upon the physiological reactions, forms those physiological reactions into a definable emotion.[32]

Think of the nervous system as an army. Sensory receptors throughout the body act like pickets and guards who may report, say, a sudden reduction of compressive stress from the soles of the feet upward through the legs and spine. Noncommissioned officers forming the lower levels of the central nervous system receive these reports, recognize that something is amiss—that your feet have lost their purchase—and sound an alarm. Adrenaline and other chemicals carry the alarm throughout the body, which goes on a high alert. The noncoms may then order a response, if the sensory reports fit a pattern of behavior that they have orders covering—either general orders of genetic programming or specific orders formed by rote practice. Finally the alarm wakes up the brass, commissioned officers forming the various departments of the cortex of the brain. These highest departments of the brain examine in detail all the information that has been sent in by the sensory receptors; they figure out what is happening; they may order some holding maneuvers; and then they sit in conference to contemplate what the alarm portends. They may conclude that your feet have lost their purchase because you have begun to rappel down the side of a mountain; or they may conclude that your feet have lost their purchase because you have slipped on a glacier and are falling into a seemingly bottomless crevasse. In the first case they would anticipate fun; in the second they would anticipate injury and pain. The mental expectation of fun would form the physiological high of your adrenaline reaction into feelings of exhilaration. The expectation of injury and pain would form the same physiological high into feelings of terror.

On the other hand, a newborn whose feet lost their purchase would feel neither. Most of the upper reaches of his nervous system are immature,[33] so they take command infrequently; and the newborn has had little experience, so at any neurological level, he cannot anticipate many consequences. As a result, his sensations and physiological reactions are unlikely to be formed into emotions. Some sensations engender vague feelings of positivity and negativity, but they do not engender anything so specific as fear. Visual sensations in particular do not, for the newborn is utterly naive visually, too naive even to guess what to expect. The newborn is not afraid of light.

However, the newborn does find light uncomfortable—so uncomfortable that it can bother him while he is sound asleep. In 1930 psychologist Edith Bryan described what happened when she played a flashlight over the faces of sleeping babies.[34] "During the first three days of life . . . the child frequently gives a start, the lids are more tightly closed, a frown appears, the lips are frequently closed more firmly and if the light persists the head is moved from side to side, [and] is thrown back or turned well away from the source of light." Silver nitrate dropped into the eyes (done routinely to prevent blindness in case the mother has gonorrhea) exacerbates this sensitivity: Perry Butterfield and three colleagues at the University of Colorado compared babies given silver nitrate immediately after birth to babies given it an hour later.[35] Those given it immediately opened their eyes less widely, followed moving objects less often, and cried more.

The newborn's discomfort in light is caused by a neurological hypersensitivity to light, a hypersensitivity born of a profound and complete neurological adaptation to the dark. This is similar to the hypersensitivity of an adult who has become adapted to the dark— the hypersensitivity that makes us squint when we switch on a lamp in the middle of the night. Adults recover in minutes, of course—but not if they have been in the dark as long as newborns. Blind adults whose sight is restored surgically remain hypersensitive for days.[36]

To a newborn, almost any light seems to be unpleasant—you will rarely see him with his eyes open in the hospital—and judging from his reaction to a flashlight while asleep, even closing his eyes does not always eliminate its unpleasantness. We doubt that the newborn feels *pain* from light in most circumstances, for as we have said, the newborn's sense of pain does seem to be dull; and he can close his eyes. But one hospital nursery that we visited was illuminated so brilliantly that we found ourselves donning sunglasses after midnight. In a room like this—typical of nurseries for premature babies—or outdoors in the sun, the baby's discomfort might be considerable. In addition, about 5 percent of full-term babies receive phototherapy for jaundice.[37] These babies spend their first days lying a foot away from a bank of fluorescent lamps. To shield their eyes, gauze is usually taped across the face. This seems a meager shield at best, and babies often pull it off. Until the nurse gets around to noticing and replacing it, this therapy would feel unpleasant indeed.

Cold

One final stimulus is as novel to the newborn as light. It is also uncomfortable—and it can be fatal. This is cold.

Inside the uterus, the temperature is always slightly higher than elsewhere in the mother's body.[38] The uterine temperature changes slightly as the rest of the mother's temperature changes— down half a degree at night, up two or three degrees during a fever, and so on—but these changes are so slight and slow that the fetus would not notice them. He probably becomes so completely accustomed to constant warmth that he feels no sensation of temperature at all.

Then he is born. He emerges soaking wet into a comparatively cool room, as though he were emerging from a bath. This would chill an adult, and it chills the newborn even more; for compared to the volume of his body, the newborn has disproportionately more surface area from which to lose heat, plus thinner thermal insulation in the forms of fat and skin. The newborn's body does generate more heat than the adult's—its metabolic rate is roughly twice as high—but this is only half enough to compensate for the extra losses in heat caused by the newborn's proportions.[39] As a result, within minutes of birth, a baby's body temperature plummets. Warm delivery rooms and incubators temper this to varying extents, but they do not prevent it.[40] The newborn is simply unable to control his temperature adequately. Indeed, it is not unheard of in Britain, where many families still heat drafty houses with coal fires, for a newborn to freeze to death slowly while being cared for tenderly, in a nursery heated to 55 or 60 degrees.[41]

Paradoxically, although a newborn may die in cold that an adult finds tolerable and even comfortable, a newborn is also less wont to shiver. This is because the newborn has a more efficient mechanism for generating supplementary heat, a highly specialized mechanism that adults lack: brown adipose tissue. This is brownish tissue underlying fat on four parts of the body, but mostly on the back of the neck. It looks nondescript, yet it acts in the newborn's body like the afterburner in a jet engine, converting food into extra energy (in the form of heat) more rapidly than any other means the body can employ. Brown adipose tissue disappears within a few weeks of birth, possibly because babies are kept warm enough that it atrophies from disuse.[42] Without it, the adult is forced to generate supplementary heat by making his muscles do busywork—that is, by shivering.

However, a newborn *can* shiver, and he will shiver if he is chilled enough.[43] Careful measurements under controlled conditions show that a normal baby is born with the full complement of adult temperature-controlling mechanisms, and all of them function properly.[44] These include not only shivering but also increasing and decreasing the amount of blood circulating between the core of the body and the skin, quickening and slowing the metabolism, and sweating (although a newborn does sweat less copiously than the adult).

A newborn not only controls his temperature much like an adult, he also acts when he is chilled and heated like an adult who feels chilly or warm. At Columbia University, Karlis Adamsons, Gilliam Gandy, and L. Stanley James observed fifty babies who were dried with warm towels and placed inside an incubator as soon as they were born.[45] When the temperature was 85 degrees, the ambient temperature that makes the least demands of a naked newborn's body, most of the babies slept or lay quietly. As the temperature was lowered to 77 degrees, the babies rarely slept, and they moved more. The lower the temperature, the more they moved. On the other hand, when the temperature was raised above 100 degrees, some babies were able to maintain a normal body temperature (99.5 degrees), but others could not. Of those whose temperatures rose, some moved and cried restlessly, appearing quite uncomfortable.

So a newborn acts in heat and cold much as an adult acts in heat and cold, both in his overt behavior and in his physiological behavior. We know from studies of animals and of babies with congenital defects of the brain that the temperature-regulating part of the body is a section of the midbrain called the hypothalamus.[46] Clearly, this is functioning in a newborn. The hypothalamus also appears to be the body's sensorium of temperature. Thus if a baby is chilled enough to act chilly, he is likely as well to feel chilly; and when the newborn's body temperature drops a few degrees, then he is likely to feel downright cold. If he is fretful at night and does not sleep, this may well be the reason.

Trauma

Judging from the information we have gleaned so far, during the first minutes after a baby emerges from the birth canal his sensations are not painful, but neither are they pleasant. He feels cold and headachy; his eyes are dazzled; he is startled by strange sibilances and screaks; his skin feels pinched and pressed; his limbs and head feel stretched and jolted.

However, although the newborn feels cold, the world does not seem cold to him, nor dazzling, nor anything else. This distinction is subtle but important. The newborn senses only chilliness; he does not perceive that there is a world that is cold that is causing his chilliness. We shall see later that such a perception is a conclusion of the intellect, a conclusion requiring logical deductions that are far beyond the newborn's capability. During his first six months, a newborn perceives merely sensations and nothing more. He does not perceive that anything other than himself and his sensations exists.

Moreover, we shall see in the next chapter that the newborn does not keep his sensations separate from one another. He mixes sights, sounds, feelings, and smells into a sensual bouillabaisse. Sights have sounds, feelings have tastes, and smells can make him dizzy. The wildest of 1960s' psychedelia could not begin to compare with the everyday experience of a baby's entry into the world.

This is one reason that a baby is unlikely to remember even one of the many sensations he felt at birth. A sensation must be repeated many, many times before a newborn demonstrates any recognition of it, and usually this recognition lasts but minutes (see chapter 10). As a result, the discomfort a baby feels at birth is not likely to have any sort of lasting effect on his psyche or on his psychological development.

Nevertheless, the newborn is a sentient being, so common humanity calls for us to minimize his discomfort. The French obstetrician Frederick Leboyer has suggested a common-sense approach toward doing this that has gained wide currency.[47] Leboyer attempts to make the transition from womb to world as gentle and gradual as possible. He disfavors delivering the baby into a brilliantly lighted, surgical delivery room in which mother is draped off from baby by sterile sheets; he prefers delivering the baby into an ordinary room that is dark and silent. He suggests not cutting the umbilical cord immediately, instead leaving the baby snuggling naked against his naked mother until the cord stops pulsating naturally, and only then cutting it. He dislikes spiriting the baby away immediately to be toweled dry and blanketed; he prescribes bathing him at body temperature. Leboyer claims that babies delivered like this act and are immeasurably happier. However, Leboyer gives no evidence whatsoever for these claims, and upon examination, both his claims and any serious concern about discomfort caused the newborn by a normal delivery seem unwarranted.

Considering what is necessary to feel an emotion, it is not likely that newborns would ever feel happy or unhappy; but let us evaluate whether Leboyer's method at least makes them feel more comfortable. If it did, they should be calmer, more quiescent, and more alert. But they are not. For a doctoral dissertation at McMaster University, Nancy Nelson compared the two delivery procedures we described in the last paragraph. First she found women whose pregnancies entailed little risk and who agreed to accept either of the two procedures that might be offered, and then she assigned a procedure to each woman by lot.[48] (This means of forming experimental groups is rare in medical research, but it is highly desirable; for when groups being compared are selected at random, there is little chance that the groups will differ significantly enough in respects not being studied to prejudice the results.) Finally, after the babies were born—thirty-six of them—she observed their movements continuously for an hour according to a standard protocol that enabled her to compare how many minutes each group of babies slept deeply, slept lightly, lay drowsily, lay quietly alert, was active and alert, or cried. She also administered an extensive battery of tests. After all this she found no difference between the babies handled Leboyer's way and the babies handled the more conventional way—with one exception: Leboyer's way let the babies get colder during the hour after birth.

Nelson's study shows that Leboyer's "gentle" method may not even lessen a newborn's discomfort, let alone make him happier. Leboyer's method might even make the newborn more uncomfortable by chilling him additionally. *Yet this is not necessarily bad.* When adults are exposed repeatedly to cold, they become better able to tolerate it;[49] and when newborns are exposed to cold, they may become better able to tolerate it too. At the University of Florida, William Whitner and Margaret Thompson bathed fifty-eight newborns *à la* Leboyer and compared their temperatures to another fifty-eight whom they toweled clean.[50] Shortly after the bath, the bathed babies' temperatures had dropped one degree lower than the others', but after a few hours they had risen five degrees *higher*. And at Columbia, Leonard Glass, William Silverman, and John Sinclair put small but healthy premature babies into incubators for two weeks, twelve babies into incubators heated to 95 degrees and twelve babies into incubators heated to 98 degrees.[51] Before and after the two weeks, the babies were put for one hour into an incubator heated to only 82 degrees, and their temperatures were taken at the beginning and end of that hour. Those who had lived in the cooler incubators showed greater improvement in their ability to maintain their body's temperature.

This improved reaction to cold is consistent with the general bodily principle that we mentioned in the last chapter: the body and its functions develop best when stressed. The ubiquity of this principle is astounding: even the stresses of labor and delivery prove helpful, serving to facilitate a healthy birth. We can see this in a study by Andrew Boon, Anthony Milner, and I. E. Hopkin in Nottingham.[52] They measured how much air three groups of newborns were able to breathe. One group consisted of babies borne vaginally by healthy women; a second group consisted of full-term babies delivered from healthy women surgically (by cesarian section) before labor had begun; and a third group consisted of babies delivered by emergency surgery after labor of normal length. During the first six hours after birth, the babies delivered vaginally breathed more voluminously than the babies delivered surgically. This was to be expected, since those delivered vaginally would have received less medication. On the other hand, all of the babies delivered surgically would have received comparable medication; yet of these, the babies who had undergone the rigors of labor breathed more voluminously than those who had not. Apparently, being squeezed toward and through the birth canal squeezes out some of the fluid that the fetus has in his lungs, enabling the baby to breathe more easily. This is no minor matter, for problems in breathing are a major cause of newborns' sickness and death.

In nature, moderate stresses are unavoidable, so over the evolutionary eons, the babies more likely to survive and produce offspring have been those who are better able to withstand stress. This tendency has bred endurance at birth, and has bred it for so long that by now babies do not merely withstand natural stresses, in some ways they actually benefit from them. Unnatural stresses like drugs and forceps are another matter, of course: evolutionary selection has not equipped babies to handle these, so they can easily cause harm. Yet normal, natural stresses merely cause the baby discomfort; they do not pain him, nor do they cause him any physical or psychic damage. There is no reason to be concerned about them; and to try to avoid them by extraordinary means is no more likely to help the baby than to cause him ill.

4

Escape into Sleep

TWENTY-THREE HOURS out of every twenty-four, a newborn baby sleeps, cries, lies drowsily half-asleep, or fusses. Only one hour does he lie quietly awake—not all at once, but five minutes now, ten minutes later, mostly at intervals of three to four hours, around feedings.[1] Only during those short moments does he appear to observe the world with all his faculties.

This frustrates researchers, because often we can study a newborn only during those moments. (Indeed, much of this book was written while waiting in the lab for some baby—*any* baby—to wake up.) It also disappoints parents who had imagined cooing at, and cuddling, a more responsive being, a baby as it will not become for six to eight weeks. And it is puzzling, for a baby is born knowing virtually nothing and with a severely limited ability to learn. One hour a day seems insufficient time for him to learn as much as he does during the first six weeks or so after birth.

Those other twenty-three hours a newborn seemingly must be putting to some use. Since twenty of those hours he is sleeping, he must in some way be learning while he is asleep. Adults cannot do this, save under special and artificial circumstances. But a newborn's sleep is different from an adult's—different to observe and different to experience.

Sleeping and Consciousness: Adults

Before we investigate the newborn's sleep, we need to understand our own. We usually think of sleeping and waking as two distinct and discrete states of consciousness: either you are awake reading this, or you have dozed off. Yet sleep and waking are neither discrete phenomena nor states of consciousness. They are sets of muscular and sensory enervations and innervations caused by systematic switchings on and off of varying numbers of neural circuits by the midbrain, a central, neurological relay station that is buried deep inside the brain. Innumerable neural circuits go through the midbrain, circuits from every part of the brain and body to every other part. Many of these circuits are connected constantly, but others the midbrain switches on and off with millions of neuronal relays, each of which is connected to many others in an extraordinarily complex network that makes widespread changes in response to slight chemical imbalances or quick hints from sensory neurons. These changes allow various parts of the body, including parts of the brain itself, to rebuild themselves or to respond to a salient stimulus.

In contrast to sleep, consciousness arises largely in the interconnections between the upper parts of the midbrain and the cortex—the outermost, "highest" layer that does most of the complex processing of information—plus interconnections among various parts of the cortex itself.[2] The more circuits involving the cortex that the midbrain disconnects, the less we become conscious of; and the more circuits it reconnects, the more we become conscious of. We are conscious of varying amounts while we are awake; we are conscious of varying amounts while we are asleep. The enervations and innervations of sleep and waking form a continuum. On this continuum, three states stand out, two of sleep and one of waking. In adults, consciousness also forms a continuum upon which three states stand out. Each adult state of sleep and waking is mirrored by a state of consciousness:*

Full Consciousness. All neural circuitry is switched on and functioning normally. You are awake and alert.

Severed Consciousness. The midbrain severs connections between the cortex and the rest of the body but leaves largely alone the other cortical circuitry. Your muscles are relaxed to an extreme—they have no tone at all—because the midbrain blocks neural signals leading to the muscles. But sometimes a barrage of signals does make it through the midbrain's blockade, causing violent twitches. You sense little of the world—few sensory stimuli evoke large responses in the cortex—because the midbrain also blocks signals from the sensory organs. This makes you difficult to arouse. These blocked sensations normally help regulate your breathing, blood pressure, pulse, and other automatic functions, so these fluctuate more than normal. Yet the neuronal activity within the cortex is lively, nearly as lively as while you are awake and alert. Some of this intracortical activity, interacting with the midbrain, forms a kind of consciousness, a consciousness severed from the sensate world: dreaming. Some of this cortical activity also causes your eyes to move frequently, rapidly, and in proper synchrony, thereby exercising the neural and muscular systems that synchronize the eyes but that would begin to lose their precision after a few hours of disuse.[4]

Suppressed Consciousness. The cortex retains its connections with the rest of the body but activity within the cortex is largely suppressed. Suppressed intracortical activity leaves you motionless and conscious of nothing except vague, inchoate sensations. However, those sensations permit your body to regulate precisely its heart, breathing, blood pressure, and so on, and they enable you to be aroused easily.

---

*These states are usually called wakefulness, "rapid-eye-movement (REM) sleep," and "non-rapid-eye-movement (NREM) sleep."[3] Yet eye movements do not form fundamental differences between waking and sleep; they are merely insignificant signs of far more important neurological goings-on. Nor have they anything to do with consciousness, which is the indirect subject of much research into sleep. Characterizing sleep (and by indirection, consciousness) in this way is like characterizing animals not by their biological differences, but according to the lengths of their tails.

Sleeping and Consciousness: Newborns

In adults, sleep and unconsciousness are both caused by the brain's organized shuttings down for bodily maintenance and repair. However, the newborn's brain is not organized like the adult's, for organization comes from physical maturation and experience. Because the newborn's shuttings down are organized less and differently than the adult's, his sleep and waking are also organized less and differently, and his states of consciousness differ.

Many researchers have made extensive, detailed, systematic observations of babies as they lay sleeping and awake throughout the day. Most notable among these are Evelyn Thoman of the University of Connecticut, Arthur Parmelee of the University of California at Los Angeles, and Heinz Prechtl of the University of Groningen, in the Netherlands.[5] They have found not discrete categories of behavior but a continuum. Researchers differ about just where this continuum should be divided and subdivided, and about how to name the divisions; but they all agree that newborns show three archetypical states of sleeping and waking (plus crying, which we shall discuss later). These are:

Waking. The newborn cannot use his eyes and his muscles at the same time, so while he is awake either he looks at the world and attends to what he sees, or he moves and stops attending. While he is looking, his eyes are bright and shining, and dart about frequently under good control. He lies quietly with his face relaxed, and does not move except to shift his arms and legs a bit. On the other hand, while the newborn is moving, his eyes are open but seem dull and unfocused. He seems to be staring into space. Much of the time that he is awake, he squirms, moving his arms, legs, fingers, hands, feet, toes, and head, sometimes singly, sometimes simultaneously, and always awkwardly, without coordination. He may moan, grunt, or whimper. His skin is flushed and his breathing is fast and irregular, as though he is exercising fairly hard—which he is.

Active Sleep. The baby's eyes are closed yet move frequently, synchronously, and periodically, with both slow, rolling motions and rapid jerks. Sometimes his eyes move like this while they are halfway open, so you can see them: they look bizarre. His muscles

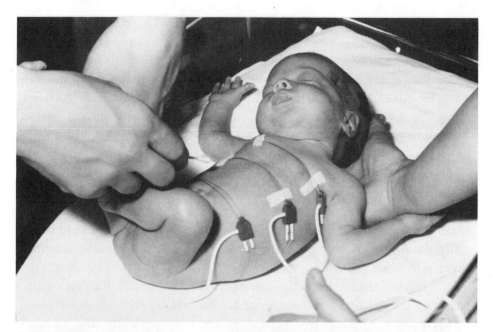

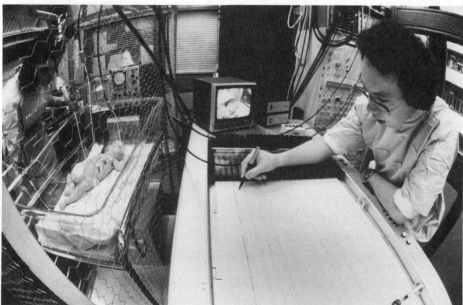

Learning what a baby's body does while he sleeps. ABOVE: To record his breathing, researchers strap on sensors that detect when his chest and abdomen are expanding and contracting. BELOW: While he sleeps, these sensors print out a record of every breath, while other sensors in the mattress record his movements. The television camera trained on the baby's face lets the researcher see when he twitches, grimaces, and moves his eyes. Photographed in the laboratory of Hans Daniëls at the Catholic University of Louvain in Belgium.

are relatively flaccid, yet he will spasmodically twitch, kick, writhe, smile, or frown, as though he is undergoing a seizure (which he is not). His heartbeat is irregular and his skin may become flushed. He breathes shallowly, quickly, irregularly, and ineffectually, contracting his rib cage with each breath. He may occasionally stop breathing for ten seconds or more. The slightest noise or touch may awaken him, even just adjusting his blanket.

Quiet Sleep. The baby lies still with his eyes closed and face relaxed, the picture of peace. His breathing and his pulse are slow and regular. His muscles are but slightly flaccid—less flaccid than during active sleep—yet he rarely moves. Occasionally he moves his mouth regularly and rhythmically, as though he were sucking on a nipple. Almost nothing will wake him up: he will move after a noise yet will remain asleep.

During these states the newborn behaves much like an adult during the various adult stages of consciousness that we described. However, the newborn's behaviors are not so clearly and neatly bundled together as the adult's, which shows that the neurological basis of these states is less organized. The newborn's quiet sleep is punctuated by frequent, massive, spasmodic jerks of his entire body, followed by bouts of disturbed breathing and a pounding heart. During active sleep, his muscle tone is relatively weak, but it is never so weak as the adult's becomes. Behaviors of the different states are far more likely to intermix.* And the states follow one another less predictably than they do in adults.[8]

Apparently, within the newborn's brain, the neural networks are not sufficiently organized to allow the midbrain to switch cortical circuits on and off *en masse* in the orderly adult fashion. Moreover, in the newborn, those waking behaviors whose disappearance marks the appearance of sleep involve but little of the cortex. The newborn's cortex is active, but it controls little of his behavior or

---

*An interesting example of the intermixing of states is penile erections. Men sustain whole or partial erections during nearly all of that portion of sleep during which their consciousness is severed. In contrast, newborn boys sustain partial erections during only two-fifths of their active sleep, but also during much of the time they are sleeping quietly or crying.[6]

Because newborn boys do sustain partial erections, many people believe that babies derive pleasure from genital stimulation from birth. There is no evidence for this. When boys are permitted to lie naked, they do not seem to discover their genitals until about six months of age, and then they play with them no more often than they play with their feet or their ears. Nor do they show any difference in facial expression when playing with their genitals or their feet.[7]

perception.[9] Almost all of his actions are reflexive kinds of action controlled by various parts of the midbrain. Thus these behaviors can be quelled, and the newborn will fall asleep, without involving or affecting the cortex at all.

The implications of this are profound. While *you* sleep, the midbrain shuts off many connections with the cortex. Consciousness lies in these connections, so you lose much consciousness. A newborn has little functioning cortex, so he is never so conscious as you are while you are awake. On the other hand, while the newborn sleeps, most, if not all, of those connections continue to be made. Thus a newborn retains more of his waking consciousness, if not all of it, all the while he is asleep.

The Electroencephalogram

Confirmation of this comes from studying the electrical activity of the newborn's brain. We have alluded to these "brain waves" several times before, and we shall encounter them often later. Let us take a paragraph to see what they are.

When a single nerve cell (a *neuron*) "fires," it produces electricity—first a quick negative burst, then immediately a slower, weaker, positive burst while it "resets." These bursts are only thousandths of a volt, and they last only thousandths of a second; but within the brain, millions of neurons fire every second, and their combined output forms a continuous, fluctuating electrical signal strong enough to be picked up by electrodes placed on the scalp. The signal picked up by these electrodes can be amplified, then fed into an electromagnet that is adjacent to a magnetized pen. The electromagnet pulls and pushes the pen from one side to the other in proportion to the signal; and as the pen moves, it draws a line on a moving sheet of paper. This forms a continuous graph of the brain's electrical activity, an electroencephalogram, or EEG.[10] A typical study involves recording from six to ten different parts of the scalp.

When leafing through EEGs recorded like this, it becomes obvious that the newborn's intracortical activity never flattens as ours does when our consciousness becomes suppressed. It sometimes lessens a little while he is sleeping quietly, but not much.[11] Awake or asleep, a newborn's cortex is active. His consciousness seems never to be suppressed.

Nor does his consciousness seem ever to be severed. This we can see from studies that have attempted to decode the newborn's EEG by noting changes in it evoked by flashing a light, or making a noise, or tapping the baby. If you do this once, you will see nothing, for the brain's overall activity masks responses to individual stimuli, just as the massed noises of a crowd mask individual voices. However, if you flash the light fifty or one hundred times, then a computer can add together just the few seconds of EEG following each flash, setting each signal on top of the ones that came earlier. Among these summed signals, those portions synchronized with the lights (and hence evoked by the lights) will reinforce each other, while those portions unsynchronized with the lights (and hence not evoked by them) will tend to cancel each other, negative fluctuations canceling positive. Thus the response evoked by the light will stand out as a measurable, *visually evoked response.* Similarly, clicking castanets fifty times will evoke a measurable *auditorially evoked response;* and tapping the skin fifty times will evoke a measurable *somatosensorially evoked response.* If all other things are equal, larger evoked responses indicate more extensive neural processing than smaller evoked responses.

In adults, lights, clicks, and taps all evoke large responses during full and suppressed consciousness, but they evoke only small responses during severed consciousness. This is one demonstration that many sensory circuits are cut during severed consciousness, yet function during other states. However, in the newborn, more or less comparable responses are evoked whether the baby is awake or sound asleep, and whether he is sleeping quietly or sleeping actively. This holds true for visually evoked responses, for auditorially evoked responses, and for somatosensorially evoked responses.[12] Hence it is very likely that a newborn's sensory circuits are connected and functioning twenty-four hours per day.

Since the newborn's cortex is never cut off from sensation, and since the newborn's cortical activity is never suppressed, the newborn's overall EEG ought to be similar during all three states. It is. EEGs recorded during wakefulness and active sleep are almost indistinguishable from each other, and those recorded during quiet

sleep would be indistinguishable too, were it not for some spasmodic bursts of firing.[13] In contrast, marked differences among the
EEGs are recorded during the three analogous adult states.

In sum, then, a newborn's sensory systems are connected
twenty-four hours per day, and his intracortical activity is maintained twenty-four hours per day. For these to happen, his midbrain
must interact with his cortex twenty-four hours per day. In these
interactions lies consciousness, so a newborn is conscious twenty-
four hours per day—although not so conscious as an adult who is
awake, since the newborn's cortex is still immature. Thus the baby
can learn while he is asleep—learn to recognize a story read to him
repeatedly, learn to expect the chiming of a clock, learn to expect
to be fed. To a newborn, sleep is not a lessening or change of
consciousness; it is merely muscular relaxation.

Energy and Sensation

This presents us with the question of just what the newborn is
conscious of. We shall answer this throughout the rest of the book,
dealing with one sensory system at a time; but here we would like
to consider a factor common to all sensory systems: energy. All
sensations and all learning start when energy from outside the body
impinges upon the nervous system. This energy takes different
forms—light, heat, pressure, vibration—but since it is all energy
impinging upon a physical system, the system reacts to it according
to the laws of physics. Because of this, we can examine the nervous
system like engineers. Our approach will be unorthodox, and it may
sound cold and strange at times; but it will provide an unusually
revealing view of the newborn's world.

A neuron fires when an impulse of energy jolts it hard enough
to force some electrically charged atoms—ions—through the membrane that sheathes the neuron. This impulse may be a sudden
increase in energy, or a sudden withdrawal; and it may be electromagnetic, thermal, inertial, electrical, vibrational, gravitational, or
chemical: any form of energy can set off any neuron, if it is strong
enough to break the ionic equilibrium. (That is why a punch in the

nose makes you see stars: the force fires sensory neurons within the eye.) However, most neurons are formed in ways and located in places that leave them more sensitive to one form of energy than to others—and more sensitive to one quantity of energy as well.[14]

The movement of ions in response to this energy forms a pulse of electricity—a burst of energy that forces adjacent ions through the membrane in turn, beginning an amplifying chain reaction that spreads along the entire cell and ripples in different forms through and around the cell, causing numerous chemical changes that carry the wave across the sea of molecules between cells, to fire more neurons. After the wave of energy passes, everything usually swings back to the way it was before; but if waves of energy pass repeatedly through the same chemical structures, they gradually change the neurochemical topography, forming neurochemical channels. These channels organize the flow of neural energy into distinct sensations and perceptions. Adults have extensive networks of these channels, so we can handle energy from a vast number of sensory neurons and organize it into many clear sensations simultaneously. However, the newborn has had little experience, so the neurochemical channels he has formed are few and ill-graved. As a result, his sensations are less distinct than ours.

We can see this in a fascinating study of the visually evoked response by Robert Hoffmann of Carleton University in Ottawa.[15] As a baby lay nursing on a bottle in his mother's arms and facing a display panel, Hoffmann flashed a light through one of four translucent panels: either a large gray square or a black-and-white checkerboard formed from two-inch, half-inch, or quarter-inch squares. The eye's sensory neurons are distributed anatomically and organized neurochemically into a complex structure that causes each of these stimuli to fire a different set of neurons. Hoffmann showed each stimulus forty times to babies between one and three months old, while recording EEGs from directly over the visual cortex and from three areas far removed from the visual cortex.

One-fifth of a second after the flash of light, the visual cortex produced a large, positive wave. This wave was recorded only over the visual cortex. It represented the visual sensation itself: the sight of squares of light and dark. Since the eyes would have sent out stronger signals in response to one stimulus than to another, this initial wave should have been stronger in response to one stimulus than to another; and indeed, Hoffmann found this among the more mature babies.[16] But in the others, each stimulus evoked a similar response. In these less mature babies, the visual cortex initially detected no differences among the stimuli. To these babies the initial sensation—the sight of squares of light—seemed always the same.

This sounds strange—and also paradoxical, for those babies could certainly distinguish among those different stimuli. Six-week-olds will consistently look longer at any of those checkerboards than at the plain gray square, and they will look longest of all at the checkerboard formed by two-inch checks. Hoffmann knew this from other studies: that is why he selected those particular sizes of check.

Synesthesia

To resolve this paradox—and to lead us into territory stranger still—let us examine the later waves of the visually evoked responses that Hoffmann recorded. These waves came through all four EEG electrodes: they welled up from all over the cortex. They were formed by energy from the eyes that was channeled throughout (and amplified by) the brain, where it would impinge upon, and mix with, energy flowing through other neuronal channels. Such impingement is the stuff of thought—not just verbal thought, but all associations, associations both meaningful and confused.

Each of Hoffmann's stimuli evoked these later waves to a different degree. This showed that all of the babies did indeed perceive the stimuli differently—but these differences came not from the direct sensations; these differences came from the impingement of varying amounts of visual energy upon nonvisual areas of the brain. There energy from the eyes might mix with energy from the ears to produce vague sounds; or it might mix with energy innervating muscles to cause a twitch—which would in turn fire sensory neurons within those muscles, causing the sensation of movement. The amount of mixing depends on the amount of energy entering the nervous system. This total amount of energy added to the nervous system is a prime determinant of a newborn baby's perceptions.

As adults, we never equate sounds with light, for our sensory channels are so well developed that our initial sensations are clear and predominant. The very notion seems bizarre, as David Lewkowicz and Gerald Turkewitz found at New York's Albert Einstein College of Medicine, when they asked adults to adjust the loudness of a loudspeaker to make it equal the brilliance of a light.[17] Yet the adults agreed remarkably closely on one level of noise that seemed as intense as the light. And a group of twenty-eight three- to four-week-olds agreed with them. Lewkowicz and Turkewitz switched on the light repeatedly while checking the babies' pulse; then they substituted a burst of noise for one of the flashes. One level of noise caused little reaction: the level that adults had decided was equivalent to the light. Every other level caused a marked quickening of the pulse, a quickening proportionate to how much more or less intense the sound was than the matching sound. Then, to make sure that this was not just a coincidence, Lewkowicz and Turkewitz repeated the study with different babies and brighter lights. These babies equated brighter lights with louder sounds.

This kind of confusion of senses is called synesthesia. It lingers into maturity in a very small proportion of people, notably the composers Rimsky-Korsakov, Scriabin, Messiaen,[18] and an anonymous Russian called S, who was studied for almost thirty years by the Soviet psychologist Aleksandr Luria.[19] Within S's brain, energy from every sensory system impinged markedly on every other. A loud, high-pitched oscillation "looks something like fireworks tinged with a pink-red hue. The strip of color feels rough and unpleasant, and it has an ugly taste—rather like that of a briny pickle. . . . You could hurt your hand on this."[20] A saw-toothed figure "is a vowel sound, but it also resembles the sound *r*—not a pure *r* though. . . . If the line goes up, I experience a sound, but if it moves in the reverse direction, it no longer comes through as a sound but as some sort of wooden hook for a yoke."[21] The numeral 8 "somehow has a naive quality, it's milky blue like lime."[22]

Usually when S's sensory systems impinged upon one another, the impingements formed specific, distinct perceptions—but then, S was adult, so he had developed a full adult complement of neuro-

nal channels. (Indeed he had developed an abnormally full complement of neuronal channels: his memory was so extraordinary that
he earned his living by exhibiting it on the stage in the Soviet
equivalent of vaudeville.) But sometimes S encountered stimuli that
he had never experienced before, and with little inherent meaning—
"isolated sounds, nonsense syllables, or words he was not familiar
with." These "evoked some visual impression such as 'puffs of
steam,' 'splashes,' 'smooth or broken lines'; sometimes they also
produced a sensation of taste, at other times a sensation of touch,
of his having come into contact with something he would describe
as 'prickly,' 'smooth,' or 'rough.' "[23] This is how a newborn's synesthesia would feel. Moreover, as we saw earlier, the diffuse energy
causing this can also impinge upon circuits that are not sensory at
all—circuits that activate muscles. Thus if you turn up the radio, the
sudden increase in sound can bend a newborn's knee.[24]

Optimal Stimulation

Energy from the world impinges upon the nervous system, rattles
around within it through chains of chemical reactions, and causes
sensations and perceptions in the process. What then? Since this
energy cannot be destroyed, it must ultimately be applied by the
nervous system to other purposes—to stimulating muscles and to
the nervous system's physical maintenance. This energy is available
to the nervous system constantly; so over the evolutionary eons, the
nervous system has not only adapted to it, it has become partially
dependent on it. For this reason, a kitten raised in the dark will grow
up largely blind.[25]

Depending on the individual nervous system's inheritance, age,
and experience, some one range of stimulation will develop and
maintain neural functioning most efficiently.[26] Within a species,
any individual that can coordinate its nervous system and muscles
to seek this optimal level has an advantage in survival; so this ability
has evolved in a number of species, including man. We do not notice
this ability in ourselves, for our everyday activities are complicated
by so many other factors; yet still, people who thrive on the stimu-

lation of cities seek out cities, and people who function best in quiet seek the countryside.

In contrast, newborns exercise this skill constantly, in the most trivial of decisions. Thus in another study, Lewkowicz and Turkewitz found that eleven- to forty-eight-hour-old babies would look longer at a middling-bright object than at a more dim or brilliant one. On the other hand, if before they were given the choice they had been stimulated by a burst of noise, then they looked longest at the dimmest object.[27] Thus the babies combined their sensations and sought a middling level of total stimulation.

Similarly, a newborn will look longest at checkerboards with a middling number of checks or at a light flashing at a middling rate; and suck longest on a middling-sweet sugar-nipple; and extend his fingers most toward a middling-loud sound; and, in general, extend his limbs toward gentle stimuli as if to embrace them, but flex his limbs away from more powerful stimuli.[28]

However, when a newborn seeks an optimal level of stimulation, his actions do not look like the actions of an adult, or even of a four-month-old (except for the sucking). They look more like the actions of a baby born with no cortex.[29] When the newborn looks at something, his eyes make minuscule movements over one part of it instead of ranging widely across and around it.[30] When he turns his head, he turns it slowly, after a delay of several seconds, like the comedian Jack Benny (we shall discuss this at greater length in chapter 7). And extensions and flexions of his limbs are ineffectually coordinated; they are not effective reachings-out or pullings-away.[31] In sum, these are not voluntary actions controlled by the cortex; they are the coarse, reflexive actions controlled by the midbrain—the same actions that the newborn's midbrain shuts off to form sleep. Hence sleep might be more than merely muscular rest and rehabilitation: it might be a way that the newborn controls from one minute to the next how much energy his nervous system takes in.

Certainly sleep does reduce stimulation. It reduces light, since the eyes close at least partially during active sleep and close wholly during quiet sleep. It reduces the number of impacts against his skin, since the baby moves less during sleep, especially during quiet sleep. Also, since he moves less, fewer forces are applied to the neurons of the inner ear that sense changes in acceleration and position; and fewer forces are applied to the sensory neurons within the joints and muscles that sense the movement of limbs. The baby vocalizes less while asleep, so the sonic energy reaching his ears is reduced. And when the baby closes his eyes and stops moving and vocalizing, his parents are less likely to rock him, feed him, talk to him, dandle him, and otherwise stimulate him. In these and other ways, the muscular enervations of falling asleep provide the mid-brain with powerful means of reducing the amount of energy impinging upon the nervous system; and conversely, the muscular innervations of awakening provide powerful means of increasing this energy.

To see if the newborn uses sleep and waking to control his stimulation, we looked at over one hundred studies of the effects on the baby's waking or sleeping of changes of stimulation. Many studies examined momentary changes in stimulation: banging a tin can, flicking the baby's feet, dropping sweetened water on his tongue, tickling him, switching lights on or off, wrapping him in swaddling cloths (or unwrapping him), and so on. All of these caused an immediate increase in activity—the kind of increase that comes with the adrenaline reaction to surprise.[32] Some fifty studies examined prolonged, moderate changes in stimulation; and all of them found that *more* stimulation led to *less* activity, and vice versa. Rocking, noise, light, or heat—reducing any of these tends to change behavior from sleeping quietly through sleeping actively toward awakening and ultimately crying. On the other hand, increasing any of these (or keeping the baby swaddled,* or holding a pacifier in his mouth) tends to quiet the baby if he is crying, or put him to sleep, or cause him to shift from active sleep to quiet sleep.[33] Up to a point, the more intense that the continuous stimula-

---

*Many people have wondered why swaddling is so effective at keeping a newborn quiet. One common explanation is that it simulates the baby's experience in the womb. Yet swaddling is much more restrictive than the womb, for even at the end of term the fetus is able to move his arms and legs. We think the most sensible explanation lies with the amount of energy that swaddling applies to the nervous system. As you wrap the baby you suddenly increase the amount of stimulation applied to his skin, so you arouse him. But after he is wrapped, the continuous pressure of the wrappings, plus the heat of his body retained by the wrappings, maintain a high level of tactile stimulation. This prolonged stimulation causes him to fall asleep. Once he is asleep, the wrappings prevent him from awakening himself through sudden movements, so he sleeps for a long time. Note that if you swaddle him loosely (in a way that more closely apes the womb), he will either remain awake or he will wake himself up shortly after he falls asleep. For then, although the wrappings increase the overall level of stimulation, they do not prevent him from thrashing about: those movements apply *sudden* changes in stimulation to his skin, so they arouse him.

tion is, the greater is the change in activity: louder sounds are more pacifying than softer sounds, and so are brighter lights and faster rocking.[34] And as we would expect from the newborn's synesthesia, a moderately intense light combined with a moderately intense sound is a more effective pacifier than either one alone.[35]

This is probably why newborns sleep more during the day than at night:[36] because the day presents more stimulation. It also explains why amplified heartbeats can put a baby to sleep—or wake him up, if they are sudden and intense enough. For as we said, stimulation quiets a baby only up to a point; excessive stimulation will obviously set him to crying, and will keep him crying until it is removed. This is a reflex that helps him to survive. Excessive stimulation can come from one intense source; but since the nervous system combines energy from all sources, excessive stimulation can also come from several concurrent, moderate stimuli. Then the baby may cry and cry and cry, yet be neither hungry, nor thirsty, nor cold, nor hurt, nor discomfited in any other obvious way. This is frustrating, especially because it is most likely to happen in the late afternoon and early evening, after a parent has come home tired from work, expecting to enjoy the baby. When this happens you can pick the baby up, rock him and sing to him, yet he will cry all the more. Nothing will pacify him—unless you give up trying to calm him and just put him to bed, closing his door behind you. Then, eventually, he will quiet down and fall asleep.* This happens when energy pouring into his nervous system throughout the day accumulates faster than his nervous system can handle it. This excess energy can inundate the reflexive channels that coordinate the muscular contractions which form crying. Then the baby cries—and the racket he makes feeds back into his nervous system, stimulating him more. However, a newborn uses proportionately as much energy to cry as an adult uses to run; so if you stop stimulating him—if you put him to bed—then soon his excess nervous energy becomes depleted. And since his muscles are exhausted, he falls asleep.

Something analogous happens now and again with adults. You drive home from work during a heat wave. You are stinky, clammy, and feel pummeled by noise from the open windows of the car.

---

*As we explained previously, earlier in the day, before the baby has absorbed this excessive amount of stimulation, his parents' tactics of rocking, singing, and so on are likely to *help* the baby go to sleep because they overwhelm him enough that his body does the biological equivalent of pulling a fuse.[37]

Tremendous amounts of energy are impinging upon your nervous system, more than it can cope with. This energy dams up within you, making you tense and edgy. You pull into the driveway, walk in the front door, and are blasted by a rock band on the stereo. This is the last straw! You explode at your children and spouse. Once you start yelling, you continue until you get it out of your system. Finally you simmer down and sink, exhausted, onto the sofa to take a nap. In this situation, "getting it out of your system" means quite literally ridding your nervous system of excessive energy taken in through your sensory organs. Between you and the newborn there is only one difference: your mature cortex. This processes the energy thoroughly on its way into your brain, so it creates more distinct perceptions; and this also modulates your explosion, so instead of crying amorphously, you form more or less sensible speech. But the inchoate currents of sensation that you can feel underneath and through all this should differ little from some of the sensations of an overstimulated baby.

Regularity of Sleep

Although a newborn uses his sleep to control stimulation, he also uses sleep for bodily maintenance. His minute-to-minute variations in sleep and waking are superimposed upon the basic physiological cycles of his body's tissues. These cycles vary from baby to baby, but on the whole, during the first month of life they form a four-hour period that looks something like that depicted in figure 4.1.[38]

Babies show this cycling when they are less than ten hours old and have not yet been fed, so it does not derive from feeding schedules.[39] Nor has it any relation to the mother's biological cycles.[40] The baby's cycling is rooted in the baby's physiology— rooted so firmly that it is difficult to shift him from one state to another more than momentarily. He reacts to a disturbance readily enough, but then he goes right back to the state he was in before: if he falls asleep while nursing, you can jiggle him awake, but a few seconds later he will be back asleep.[41] It takes a prolonged change in stimulation, like a bath, to shift him into a different place in his

FIGURE 4.1
Four Hours of the Newborn's Day

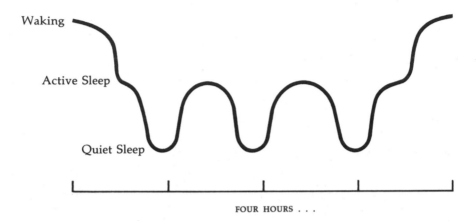

FOUR HOURS . . .

cycle. Prolonged changes occur sufficiently often that the period pictured in figure 4.1 varies considerably from one day to the next as well as from one baby to another. Rarely can a mother predict accurately when her baby will next wake up. Yet averaged over a number of days, the regularity is evident.

If this regularity is not evident, then something is likely to be wrong with the baby's physiology, either in his nervous system or elsewhere. As a result, the baby is likely to evince problems later. One of Evelyn Thoman's studies shows this chillingly.[42] Once a week, for five weeks, she and four colleagues observed for seven hours how long each of twenty-two seemingly normal babies slept quietly, slept actively, and so on. Next, they listed the babies according to how consistently each had slept from week to week. Finally, they followed the babies' mental and physical development for the next two and one-half years. The thirteen who had slept the most consistently seemed normal. Three of the next five proved to be developing slower than normal mentally. And of the least consistent four, one became hyperactive; one proved to be severely retarded from brain damage; one proved to have aplastic anemia; and the fourth died of "crib death" during his fourth month.* (In

---

*Babies whose mothers drank heavily during pregnancy, or whose mothers used methadone or heroin, also sleep abnormally. They have trouble shutting down enough to reach quiet sleep, and their active sleep is interrupted by frequent movement and awakenings, so that they do not show the normal, periodic cycles of sleeping and waking. These babies must feel fatigued and dazed by overstimulation.[43]

the United States, two babies in one thousand die of crib death during their second through fourth months. Nobody knows why. They just stop breathing in their sleep, as newborns commonly do—but then they do not resume again.*)

Learning While Asleep;
Forgetting While Awake

We began this chapter by speculating that the newborn must somehow learn about the world while he is asleep. Adults cannot do this, because while we sleep, our consciousness is either severed from our senses or suppressed. But since a newborn maintains consciousness during sleep, his sleeping need not impede his learning. In fact, *waking* is more likely to impede it.

Roderick Ashton, an Australian psychologist, learned this accidentally while studying other things about three-day-olds at the University of Sheffield.[45] Ashton placed babies in an incubator, sounded a noise for two seconds, and noted any movement or quickening of the pulse. Then he waited at least two minutes and repeated the process; and waited another two minutes, and so on, until he had sounded the noise six times. Ashton thought that by spacing the noises so far apart, the babies would not habituate to them; and indeed, while the babies were awake, they did not habituate: their movements and pulse increased after each blast of noise.[46] However, while the babies were asleep, they did habituate, no matter whether they were sleeping actively or sleeping quietly.

*Sudden infant death is more common in boys, at night, during the winter, and among babies who are recovering from a cold. It occurs between ages one and four months, when many physiological systems are changing dramatically: heart rate and a number of metabolic substances that increased during the first month are now decreasing; the baby is growing more rapidly; he is beginning to show voluntary behavior; and he is beginning to sleep much more at night than during the day. It is a time when his physiology is topsy-turvy.

Most of the information on sudden infant death comes from studies of the siblings of babies who died, in whom the risk is greatly increased (although it is still only about 2 percent) and from studies of "near-miss" babies who were resuscitated. These babies tend to wake up less during the night when sleeping normally and to be less likely to wake up when exposed to reduced oxygen or increased carbon dioxide. They also tend to stop breathing more often and for longer. Autopsies of babies who died of sudden infant death show that many were chronically hypoxic—short of oxygen. However, there are no signs of such abnormalities in about one-third of the babies who died; and in one study, the baby who had had the lowest rate of apnea (arrest of breathing) ultimately died of sudden infant death. So the cause of these deaths remains a mystery.[44]

Certainly this kind of habituation is but a rudimentary form of learning; yet it is the way a baby begins to perceive the consistencies that he must perceive if he is to understand anything of the world at all.

Of course, a newborn can habituate to things while he is awake. We shall see this repeatedly throughout this book. But he often habituates more readily while he is asleep.[47] For while a baby is awake, energy is likely to flood in faster than the nervous system can handle it, especially in the form of light impinging upon dark-adapted eyes. Indeed, after a newborn awakens, energy floods in so quickly that he falls asleep again within minutes. Such an inundation can easily overflow neurochemical channels and possibly erode them rather than create them. Since learning is the creation of these channels, his learning suffers.

When a newborn does habituate to something, he habituates to a combination of the original sensation plus the total amount of energy entering his nervous system. And when a newborn shifts from active sleep to quiet sleep or waking, this total amount of energy changes. Thus when a newborn habituates to something in one of these states and then shifts states, he loses this habituation. Several studies have demonstrated this formally,[48] and it was strikingly obvious recently in one of our own labs when workmen were remodeling some rooms nearby. Early in the morning, whenever the masonry saw began to cut, the babies in the newborn nursery started and shifted in their sleep. Then they habituated to the racket. Later, after they awoke, we brought them into our lab—and saw them fidget again after every cut. The implications of this are clear: each time a newborn wakes up or falls asleep—or shifts from quiet to active sleep—he suddenly begins again to perceive things that he had just stopped noticing. Each of the forty-five to fifty times a day that he shifts from state to state, he perceives much of his world anew. The noises around him suddenly sound different—and feel and smell different too. Every time he wakes up or falls asleep, he begins to learn about the world all over again.

How Sleep Develops

When a baby is first born, his body's clock does not run synchronously with the clock on the wall. This discrepancy causes the equivalent of jet lag—a jet lag that usually happens twice: after he emerges from the womb into the hospital, then after he leaves the hospital for home. We cannot isolate the jet lag of birth from the many other factors that occur when he is born, but all parents see and feel the baby's jet lag after he leaves the hospital: during his first day or two at home, he sleeps poorly and irregularly, and cries a lot. The baby has a still more difficult time fitting into his new family if he has spent his first days in the common sort of hospital nursery where babies are fed on schedule, and lights burn continuously day and night. Louis Sander and associates at Boston University compared eight babies who lived their first ten days in such a nursery to eight babies who lived their first ten days in ordinary hospital rooms, with surrogate mothers to care for them and feed them on demand.[49] (All the babies studied were up for adoption.) Within a few days of birth, those babies who were rooming in with surrogate mothers began to be quieter at night than during the day. On the other hand, those babies who stayed in the nursery were as active through the night as during the day until they left the hospital.

Between one and three months after birth, a baby's sleep, waking, and consciousness gradually begin to change. His four-hour cycling begins to shift toward twenty-four hours: he stays awake longer during the day and sleeps longer at night.[50] His parents begin to be able to predict when he will be asleep. During quiet sleep he stops twitching and making other spasmodic movements, and his EEG begins to slow and to show the forms seen during an adult's suppressed consciousness. He becomes less likely to react then to noises or to handling. By three months, he probably sleeps through much of the night, and his behavior and EEG during quiet sleep look substantially like those of the adult whose consciousness is suppressed.[51] His waking also changes then: his EEG develops a new rhythm ("alpha"), the rhythm that typifies the adult's waking EEG; and for the first time he becomes able to look at the world and move simultaneously. He can even reach out to grab an object, or kick the mobile he sees above his crib, then watch it move. Clearly, the cortex has now become involved in his waking activity.[52] Also by three months he has begun to respond to the *qualities* of a stimulus as well as to the quantity of energy that it imparts to the nervous system: for the first time he will look at his mother in preference to a stranger, even if she is farther away and hence is reflecting less light into his eye.[53] In short, by three months a baby's nervous system is beginning to become organized like the adult's. His consciousness is becoming more acute while he is awake and partially suppressed while he is asleep.

However, throughout twenty-four hours the three-month-old still sleeps every bit as much as the newborn; his EEG during active sleep is still much like the newborn's; and his visually evoked responses are still the same while he is asleep as they are while he is awake.[54] He will still start when you talk to him while he is sleeping. The three-month-old's consciousness seems not yet to be severed from his senses.

This changes only gradually through the next six months; but when he is around nine months old the baby begins to take on a wholly different aspect. During active sleep, his EEG, behavior, and visually evoked responses begin to look like those of an adult whose consciousness is severed.[55] His sleep becomes harder to disturb. Now, too, his periods of active sleep are much shorter toward the beginning of the night than toward the end, like the adult's periods of severed consciousness.[56] For the first time he begins to sleep less than he did as a newborn.[57] We shall see in chapters 9 and 10 that at this time he experiences many other profound changes as well, changes more profound than any he will experience again in his life—changes that allow him to perceive our adult world. For the first time he begins to develop adult consciousness, and with it adult waking and sleep.

Yet even then he does not understand sleep and waking as adults do. For although he probably dreams like us, he does not distinguish dreaming from waking. Even a three-year-old does not make this distinction: he may awaken puzzled that you are not crying, because he just saw a dog bite you. Not until age five or six does a child begin to understand that his consciousness while dreaming is severed from reality.[58]

5

A Question of Taste

THE WEEK-OLD BABY nursing on his mother's breast looks utterly pleased, quite the hedonist. Yet just minutes earlier he was crying in full voice, as though he were being driven to eat. The abruptness of this change makes us wonder whether a baby is indeed the hedonist that he looks, or whether he is merely a human machine that squeaks and cries when insufficiently greased by food.

Every new mother realizes quickly that her newborn baby does not eat automatically. He can suck as soon as he is born, of course; but he cannot draw anything from the breast then, for he sucks in short bursts with pauses between each pair of bursts.[1] Sucking like this on the breast is as ineffective as trying to suck soda through a straw in short bursts: the vacuum collapses with each pause, so that nothing comes out. Moreover, nursing involves three coordinated actions: (1) squeezing milk from the breast tissue into the nipple, (2) sucking milk from the nipple into the mouth, then (3) swallowing. A newborn baby cannot coordinate these actions efficiently. He needs hours, if not days, of practice, and may have trouble even then.[2] He may squeeze without sucking, or suck without swallowing; he may keep his mouth open so that he sucks in air while milk seeps out; he may lose the nipple or suck on a finger; or he may turn away or fall asleep. The baby's inability to suck efficiently makes nursing him on the breast difficult for the first few days. Nursing on a bottle is easier because milk flows into the nipple on its own.

Also unlike a machine, the newborn is a little lazy. Breast tissue has the texture of a sponge. When the breast is full, it is saturated so thoroughly that milk comes out on its own. But when the breast is partially empty, the milk must be sucked out, and the emptier it is, the more effort this takes.[3] Moreover, the milk that comes out readily is relatively thin: richer, thicker milk is less likely to run out on its own, and is more difficult to extract.[4] This further increases the effort required of the baby. The actual amounts of force that are required vary greatly from one mother to the next and from one day to the next, but are low enough that the youngest baby can handle them: if you let a baby nurse for ten minutes on one breast, then take him off it and put him back on, he will resume nursing.[5] But he will continue for only a short time. He does not stop then because he is tired: if you take him off the breast and give him a pacifier— which resists his efforts infinitely harder than his mother's "empty" breast—then he will continue to suck indefinitely.[6] Nor does he stop because he is full: he will nurse at full tilt on the other breast.[7] Nor does he stop because he dislikes the richness of the milk that the breast yields after ten minutes: babies will drink whole bottlesful of that rich milk.[8] A baby stops nursing simply because he finds that the reward is not worth the effort.

This is an interesting paradox. The newborn will stop sucking on a breast because it becomes difficult to draw out milk—yet he will continue sucking on a pacifier through which it is impossible to draw milk. This would be peculiar behavior for either a hedonist or a machine. Clearly, the newborn is unlike either, all the while he is very like both.

The Sense of Taste

To illuminate this paradox, we must look at a baby's senses of taste and smell and at his sensation of hunger and satiety. Let us begin in Jerusalem at the Hebrew University, where Jacob Steiner has executed a fascinating series of studies on facial expressions in response to taste and smell. Steiner's studies were simple: he put a drop of some chemical on a baby's (or adult's or animal's) tongue or beneath the nose; he recorded the facial reaction on film; he analyzed the filmed reactions; then he related the chemicals to his analyses, to see which chemical caused what reaction.* The reactions proved to be surprisingly similar in adults and babies.[9]

Steiner started his work with adults. He noticed that when he gave people drops of various substances to taste, immediately they made some kind of face: sugar brought a slight smile; sour salt (citric acid) caused a pursing of the lips; quinine caused a foul grimace that looked like a presage to vomiting. The expression might be fleeting, but it would appear almost instantaneously, and the expression elicited by any one substance was always similar: it was recognizable in men or women of different age, from different cultures, with different amounts of education, no matter whether they were sick or well. This led him to hypothesize that some facial expressions in response to tastes are universal, and hence innate.

To confirm this, Steiner tested 175 newborn babies much as he tested adults, including 75 babies who were so young that they had never yet been nursed or fed.[10] Those babies reacted much like the adults—except the babies' reactions were anything but fleeting. Drops of sugared water caused the babies to break slowly into a slight, lingering smile something like the Mona Lisa's, and induced bursts of "joyful, loud" sucking, with the babies often licking their lips. Citric acid brought a long-lasting pucker to their lips. And quinine made them open their mouths into a contorted grimace, and often retch, in a "dramatic, violent" reaction. You can see typical reactions from the photographs on page 80; or try a drop of vinegar

*Note that Steiner analyzed the film without knowing which chemical was being tested. Although this is a small detail, it is of considerable importance, for if Steiner had known which chemical was being tested, then his analyses could not have been so objective. This is typical of the care Steiner took in designing these studies. One can pick a few nits here and there in Steiner's work, as one can in anybody's; but by and large it is a model of what science ought to be but rarely is. In psychology—indeed, in any field of science—broad findings are almost always tenuously proved, while "solid" findings are usually minutiae. This tendency is built into the scientific approach; for the larger the ballfield in which a scientist plays, the harder it is to cover every base. Modern technology has exaggerated this difficulty: it has become difficult to cover the bases in even sand-lot leagues without vast sums of money for equipment. By North American standards, Steiner has had barely the resources of a high school science lab, yet he has managed to produce work that is a rare combination of solidity and scope.

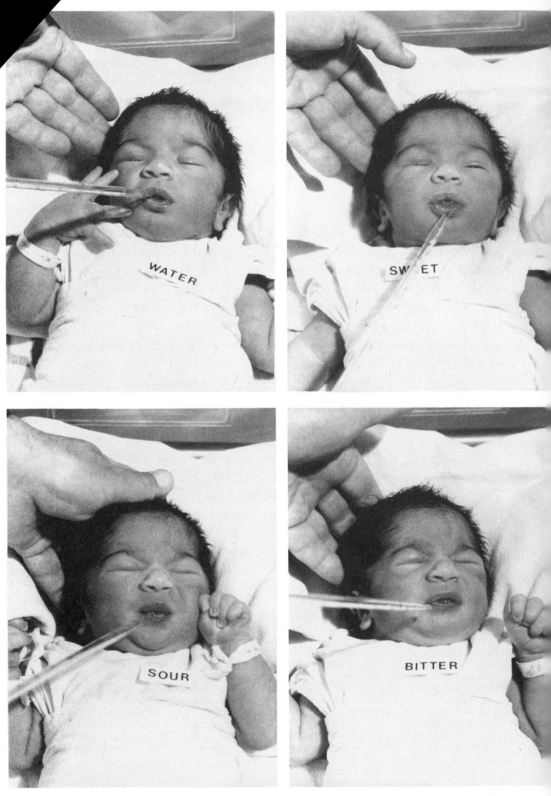

This baby is only a few hours old and has never tasted milk. He is showing for the camera that a newborn reacts to tastes much like an adult. This is a demonstration by Jacob Steiner of his work at the Hebrew University of Jerusalem.

on your own baby's tongue, then a drop of corn syrup. In a later study with Judith Ganchrow and Munif Daher, Steiner also found that increasing the concentration of sugar or urea (a bitter substance that is the chief constituent of urine) increased the intensity of the babies' expressions.[11]

This is clear evidence that the newborn differentiates among some tastes like an adult. However, Steiner's work tells us nothing about saltiness, for neither adults nor babies make faces in response to saltiness. We do know that, at some level, the newborn does sense saltiness; for at Brown University, Charles Crook found that two- to three-day-olds suck differently if you place a drop of salt-water on their tongue than if you place a drop of water on their tongue.[12] However, these babies' sensation of saltiness—and Steiner's babies' sensation of sweetness, sourness, and bitterness— may have been at such low neural levels that the babies were un-conscious of them. Indeed, Steiner found similar reactions in four newborns who were born with no functioning parts of the brain higher than the midbrain.[13] These reactions to tastes seem to be low-level, reflexive reactions akin to the jerk of your knee to a physician's hammer. Now it happens that you can feel the physi-cian's hammer instigate this reflex; yet if a comparable reflex is triggered from within your knee—if you have a bit of loose tissue inside that catches in the joint—then your knee may reflexively give way to avoid straining itself, yet you might not perceive anything wrong at all. As the possessor of a trick knee like this, one of the authors of this book can assure you that this phenomenon is not caused by any insensitivity of the knee to things inside it. It can hurt a lot. But it does not *necessarily* hurt; and that is the point here: the presence of a reflex like the baby's expressions does not *necessarily* indicate the presence of any conscious perception.

Moreover, we have evidence that the newborn does not react to tastes—in particular, to saltiness—as we do. Three newborns died in the Binghamton General Hospital in 1962 after being given for-mula accidently mixed with salt instead of sugar. They drank it contentedly until they literally drank themselves to death.[14]

The Perception of Flavor: Background

Clearly, something about the newborn's gustation differs from an adult's. To figure out what differs we shall need to leave Steiner temporarily. First we shall cover some background material on the perception of flavors; next we shall look at aspects of flavor other than taste; then we shall return to the newborn's sense of taste; and finally we shall fit all that we have learned together.

All of us were taught in school that flavors have little to do with taste; that we perceive flavors mostly through odors; and that tastes are restricted to sweetness, sourness, saltiness, and bitterness, intermixed to varying extents, but readily extricable from odors and extricable from each other, like the greens of a salad, by the discriminating palate of a gourmet or the discriminating tests of a psychologist. However, the perception of flavor is much more complicated than this. For the perception of taste is far more subtle than a simple salad tossed of mixed sensations. Tastes are subtle stews—*boeufs à la bourguignonne*—combining sweetness, sourness, saltiness, and bitterness into forms that usually differ substantially from their ingredients. In this way tastes are like colors, which are blended by the nervous system from four primary colors, red, green, yellow, and blue (for a discussion of primary colors, see the footnote on page 126). To say that sucrose (table sugar) and fructose (fruit sugar) taste the same but merely have different amounts of sweetness is like saying that brown and pink are similar in hue and differ merely in saturation. Moreover, opposite tastes can run into one another: extreme sweetness can taste bitter. Sweetness, sourness, saltiness, and bitterness do indeed function to some extent as primary sensations, and it will prove useful for us to deal with them as such. But they are actually far more.*

---

*One reason people believe that there exist only four tastes lies in an extensive literature of biased experiments. To avoid wasting time, psychologists and physiologists who study taste commonly pretest their human guinea pigs, to try to eliminate those with insensitive palates. Thus they ask, "Here is a substance: is it salty, sour, sweet, or bitter?" They select to study only those people who are willing to categorize what they taste like this—and who agree in their categorization with the experimenters. This is like studying the perception of colors by testing only people who might be willing to admit that yes, oranges can be described as either red or yellow, and who will agree with you that this one here is red.

Besides the senses of taste and smell, the senses of touch, temperature, hearing, and sight also contribute to our perception of flavors.[15] And quite as important as taste and smell is a third chemical sense, one that is usually ignored because it has no specialized organs of its own. This is our sense of chemical imbalance.

Innumerable things can cause chemical imbalances to occur in one part of the body or another. Many of these imbalances we sense unconsciously; yet others we perceive consciously, and we perceive these in a variety of ways, depending on the chemical and the part of the body it contacts. Acidity at the bottom of the esophagus feels like heartburn. Histamine within the skin (released in an allergic rash) feels itchy. Gaseous allyl disulphide, carried from onions into our eyes, makes us tear.

Gaseous allyl disulphide can also enter the nose through either the front or the rear (from the mouth); or it can touch the mouth and tongue. In these cases we perceive it as the sharpness of an onion. Other chemicals impinging on the nose and mouth cause us to perceive the heat of mustard and horseradish, the piquancy of garlic, and the raw edge of espresso.

Note that we are not talking now about the entire flavor of these foods; we are talking only about attributes that can be described as "heat" or "piquancy" or "rawness." Unlike the senses of smell and taste, this more general sense of chemical imbalance is not sufficient to let us distinguish one substance entering the mouth and nose from another. But it does add intensity to odors and tastes, and it sharpens flavors by its addition. When this sensory system's nerves are destroyed, odors seem less pungent.[16]

The sense of chemical imbalance differs from the senses of smell and taste in another way as well: the senses of smell and taste habituate to chemicals quickly, but the sense of chemical imbalance does not.[17] After you eat a bowl of hot chili, you habituate rapidly to the residue of tomato and beans left in your mouth, so that after a few minutes you neither smell nor taste it; but the residue of chili pepper continues to stimulate your sense of chemical imbalance, so that the heat of the chili lingers long after all smell and taste of it are gone.

For a baby to perceive flavors like an adult, his sense of taste, his sense of smell, and the oral and nasal portions of his sense of chemical imbalance must all be more or less adult.

The Sense of Chemical Imbalance

Within the nose and mouth, the sense of chemical imbalance is based on the undifferentiated endings* of the trigeminal nerve,[18] so physiologists call that portion of this sense the trigeminal system. It is difficult to isolate the trigeminal system for study, because within the mouth and nose, almost every chemical that stimulates it stimulates the sense of taste and/or smell as well. However, one class of chemical does allow us to see that the newborn's trigeminal system functions in some ways like the adult's. This class is the alcohols.

Molecules of one alcohol differ from molecules of another in the length of a chain of carbon atoms that forms an alcohol's backbone. Methanol has only one carbon atom; ethanol (vodka) has two; propanol has three; butanol has four; and so on. In adults, the shorter this chain is, the more concentrated the alcohol must be to stimulate the sense of smell. At relatively weak concentrations, all of these alcohols stimulate our sense of smell without stimulating the trigeminal system: their odor is fresh and medicinal. However, stronger concentrations begin to stimulate the trigeminal system, and soon the trigeminal system becomes predominant: then we feel a sharp pungency more than we smell an odor. Moreover, at these concentrations, shorter-chained alcohols feel sharper than longer-chained ones.

This holds for adults, and it seems to hold for two-day-old babies as well. At Brown University, Trygg Engen, William Cain, and Carolyn Rovee studied the reactions of sleeping babies to swabs

*The sense of chemical imbalance has not evolved so far that its receptors differ visibly from ordinary nerve endings, so its receptors are usually described as undifferentiated nerve endings. However, they actually differ widely in the chemicals to which they respond, and sets of "undifferentiated" nerve endings that are differentially sensitive to various chemicals are concentrated in different parts of the body. Thus, at a molecular level, these nerve endings are not undifferentiated at all; they are quite specialized.

of alcohol held beneath their nose.[19] The shorter the alcohol's chain of carbon atoms, the more strongly the alcohol had to be concentrated before the babies changed their rate of breathing or wriggled—yet when the alcohol was concentrated 100 percent, then the shorter the chain, the more responses the newborns made. In addition, when the alcohol was concentrated 100 percent, then the newborns began to habituate almost immediately to long-chained alcohols, just as adults do when we smell something—but they did not habituate readily to short-chained alcohols, again just like adults using their trigeminal system. In sum, the trigeminal system and the sense of smell seem to interact in newborns as they do in adults.[20]

The Sense of Smell

Since the newborn's sense of smell interacts with his trigeminal system in an adult way, we would expect him to smell everything more or less as we do. Up to a point, he does.

To see this, let us return to Steiner's work. Steiner asked a panel of adults to select, from among a large collection of food flavorings, those that had fresh "odors" and those that had rotten "odors."[21] (We are using quotation marks here to remind ourselves that in this context, "odors" come not from the sense of smell alone but from the sense of smell intermixed in varying and unknown amounts with the trigeminal system.) The adults said unanimously that rotting eggs and shrimp "smelled" foul; they found that a milky aroma like margarine was "acceptable and fairly pleasant"; and they found that banana, vanilla, chocolate, and, especially, honey were "pleasant" and "enjoyable." Next Steiner held swabs of these flavorings under the nose of babies—babies tested in the very first hours of life, before they had had any contact with food or with the odors of food. The babies grimaced while smelling the rotten flavorings just as they grimaced while tasting quinine, and they smiled while smelling the pleasant flavorings just as they smiled while tasting sugar. Among all of the flavorings, rotten eggs evoked the clearest response. Among the flavorings that adults found to be pleasant, the one they found most pleasant—honey—evoked the clearest positive responses from the babies as well.[22]

The similarities between adult and baby are so striking, it is tempting to conclude that both adult and baby perceive "odors" similarly. But this conclusion would be premature, for Steiner also found that a baby born with no functioning cortex reacted similarly.[23] As he points out, these reactions to "odors"—or more precisely, these reactions to chemicals borne upon the air—are analogous to the reactions of a housefly buzzing toward and away from different kinds of ordure. These reactions may indicate conscious perceptions, or they may not. From Steiner's work alone we cannot tell.

However, clearer evidence comes from a study by Aidan Macfarlane at Oxford.[24] Macfarlane tested whether a newborn would discriminate between, on the one hand, the smell of his mother and her milk, and on the other hand, the smell of another mother and her milk. The smells came from gauze pads that the mothers had kept within their brassieres to absorb any milk seeping out. Along one side of the baby's face, Macfarlane draped a pad from the baby's mother; along the other side he draped a pad from another mother. Thirty-two two-day-olds showed no sign of discriminating one pad from the other: roughly half of them turned toward each pad. However, more than two-thirds of the six-day-olds he tested turned toward their mother's pad, as did more than three-fourths of the eight- to ten-day-olds. Young babies prefer the familiar to the unfamiliar: here they recognized their mother's odor, and turned toward it. We cannot say from this that the two-day-olds did not distinguish between the two odors, for they may have realized that the odors were different yet not have learned to recognize one of them. There also may have been less of a difference in odor at two days, for many of the mothers might not yet have begun to produce enough milk to seep out. However, the older babies certainly did smell a difference—a difference that Macfarlane, when he smelled the pads himself, was unable to detect.

Now, we should not read too much into this. We cannot say that newborns are more sensitive to odors than adults, for we do not know whether Macfarlane was a representative adult. In any case, he probably could have learned to make the discrimination, given as much exposure to one of the odors as each baby had had: college students have no trouble recognizing the odors of classmates and members of their family, and mothers learn to recognize their baby's odor quite as their baby is learning to recognize theirs.[25] However, Macfarlane's study does make it look as though the newborn's sensitivity to smells is close to being adult.

Moreover, Macfarlane's babies did not just detect an odor, they *recognized* one. To recognize something requires high-level processing within the brain—some kind of conscious processing beyond the reflexlike processing of the midbrain. Thus when a newborn smiles or grimaces reflexively to an odor, he probably does perceive it as more or less pleasurable.

On the other hand, although the newborn is nearly as sensitive as the adult to odors and other chemically caused sensations in the nose, and although the newborn and adult would often agree in their assessment of pleasantness and unpleasantness, still, a newborn has less clear and distinct perceptions of odors. During the first day of life, this is simply because his nose is still clogged with amniotic fluid, like an adult whose nose is stuffed by a cold.[26] But more than this, an adult's perceptions are formed and clarified by decades of experience, while a newborn perceives odors with all the disorder and synesthesia with which he perceives everything else. His world smells to him much as our world smells to us, but he does not perceive odors as coming through his nose alone. He hears odors, and sees odors, and feels them too. His world is a mêlée of pungent aromas—and pungent sounds, and bitter-smelling sounds, and sweet-smelling sights, and sour-smelling pressures against the skin. If we could visit the newborn's world, we would think ourselves inside a hallucinogenic perfumery.

Within this perfumery, some odors come to stand out—those that are present most often: the odors of baby powder, his mother's body (if she breast-feeds her baby),[27] and dirty diapers. These odors may change their sound as the baby opens and closes his eyes; yet a constancy about them remains. This constancy he comes to recognize. Given the chance, he turns toward them, attracted to them as to islets of familiarity amidst a sea of chaos. This recognition is musk to the newborn baby. Within the newborn's world, it forms the finest perfume.

Taste and Flavor Concluded

Now we can return to the baby's sense of taste. When we left it, we had seen that at some level the newborn senses sweetness, sourness, bitterness, and saltiness, but that something about his reaction to saltiness differs from ours.

Much of this difference may be a carryover from the womb. Sodium is the most common chemical that causes the sensation of saltiness. From the taste buds' perspective, it is the active ingredient of table salt. Amniotic fluid contains a lot of sodium; so whenever the fetus has his mouth open, his mouth and tongue are bathed with sodium.[28] Thus his mouth and tongue become adapted to sodium—sufficiently adapted that his nervous system will confuse saltwater with saliva, allowing him to inhale saltwater as though it were air.[29] (This is not because he lacks the adult reflex that prevents us from inhaling while we drink: a newborn does not inhale milk or water.) Possibly because of this adaptation, the newborn's body maintains levels of sodium in his saliva that are two to three times the levels of sodium in the adult's saliva.[30] This distorts his sensation of saltiness.

If we assume that a newborn's sense of taste is adult, then we can see how this excess sodium would affect him by bathing an adult's tongue with similar concentrations of sodium. This has been done scientifically in the lab, but you can see the effect yourself by eating popcorn. You taste saltiness at first; but soon you get used to the saltiness, so to taste it anew you must either add more salt, or you must wash away the taste with a glass of water. This dilutes the sodium, leaving a slight but distinct sensation of sourness and bitterness. Alternatively, if you wash down the popcorn with tepid water to which you have added a minuscule amount of salt—a fraction of a pinch—then this minuscule increase of sodium makes the water taste slightly sweet.[31] (This is less noticeable with cold water, for cold numbs the sense of taste. Also, if your tapwater is heavily chlorinated, the chlorine may mask the sweetness. But you will find that a pinch of salt also sweetens beer.*)

---

*What is happening here? Each time you throw a handful of popcorn in your mouth, your saliva dissolves some of the popcorn and some of the salt you have sprinkled onto it,

If the newborn's sense of taste is fundamentally adult, then the sodium in his saliva should have a similar effect: he should need to take much more salt than you normally take to notice it; slightly salted water should taste sweet; and plain water should taste unpleasant. Babies act as though this is exactly the case. Young ones will rarely drink much water,[33] as though water tastes sour and/or bitter to them.

We cannot know whether a newborn experiences all tastes like an adult, but we can see that within his mouth the extremes— sweetness and bitterness—do seem to act and interact as they do in adults. Most adults prefer sweet drinks to water. Up to a point, the sweeter the drink is, the more we prefer it. Thus we prefer drinks concocted of the sweeter fructose (fruit sugar) or sucrose (table sugar) to the less sweet lactose (milk sugar) or glucose, when the sugars are mixed at comparable concentrations.[34] So, apparently, do newborns. At the University of Pennsylvania, Jeanette Desor, Owen Maller, and Robert Turner gave water and sugared water to 192 one- to three-and-one-half-day-olds.[35] During three-minute periods, the sweeter the sugar tasted to adults, or the more concentrated the sugar was, the more the babies drank.* Charles Crook then extended these findings at Brown University.[37] Crook tested only sucrose, but he tested higher concentrations than Desor, Maller, and Turner, and he used a much better test, a test that did not use ingestion as a measure of pleasure; for as we shall see, a newborn's sense of taste does not necessarily influence how much food he takes in. Crook's method was to place single drops of water or sugared water onto the baby's tongue, then to measure the duration of the baby's next burst of sucking. He found that the sugared water prolonged bursts of sucking—and up to a point, the higher the concentration of sugar, the more it prolonged the bursts. The

thereby bathing the taste buds covering your mouth and tongue with an assortment of chemicals other than those normally in your saliva, and/or chemicals in different concentrations. Taste buds are stalks of cells containing neurons whose structure makes them easily fired by the changes in energy accompanying these chemical changes. Any change will fire any of these neurons if the change is great enough, but the neurons are sufficiently different in structure that any one chemical change will fire some neurons more readily than others. Cold reduces the amount of energy impinging upon the neurons as heat, so greater concentrations of chemicals are required to fire them. What you taste depends on which neurons fire.[32]

*Many other studies report similar findings. In general, the sweeter a solution tastes to adults, the more of it a newborn drinks, the more frequently he sucks, the harder he presses his tongue against the sides of his mouth, the longer he pauses between sucks (as if to savor the solution), the faster his heart races, and the more widely he smiles.[36]

concentration that prolonged maximally the babies' sucking corresponds roughly to the concentration that adults find most pleasurable.[38] Finally, Robert Milstein at Yale confirmed this, and found that when he gave newborns plain water after sugared water, they sucked the least hard for water after the moderate concentrations.[39]* Apparently with babies as with adults, water tastes bitter after moderate sweetness.

The similarity between newborn and adult is so strong, we suspect that the newborn's primary tastes combine to form secondary tastes much as they do in the adult. Since the newborn's sense of smell and trigeminal system are roughly adult too, he probably perceives flavors to a certain extent like adults—adults who have just eaten salty food, like a bag of potato chips or popcorn. But like everything else in his world, flavors are affected by his synesthesia. He savors milk differently when his eyes are open or shut, when the radio switches from Tchaikovsky to news, when his mother is rocking or sitting still.

Moreover, a vast proportion of our adult perception of flavor is learned. Indeed, the bulk of it is learned. Although a baby resembles most adults by liking sweets and by disliking sour and bitter foods, still, many an adult enjoys a morning's eye-opener of grapefruit juice and black coffee. An adult can learn to enjoy whatever he wants to enjoy, even if it goes against some genetic disinclination—and he can learn to dislike asparagus for no good reason at all. In contrast, all a newborn knows is his inheritance. Sour smells and bitter medicine he finds repugnant; the sweetness of the breast or sugar he enjoys.

Hunger

Although a newborn savors food much like an adult, in other ways he reacts to it quite dissimilarly. Thus he will kill himself drinking saltwater, not gag. And although he dislikes sour and bitter flavors,

*It is intriguing that this was especially true of babies whose parents were obese. Fatter babies also showed a stronger sweet tooth: they sucked hardest for a high concentration of sugar (85 percent), while thinner babies sucked hardest for a lower concentration (40 percent).[40]

he will drink water fouled by sour salt or urea as readily as he will drink plain water (which also tastes sour and/or bitter to him because of the sodium in his saliva, but very much less so). A number of studies have found peculiarities like these, and many of these peculiarities are paradoxical. A one- to five-day-old will drink sour salt in water as readily as plain water, for instance—unless you add sugar to both. Then he will drink more of the plain water.[41]

Apparently, taste does not control ingestion in babies as it does in adults: babies will drink the foulest poison that may enter their mouth, even ammonia or lye. Of course, taste does sometimes affect what babies eat. As we have seen, the newborn has an adult sweet tooth. But by and large, what induces a newborn to eat is very different from what induces an adult to eat. This is especially true during the first few days of life. To a baby that young, the mixture of feelings that we know as hunger is unknown.

Physicians and physiologists used to think that our feelings of hunger come primarily from an insufficiency of food, and that they are caused by contractions of the stomach. However, neither is normally true. Any healthy adult can forgo a meal without creating a physiological insufficiency; and adults without stomachs experience normal hunger and have the normal ability to regulate their eating. Adults sense hunger not from any one physiological event but through a complicated, poorly understood, and variable confluence of physiological and environmental events that, they have learned, portend food. Consider what happens daily in the office, for instance. Several hours after you arrive, your stomach has emptied itself of breakfast; the caffeine from your morning's coffee has stopped stimulating your nervous system; the aroma of french fries wafts in through the window; people begin to leave their desks; a carillon chimes. The confluence of these events implies to the body that it is lunchtime, so you feel hungry. The significance of this confluence is learned.[42]

A newborn baby has learned nothing like this. He does not know enough to connect sensations from his stomach and ears and eyes and nose with food. He can have vague sensations of discomfort, but he feels nothing akin to what we know as hunger.

We can see from the newborn's stomach contractions how little he knows about food. Although stomach contractions do not cause sensations of hunger, they do tell us whether the body expects to receive food. In adults they are like salivation in reverse: a morsel of food in the mouth simultaneously starts salivation and calms the stomach. But this is not true of newborns. In 1917, at the Mayo Clinic, Rood Taylor studied babies' stomach contractions.[43] He inserted a tube through the mouth and down the esophagus into the stomach. (Babies less than three weeks old did not seem to mind the tube at all—as we would expect from our discussion in chapter 2 of the newborn's insensitivity to pain.) Then he blew up a small balloon inside the stomach and measured the pressure of the air that the balloon contained. Whenever the stomach contracted, it raised this air pressure. Taylor found that young babies' stomachs contract much more often than adults'—and in babies less than three weeks old, quite unlike adults, the stomach continues to contract even while food is in the mouth, until it actually reaches the stomach. The newborn's body does not yet know that milk in the mouth means food is coming.

Just as the newborn does not connect milk in the mouth with food in the stomach, neither does he associate sucking with milk. He sucks indiscriminately on everything he can get to his mouth, and not for a month will he begin to suck before a meal, in anticipation of it.[44]

Although the newborn's body undergoes many if not most of the physiological events surrounding the intake of food that an adult's body undergoes, these events are not so well coordinated as they are in adults, nor has his body had enough experience to interpret them the way adults do, as meaning "I am prepared for food, hence I am hungry." His stomach is unprepared for the onslaught of food, so he spits up.[45] He needs several weeks and hundreds of meals to tie his belly to the dinner bell.

For this reason, studies of newborns have found no relationship between how long it has been since the baby last ate and how much he eats; or between how much the baby last ate and when he awakens or "demands" to eat again; or between any behavior of the baby immediately before a meal and how much he eats.[46] Nor, during the first day or two of life, do babies cry for food. This last is impossible to prove, of course, but every nursing mother has seen evidence of it: the baby seems hardly to notice when he loses the breast. Additional evidence comes out *en passant* in study after study, even in studies claiming the opposite. For example, Dorothy Marquis at Yale claimed to find evidence that newborns cry if a meal is interrupted in midbottle; yet when we looked closely at her data, we noticed that seven of the nine babies she studied were so loath to cry, either before, during, or after a feeding, that their data ended up not figuring at all in the statistical analysis. Only two babies actually counted in Marquis's analysis—and they took at least seventy-five seconds to begin to cry after the bottle was removed, ten times as long as a one-month-old would have taken.[47]

We can see this as well in an oft-cited Swedish study by Ole Wasz-Höckert and associates.[48] These researchers executed an admirable, sophisticated analysis of the harmonic and melodic structures of babies' cries, including "hunger cries." However, they did not examine babies' cries first and then identify those slaked by milk and only milk, and call these hunger cries. Instead they *assumed* that newborns cry from hunger, and they assumed that in the absence of any obvious cause of discomfort, whenever babies cried four hours after feeding, they felt hungry (why not thirsty?). Yet when a newborn is crying four hours after feeding, he will usually stop if you merely pick him up and hold him, or if you give him a pacifier.[49] Hence, they wrote:

> It is not . . . possible to be certain that the cry is given entirely because of hunger. It might be that the baby wanted handling. . . . Although hunger cries were collected as early as 12 hours, *it is difficult at this time to be certain that the situation truly represents hunger.* Relatively few cries therefore have been collected in the first three days of life.[50] [Italics added.]

And these "hunger cries" after the first three days? In 1936 at the University of Iowa, Orbis Irwin wired a special crib to measure continuously how often four babies wriggled and squirmed during the first ten days after birth.[51] These babies were fed about every three hours, save for two feedings skipped overnight. By the second day they had learned this schedule and had begun to wriggle and squirm (and cry, we can certainly assume) around the time that they were due for their missed nighttime feedings. But then, a few minutes later, they calmed down. If their squirming had come from hunger, then they would have become hungrier and hungrier as the night passed without a feeding, so they would have squirmed ever more. Instead they calmed down just as if they had been fed. As we saw in chapter 4, a newborn moves and cries to control the amount of energy he takes in through his senses; so the rhythms of his movements and crying are bound to be controlled by the rhythms of his sensory stimulation. The rhythms of his sensory stimulation center around mealtimes. After the first few days of life, when babies begin to cry a little around mealtimes, that is the cause: the increase in sensory stimulation occurring around mealtimes. This changes completely by the end of the baby's first month, but during his first weeks of life his "hunger cries" have only an indirect connection with food. During his first month, he feels vaguely uncomfortable when mealtimes roll around because of the increased sensory stimulation occurring around them, but he does not yet feel hunger as we know it.

Why Babies Eat . . . and Stop Eating

If a newborn baby is not hungry, then why does he eat—and why does he stop eating? At first he eats merely because he is fed. Many parts of the newborn's body are wired by his nervous system to act reflexively—automatically—just as your leg is wired so that a tap on your knee makes you kick. If a newborn is awake, then when a finger (or his mother's nipple) touches his cheek, he turns toward it reflexively. When something presses his palm— like his mother's breast—then his mouth opens reflexively. When a nipple (or a pacifier) touches the inside of his mouth, then he sucks reflexively. And when milk (or anything else) touches the back of his mouth, he swallows reflexively.[52] He does none of this intentionally, just as you do not kick your leg intentionally when a physician taps your knee. Neither can he control what he is doing, just as you cannot control your leg. He does it like a machine. Like a turning, mouth-opening, sucking, and swallowing machine—albeit like an inefficient machine at first, as we have seen: a machine that works imperfectly and cannot yet extract significant amounts of fluid, but primarily collects what seeps out from the nipple on its own.

On the other hand, when the baby tastes what seeps out, he enjoys it. The flavor is sweet and pleasant.[53] Soon he discovers that certain manipulations of his lips and cheeks bring forth more of this sweetness. Thus within a day or two he learns to nurse. (During this time the mother's breasts produce a very thin milk in small quantities: its thinness facilitates the baby's learning to nurse by enabling him to extract milk more easily.)

But the end of a meal makes a more complicated story. As adults, we do not feel sated because our stomachs are full: we can stuff ourselves with roast beef until we feel as if we are ready to burst, yet still find room for dessert. Neither do we feel sated because we have taken a physiological superfluity of food: any food that we have just eaten is not yet in a form that is useful physiologically—and as soon as it is put into a useful form (when it is digested), we no longer feel sated. Feelings of satiety come instead from a confluence of physiological events involving food in the stomach, food in the intestines, and food's passing through the mouth. These three areas are tied together intimately: after a meal rich with butter and fat meat, a sweet pecan pie topped by whipped cream can actually turn bitter to the mouth—if you are not used to this kind of meal. On the other hand, if you are used to it, then your body prepares for it physiologically, so you are dissatisfied without it. In short, you feel sated with food only when you have eaten what your body, from experience, has learned to expect you to eat.[54] Since a newborn has no expectations about eating, he never feels sated as adults do.

More likely than not, during his first few days, a baby being breast-fed will stop nursing simply because he falls asleep: because the tactile stimulation of nursing has oversupplied his nervous system with energy, and because the effort of extraction fatigues him.[55] Bottle-fed babies are less likely to fall asleep because taking milk from a bottle is easier, although it still requires sufficient effort that their sucking slows down after a while, until they have rested while being burped.[56] Bottle-fed newborns stop almost solely when and because the bottle runs dry.

Of course, much of the time even a breast-fed newborn will

stop nursing before he falls asleep. He does this not by actively refusing the breast like a one-month-old, but by placidly withdrawing his head.[57] As we have seen, this is not because he feels sated. Neither is it because some physiological equivalent of a calorie counter tells him to stop: babies do not regulate their intake based on the richness of food until they become a month old. Until then, richer food merely makes them grow faster.[58] The newborn who withdraws from the breast does so, as we said at the beginning of this chapter, simply because he finds the reward not worth the effort.

We can see this from the pattern of his feeding. As we saw earlier, breast tissue is like a sponge. When the breast is full, milk drips out on its own; but when it is partially empty, the milk must be sucked out, and the emptier it is, the more effort this requires. As a result, when a newborn nurses on a breast, he takes half of what he will ultimately take from that breast in the first two minutes, and he takes 80 percent of the balance in the next two minutes. During the last 60 percent of his time on the breast he draws only 10 percent of the milk he takes in all.[59] As the flow of milk ebbs, he rests longer and more often between bursts of sucking, as though the sucking becomes more and more difficult. On the other hand, if you put him on a fresh breast, he will continue at his original speed—and if you put another, unfed newborn on the "empty" breast, he will feed just as slowly as the newborn who "emptied" it.[60] But in fact the breast is not empty. Much milk still remains when a newborn stops nursing; it is merely too effortful to draw it out.

On the other hand, if the newborn is awake when he finishes nursing, he will happily suck on a pacifier, from which it is infinitely harder to draw milk. This is the paradox we presented at the beginning of this chapter. It is perfectly sensible from the newborn's point of view, however. For whenever something touches the inside of his mouth, he sucks reflexively—and when this something inside his mouth is not delivering food, he sucks on it as he originally sucked on the breast before he learned to nurse. This kind of nonnutritive sucking is very powerful, as you know if you have ever removed a pacifier from a baby's mouth. Yet nonnutritive sucking is not as intense an effort as nutritive sucking, for the newborn pauses momentarily after every few sucks—he does not maintain long, continuous bursts of sucking—and he does not squeeze with his lips.[61] Hence even when a newborn is tired of nutritive sucking, sucking on a pacifier is not onerous.

Indeed, he finds that this kind of sucking feels good. Adults find that moderate pressures applied to the lips and mouth are pleasurable. It feels good to roll the tongue around the mouth and to squeeze the lips gently with the teeth. It feels even better when the mouth is stimulated and the lips are squeezed by a foreign object, such as a spouse's lips and tongue. Children take pleasure in similar stimulation, though it is usually provided by other things, like a pencil or a thumb. Older babies seem to enjoy it too: they will suck their fingers for several hours during the day. And so, to look at them, do newborns—even newborns who have not yet nursed. Herbert Davis and colleagues at the University of Kansas studied sixty babies through their first ten days of life.[62] Of these, twenty were nursed, twenty were fed by bottle, and twenty were fed by cup. Those babies who were fed by cup tried to suck on the cup at first, but they learned not to suck on it after a day or two. Between meals they sucked spontaneously on anything and everything—or on the air—just like the babies who took their meals through a nipple. Clearly, sucking as a pastime is innate; it is not created by any association with food. This does not prove that newborns find it pleasurable, of course. They might just suck reflexively, and derive pleasure in it only later in life by virtue of its learned association with food. Yet while a newborn is sucking on a pacifier, he reacts less to irritants. He objects less to cold metal against his bare belly, to rubber bands flicked against his feet, and to circumcision.[63] All this makes sucking look like no mere pastime. To a newborn, sucking is a primary source of pleasure.

Bonding and the Breast

Traditional psychology and psychiatry have held that pleasure from oral stimulation is learned in infancy through its association with the innate pleasures of the breast or bottle. But as we have seen, this association is quite the reverse: sucking is the innate pleasure; the others are learned. Neither does nursing represent the satisfaction of any primeval urge: it is learned. Consequently, there is no reason to expect, as many do, that if a baby is allowed to indulge this "urge" on his mother's breast immediately after he is born, then he will immediately feel loved and loving, and become attached to her emotionally. However, his mother is likely to enjoy holding him and nursing him, and to undergo an emotional reaction that will affect for some time her behavior toward her baby. So although early contact does not make the newborn feel attached to his mother, it may help to make his mother feel strongly attached to him. She may then behave differently toward him as a result, and he may respond in turn by behaving more equably and becoming strongly attached to her.

We shall examine the end of this process in chapter 11, but we can see the beginning here in an excellent study by Zulaika Ali and Michael Lowry of one hundred mothers and babies in a large maternity hospital in Jamaica.[64] None of the mothers had received narcotics for the delivery, nor had the babies received silver nitrate in their eyes afterward. Half of these mothers (chosen at random) were allowed "a glimpse" of their baby immediately after delivery; the other half were allowed to handle him "in any way" for forty-five minutes. We can safely assume that most of these women held their baby to the breast. Afterward the babies were removed to the nursery and not returned to their mothers for nine hours. From that time on, all the mothers were treated similarly. Twelve weeks later, most of the women returned with their babies to a clinic for routine medical exams. At this clinic, the mothers and babies were observed surreptitiously by someone who did not know whether any particular mother had been given only a glimpse of her baby or had been given her baby to hold. At one point during the (rigidly structured) examination, the physician undressed the baby. Half the mothers who had been given only a glimpse rose to watch the physician, while half remained seated; but of the mothers who had been given the baby to hold, nearly all rose to watch. The mothers who had been given only a glimpse were far more likely to have stopped feeding the baby solely by the breast. Their babies were less likely to be quietly awake. And the babies who had been held immediately were less likely at any one time to be sleeping, crying, or restless, as though they were running on a more even keel.

These data do not of themselves allow us to tell whether differences in the mothers' behavior reflect differences in the babies' behavior, or vice versa. Even as early as six weeks, there is undoubtedly a mixture of the two. But certainly these differences stemmed from the difference in delivery-room procedure: the mother's handling (and probably nursing) the baby immediately after birth. There is no reason to think that this handling affected the babies directly: it affected the mothers instead, making them feel more firmly bonded to their babies. As a result, they were more responsive to their babies' needs, so their babies acted more equably. Since these women also kept in closer contact with their babies, their babies doubtless learned to recognize their odor sooner; and as we shall see, this recognition does develop into attachment. So early nursing may eventually *lead* to a baby's earlier and/or closer attachment. (It may also be more healthful; for since a newborn is more alert immediately after birth, and sucks more then than he will for several days, he learns quicker to extract milk if he is nursed then, and is less likely to have to be fed by bottle later.[65]) However, being put to the breast immediately after birth does not make the newly born baby feel loving and wanted; it makes the mother feel loving and wanted instead.*

Maturation

So far in this chapter we have dealt with babies in their first week or two of life. For when it comes to food and flavor, babies mature fast. They can take three meals a day with semi-solid food almost as soon as they are born, if not as soon. In the early 1950s, Walter

---

*Ever since pediatricians Marshall Klaus and John Kennell claimed in the early 1970s that contact between baby and mother immediately after birth facilitates their attachment to one another, popular North American belief has had it that such contact is *necessary* for attachment to develop properly. This is nonsense. Most mothers and babies who have no early contact because the hospital does not allow it, because the mother delivers under general anesthesia, or because the baby is adopted, become just as close to each other. Under some circumstances, early contact can facilitate the process, especially if the mother is ambivalent about the new arrival; but it is certainly not necessary.[66]

Sackett, a general practitioner in Florida, routinely advised his obstetrical patients to begin to wean their babies at two to three days of age.[67] He also suggested feeding them only four times a day at first, and changing as soon as possible to an adult schedule of three meals a day. (Actually, he preferred to begin with three meals a day, but he added a midnight feeding "to placate . . . neighbors, relatives and apartment house dwellers" whose disapproval of the plan rendered them somewhat crabbier than they might otherwise have been when awakened by a crying baby at night.) Sackett used this feeding program for six hundred babies during five years, and he claimed that these babies not only thrived, they were "far happier and more contented" to boot. Whether they were indeed happier and more contented is open to question—his evidence for this is weak—but his feeding schedule is an interesting demonstration that physiologically, no age is too young for weaning (see figure 5.1).

By the time a baby is one month old, he has learned to associate the preparations for a meal with food: he quiets down and begins to suck as soon as you put on his bib.[68] Often he will suck even before you put on his bib, for now his physiological systems have come to expect food in discrete meals. These expectations make him feel hungry when mealtime rolls around. This is true not only of babies who have been fed by the clock, but also of babies who have been fed on demand.[69] For even babies fed on demand are fed not continuously but in batches, so the baby's body learns quickly to handle one batch first, then to prepare for the next—and these physiological preparations generate feelings of hunger. Because of the time it takes to process a stomachful of milk, these feelings usually occur at intervals of three and a half to four hours. Thus, just like his schedule-fed cousin, every three and half to four hours a demand-fed one-month-old begins to hunger for a meal.

Not only does a one-month-old feel hungry before a meal, he probably feels sated after it. For now he regulates his intake, taking less milk or formula the fattier it is[70]—and now, for the first time, he will refuse to take a nipple after he has been nursing for a while.[71]

Toward the end of his first year of life, a baby's chemical sensors are so well developed that he will actually select a wholesome, nutritious diet for himself, if you allow him *always* to select *all* the food he eats. Under these conditions, he will even take cod

FIGURE 5.1
Sackett's Feeding Schedule

Feedings at 6 A.M., 12 noon, 6 P.M. and 12 midnight. Breast or bottle. Offer water between feedings but nothing between midnight and 6 A.M.

AT 2 TO 3 DAYS: Cereal at 6 A.M. and 6 P.M. (Oatmeal and barley to start.)

AT 10 DAYS: Strained vegetables at 12 noon. (Peas, beans and/or carrots to start.)

AT 14 DAYS: Strained meats at either noon or 6 P.M.

AT 17 DAYS: Strained fruits at 6 P.M. (Applesauce, peaches and/or pears to start. May decrease cereal.)

MIDNIGHT FEEDING may be dropped at any time. Aim toward this adult schedule:

Breakfast: 7 A.M. to 9 A.M.
Lunch: 12 noon to 2 P.M.
Dinner: 5 P.M. to 7 P.M.

AT WEEKLY INTERVALS ADD:

3 weeks: Equal parts orange juice and sterile water, up to 2 ounces of each at 6 A.M.
Try other juices later.

4 weeks: Concentrated cod liver oil, 2 drops a day to start. Increase by one drop per month up to 5 drops daily.

5 weeks: Scrambled or coddled egg, or hard-boiled egg yolk.

6 weeks: Soups.

7 weeks: Mashed bananas, very ripe.

8 weeks: Custard puddings.

9 weeks: Crisp bacon.

BEGIN ALL NEW FOODS at one teaspoonful, then increase rapidly. Not more than one change daily—new food or change in formula.

NOTE: Adapted from Sackett, W. W., 1956. Use of solid foods early in infancy. *G.P.* (now *American Family Physician,* published by the American Academy of Family Physicians) 14 (September): 99.

liver oil of his own volition, if (and only if) he has a vitamin deficiency.* Yet even at one year a baby's sensation of flavor is not

*If you allow a baby to eat whatever he will, what will happen to him and what will he eat? Before and during the Depression, at Cleveland's Mount Sinai Hospital, a physician named Clara Davis set about to answer this question by setting out a buffet for eight- to nine-month-olds.[72] She allowed fifteen of them to eat whatever foods in it that they wanted, and as much of each as they liked.

Nurses fed the babies from a tray, and were instructed "to sit quietly by, spoon in hand."[73] If the baby reached for or pointed to a dish, the nurse was to take up a spoonful of it; if he then opened his mouth, she was to put the food into his mouth. Suggesting foods or refusing him foods were not allowed, nor were comments on his table manners, nor corrections of them. He was allowed to eat all that he wanted to before the tray was taken away.

Milk, soured milk, sea salt, apples, bananas, orange juice, fresh pineapple, peaches, tomatoes, beets, carrots, peas, turnips, cauliflower, cabbage, spinach, potatoes, lettuce, oatmeal, wheat, corn meal, barley, Ry-Krisp crackers (that is, rye flour and water baked with a bit of salt), beef, lamb, bone marrow, bone jelly, chicken, sweetbreads, brains, liver, kidneys, fish: these were the foods offered three or four times per day—not all at once, yet a considerable selection each time, always including water, milk, soured milk, cereals, cooked and raw meats, cooked and/or raw fruits and vegetables, and water. No two foods were mixed together in the cooking or in the serving. Rather, each food was served in a separate dish.

From the first, all fifteen babies chose their own foods. "Earl H. did this at first by plumping a whole hand into the dish," then later by touching the dish and looking at the nurse. "Abraham . . . fed himself without aid from the nurse other than help in holding the glasses. . . . At the first meal he first tried to eat directly from the dish by putting his face in it. Not having much success, he picked up a dish and tried to pour its contents into his mouth, with little better success. He then resorted to his fingers. . . ."[74] Other children tried different tacks, and their methods varied as they aged.

"We have no clue as to what influenced these infants in choosing the foods they tried first,"[75] wrote Davis. Their choices looked random.

> They tried not only foods but chewed hopefully the clean spoon, dishes, the edge of the tray, or a piece of paper on it. Their faces showed expressions of surprise, followed by pleasure, indifference or dislike. All the articles on the list, except lettuce by two and spinach by one, were tried by all, and most tried several times, but within the first few days they began to reach eagerly for some and to neglect others, so that definite tastes grew before our eyes.[76]

Despite these tastes,

> it proved impossible to predict what would be eaten at a given meal. An infant might eat from one to seven eggs or none, or from one to four bananas. Even the daily consumption of milk was unpredictable, varying [with three babies described in detail] from 11 to 48 ounces. Salt they ate only occasionally, often spluttering, choking or even crying bitterly after getting it in the mouth but never trying to spit it out and frequently going back for more, with a repetition of the same spluttering, etc.[77]

They tended

> to eat certain foods in waves. After eating cereals, eggs, meats or fruits in small or moderate amounts for a number of days, there would follow a period of a week or longer in which a particular food or class of food was eaten in larger and larger quantities until astonishingly large amounts were taken. After this, the quantities would decline to the previous level. . . . In the diet kitchen such waves came to be known as "egg jags," "meat jags," "cereal jags," etc. Symptoms of overeating did not accompany them, nor were the waves followed by a period of temporary disgust for and neglect of the particular food as is usual [in adults] when appetite is surfeited.[78]

In general the babies showed no clear preference between raw and cooked foods, although they did in the case of some specific foods: oatmeal, wheat, and bone marrow they preferred cooked, and bananas and beef they preferred raw—unless the beef was cooked rare.

completely adult: a six-month-old prefers saltwater to plain water, and he will not reverse this preference until he is one and a half to three years old.[81]

Practical Implications

Three concerns devolve about feeding a baby: his health, and the parents' and baby's comfort. To a certain extent, these three concerns are interrelated. A sick baby feels uncomfortable and cries, making his parents uncomfortable too; while peckish parents are likely to be insensitive to their baby's hunger, thereby making the baby feel uncomfortable by neglect.

Breast-feeding a baby on demand is normally the best approach to the baby's health and to the comfort of all. Milk from the breast contains nutrients and antibodies that synthetic formulations lack, so the breast-fed baby becomes ill less often. And a mother who is breast-feeding usually gets to know her baby quicker, so she ministers to him more appropriately, minimizing his discomforts. Breast-feeding also gives the mother pleasure through the sensuousness of the act; and it gives the baby pleasure because, through contacting his mother's body so often, he comes to recognize her odor. As we saw earlier, to a newborn baby, the recognition of an odor—*any* odor—is more pleasing than the finest perfume.

Some of the babies had not been healthy when they began the experiment. Four were undernourished, and five had rickets, two of them severely. For one of those two, Davis put a small glass of cod liver oil on the tray. The baby took this frequently until he was healed, after which he took no more. The other babies with rickets also healed (*sans* cod liver oil) in about the same time, and by the end of the study, all fifteen babies seemed perfectly healthy—extraordinarily healthy in fact, according to Davis.

> All had hearty appetites; all throve. Constipation was unknown among them and laxatives were never used or needed. Except in the presence of . . . infection, there was no vomiting or diarrhœa. Colds were usually of the mild three-day type without complications of any kind. There were a few cases of tonsillitis but no serious illness.[79]

All in all, the babies showed themselves remarkable judges of what foods were good for them. This is certainly not from any knowledge of what is supposed to be healthful. Not one baby chose the "proper" diet of cereals and milk supplemented by small amounts of fruit, eggs, and meat. Their meals were "a dietitian's nightmare."[80] Breakfast might be liver and a pint of orange juice; supper might be several eggs, bananas, and milk. Apparently, if a foodstuff contained a nutrient that the baby needed, his physiology caused it to taste good— even cod liver oil.

Feeding a baby when his body wants to be fed is obviously more pleasant to the baby (and to everybody around him) than feeding him according to a schedule—nor is there any reason to put him on a schedule, regardless of whether he is fed by breast or bottle. During the first few weeks, no matter how regularly his parents feed him, the baby will not behave predictably, for his physiological systems are not adapted to the rhythm of eating and digesting. As soon as the baby is able to be comfortable on a schedule—to feel hungry by the clock—then his body will develop a comparably regular rhythm of its own whether he is fed by schedule or on demand.

For the first few days after his birth, a baby is difficult to feed, both because he is difficult to rouse (especially if he was delivered with drugs) and because he does not know how to extract milk. As we have said, immediately after his birth he is more alert than he will be for several days: if he is put to the breast right away, he will find it easier to learn to nurse. Trying to rouse a baby to feed him may be counterproductive; for if you make him cry, he will have additional difficulty in coordinating sucking, squeezing, swallowing, and breathing. Not only will his crying make feeding him difficult of itself, it will also cause him to swallow air: air in his belly may then make him active and restless, and cry all the more. If you must rouse a newborn, the most effective way is the gentlest. Just undress him or dab some cold water on his forehead. To keep a baby awake and to reduce distractions, reduce the sensory stimulation he is receiving. While you feed him, turn down the lights, turn off the television, and do not bounce or jiggle him.

Since a newborn learns to nurse through his reflexes, you can facilitate his learning by facilitating his reflexes. If possible, do not try to feed him just after he has been crying, for he will be too tired for his reflexes to work well. Quiet him first. To give him a nipple, do not put it in his mouth or try to guide him toward it, but touch it to his cheek instead—*one* cheek. His rooting reflex will make him turn toward it. Do not touch both his cheeks, or this rooting reflex will not work. If you are breast-feeding him, be sure he takes into his mouth not just the nipple but also some of the surrounding breast, for to extract milk he needs to apply pressure on breast tissue with his gums. If enough milk comes out to choke him, reduce the flow by pressing on the areola or, if you are giving him a bottle, by exchanging the nipple for one with a smaller hole. You will be able to tell when a baby has learned to draw milk, because his sucking will become rhythmical: a burst of sucking, a stop for breath, another burst, and so on.

After a month or two, a baby can handle much more sensory stimulation, so he is awake much more often. Now, too, he feels hungry and full: he makes it obvious when he wants to be fed, and he leaves the nipple when he has had enough. Soon he will be able to handle sufficient stimulation that he will remain quietly awake at the end of a feeding. This is the perfect time to play with him.

During the first month of life, there is no clear way to tell when a baby is ready to nurse or when he is finished. A baby cries reflexively from any form of discomfort and does not modulate his crying to the degree of his discomfort; so there is no way to tell whether the cause of his complaint is an empty stomach or gas, bright lights or cold. All you can do is try to feed the baby and see if he settles down. If the feeding goes badly, try burping him. If he is on the breast, feed him until he stops sucking, then give him a rest and see if he will take more. Do not do this with bottle-fed babies, for babies do not begin to regulate their own intake until the second month: until then, even if they are bloated from excess fluid, they will drink from a bottle until it runs dry. (The breast-fed baby will quit before this, when it becomes difficult to extract milk.)

During the first month, you will not be able to tell when the baby has had enough. The rule of thumb is ten minutes on each breast; but in feeding as in every other respect, babies differ greatly from one to another. Some will extract significant amounts of milk from the breast long after others have stopped. The best way to tell if a baby is getting sufficient milk from the breast is to weigh him every few days. He should lose weight during his first few days, then steadily gain. Most babies exceed their birth weight around the end of the second week.[82]

Even if a baby is a prodigious eater, he will still suck whenever he can—on his blanket or fingers, or on a pacifier if one is available. This indicates a desire to suck, not hunger or an insufficiency of food. Note that during the first six months of life there is no need to be concerned about the pacifier's becoming a crutch; for a baby this young will not remember that the pacifier exists when he is not sucking on it (see chapter 10).

There is really no way to tell when a baby is being fed too much, for we do not know how to define "too much." In different countries and cultures at different times, physicians have held different opinions about how fat a healthy baby should be. The range has varied from relatively gaunt to something very like a blimp. We have searched for a sound, scientific basis for any such pronouncement but have found none. There are clear medical advantages to breast-feeding a baby, but nothing else about feeding babies has been shown to be an asset or a detriment. A baby's body seems to be sufficiently plastic that, provided it receives a minimum amount of nutrient, it will thrive on almost any regime.

6

Bright Sights

THE NEWBORN BABY lies quietly in his mother's arms. He is awake, but he looks glassy-eyed, in a trance. He stares vacantly in front of him with his left eye shut. Now, slowly, his left eye opens—and while his other eye looks forward, it ranges toward the side. His eyes are moving as if he were blind. He looks as though he can make out lightness and darkness perhaps, and maybe a little movement, but nothing more.

In fact this baby does see much more than this—but not as we see. His world looks very different from ours, so different that we can hardly imagine it. If we could see through his eyes, we would think we were in a dream.

An Eye Chart for Babies

Much of the knowledge about what newborns see comes from our own laboratory at McMaster University, where we have been studying babies' vision since 1973. Whatever a baby (or an adult) is looking at is reflected off the center of his eye: we use these reflections to determine what babies watch.

Initially we just put things in front of babies and observed whether they looked at them. Always they did, even babies only one day old. As long as the light was dim, no matter what we put in front of them or where we put it, they found it and stared at it, sometimes for minutes.[1] Lines, triangles, circles, wheels, bull's-eyes, checkerboards, golf balls—all fascinated the babies. Occasionally, in play, we wiggled the object. This fascinated them even more.[2] Nor were the babies responding merely to the presence of light. If we put a sheet of black-and-white striped paper beside a sheet of gray paper reflecting the same amount of light overall, then nearly always the babies stared at the stripes.

This "preferential looking" has let us use striped paper as an eye chart: the smallest stripes an infant looks at in preference to gray are probably the smallest stripes he can see. We have tested older babies using this "eye chart," and at Erasmus University in Rotterdam Jackie van Hof-van Duin and Gesine Mohn tested babies as young as one week old.[3] Van Hof-van Duin and Mohn found that the finest black-and-white stripes a typical one-week-old can see are thirty times wider than those a normal adult can see—stripes roughly one-tenth of an inch one foot away (see figure 6.1).

Their work, conjoined with our own, shows that from this beginning the baby's vision improves rapidly at first, then more slowly.[4] By two months he can see stripes half this thick; by four months he can see stripes one-quarter as thick; and by eight months he can see stripes one-eighth as thick. That is comparable to many adults who would benefit from weak eyeglasses, but do not bother to wear them. For four more years thereafter his vision improves very slowly. Normal adults can see stripes one-thirtieth this thick, an acuity the child develops around the time he enters school.*

---

*Of course, a baby might actually be able to see finer lines than this but find them too dull to bother with. We doubt that this is so, however. At Cambridge University, Janet Atkinson, Oliver Braddick, and Jennifer French showed stripes to ninety-seven one- to ten-day-olds while recording the babies' visually evoked responses to them. They looked for the finest stripes that would evoke a response different from the response evoked by a similar amount of plain light. Visually evoked responses can occur when the cortex is responding to things that we are not conscious of, so that they form a yardstick likely to err in the opposite direction from preferential looking. Nonetheless, when measuring the limits of newborns' vision, both of these techniques agree almost perfectly.[5]

Testing how sharply a five-month-old can see toward the side. In the photo above we attract his gaze to a toy straight ahead of him, then in the photo below we uncover a set of stripes. If he repeatedly turns toward the stripes, he must be glimpsing them out of the corner of his eye.

FIGURE 6.1
The Finest Stripes a Newborn Can See From One Foot Away

Vision as bad as a newborn's would handicap an adult severely—so severely that in most jurisdictions he would be deemed by the law to be blind. However, what is a handicap to an adult can be a boon to a baby. Babies do not need to read or sew, or to see much of anything at all beyond the barest shapes of things. A newborn is quite able to make out the form that walks through the door, comes toward him, and picks him up. He certainly can see the spindles forming his crib plus the rail at the top; and these simple shapes fascinate him. You will often see him freeze and examine them. But to the baby who has never seen anything and has gained no understanding of the world through other senses, seeing more than this soon becomes overwhelming. During his first weeks, you will see him close his eyes shortly after he opens them whenever the scene before him is in the least complex. Thus unsharp vision does not handicap the baby in the slightest. Instead it helps him by preventing excessive visual stimulation.

Sensitivity to Contrast

We can learn more about how the world looks to a newborn by examining the cause of his unsharp vision. When you look at something—say this dot:

●

—rays of light coming from it reach the lens of your eye and are focused by the lens onto the inside back surface of the eyeball, the retina. The retina is covered with special neurons, light-sensitive cells shaped like rods and cones, and called rods and cones accordingly. Rays of light shoot into these neurons, which react by shooting electrochemical impulses into a chain of neurons leading into the brain.[6]

In the newborn's eye, the rods are fairly mature. But rods are good only for gross, black-and-white vision; they are basically roughnecks hired for quick and dirty jobs in low light. The eye's craftsmen are its cones; it is they that respond to fine lines and color. Your eye employs more than fifty thousand of them in the fovea, a 0.7-millimeter spot in the center of the retina. You do most of your seeing with the fovea. In the adult it is highly specialized: no rods or other types of cell are present. But in the newborn, the fovea is not fully formed. It is like a messy construction site that has spilled out onto the street: the area is actually twice as far across as the finished product will be, but it is littered with other kinds of cell; the cones are spread over a larger area, so they are less densely distributed; and the cones are not elongated yet. They look more like stumps than cones.[7]

This immature fovea—not the lens—is what limits a newborn baby's acuity. Even when his lens does occasionally focus light on his retina reasonably well, his immature fovea blurs lines and edges, and limits his perception of textures and detail. Since this is not an optical problem, eyeglasses cannot correct it.[8] Yet it is the major cause of a second kind of unsharpness, a far more important kind: poor sensitivity to contrast.

To understand this, think of the rods and cones as machines that convert light into neurochemical impulses.[9] The brighter the light, the more photons hit the rods and cones in a given time and the more frequently impulses shoot out. Other neurons in the retina and brain receive those impulses and note how frequently they arrive. On this basis—by frequency of firing—the brain determines how much light is present. If the brain detects two different frequencies of firing, it registers two different levels of light.

In dim light—outdoors at night—the retina works solely with its rods, not with its cones. Studies of the newborn's preferential looking show that his rods work only a little less efficiently than an adult's:[10] he sees nearly as well as you do when you get up to feed him in the middle of the night. The difference between the dimmest glow that you can see and the dimmest glow that a newborn can see is comparable to the difference between a dark and a light object on a starless night. Considering the enormous range of illumination to which our eyes are sensitive, this difference is trivial. However, most illumination is brighter than this, bright enough to stimulate the cones; so in adults it is processed by the fovea. But in the newborn, the fovea is where the cones are immature. Hence most of the time a newborn's retina is working inefficiently. This means that normally a newborn requires more light than an adult to produce any given frequency of firing—and to produce any given *difference* in frequency of firing a newborn requires a greater *difference* in the amount of light. So before a newborn can see a difference between two levels of light—or between two shades of gray, or between two shades of the same color—the contrast between them must be greater. Judging from our own tests of newborns and two-month-olds, and from comparable tests by others (all done using preferential looking), young babies are less than one-tenth as sensitive to contrast, and to differences in contrast, as adults.[11] They improve to nearly the adult level by around one year, much as their ability to see lines is improving.[12] However, when they are born, the difference between white bond paper and clean newsprint is about the smallest difference in contrast that they can see.

If an adult suddenly lost this much sensitivity to contrast, the effect would be profound. Textures would suddenly disappear: on a cloudy day, concrete would look as smooth as porcelain. Parts of many objects would meld into the areas surrounding them, so objects would merge together. People's faces would lose their modeling. Sometimes whole objects would disappear into their surroundings. You would feel as if you were living in a drawing by Escher—a faded drawing with all the subtlety washed out. Like the newborn baby lying in his crib, you would pay no attention to pastel animals on the wallpaper or to other subtleties. You would find coarse contrasts far more interesting, especially black on white. Like the baby, you would pay little attention to what the sunbeam illuminates; you would watch instead the line where sun shifts to shadow. We would see you, as we see the baby, staring not at the sunbeam but at where the sunbeam ends.

Accommodation to Distance

Vision as poor as a newborn's would seriously handicap an adult, but it does not handicap a baby. He does not notice the Escheresque absurdities, for he has developed no understanding of how objects ought to look. (Indeed, we shall see in chapter 10 that he has no understanding even that the things he is seeing *are* objects.) Nor does he miss seeing additional lines and textures, for he is forced to see more than he wants to see as it is. Rather than handicapping him, the newborn's poor vision actually helps him to see. It partially compensates for his poor ability to focus his eyes at different distances.

When you look up from this book to the wall beyond, the wall looks blurred for a split second until your eyes accommodate to the new distance. They do this automatically, reflexively: a rudimentary part of the brain sees that the image is no longer in the clearest focus and "instructs" certain muscles to make an optical correction by changing the lens's shape.[13] But in the young baby, especially the newborn, this system works sluggishly and inaccurately. Optical measurements show that a newborn's eye usually ends up focused not on the object that he is staring at but closer.[14] What he is looking at is usually misfocused optically. However, his poor eyesight mitigates the effect of this misfocusing.[15]

To visualize what happens, lay this book on top of a newspaper on your lap, stare at the newspaper with one eye closed, and while you are focusing on your lap, draw the book toward your face.

Notice how quickly the book becomes blurred. Now do the same thing while looking through a sheet of cellophane or some other kind of transparent but unclear plastic. (Again, be sure to shut one eye: if both eyes are open, certain adult reflexes will vitiate the demonstration.[16]) The plastic makes everything look somewhat blurred, but now you can move the book farther before it looks more blurred than the newspaper. Looking through the plastic is like looking through a newborn's eyes: his retina prevents anything from appearing as sharp as it appears to you, but this blurring allows objects over a greater range to seem in best focus. And he accommodates to distances well enough—*just* well enough—that usually he can focus his eyes somewhere within this range.[17]

A baby's blurred vision also helps him to focus by amplifying the difference in sharpness between objects that are in best focus and objects that are not. Again, close one eye and stare at this book; but this time hold up the book so that you can see the far side of the room. While you are focusing on the book, notice how blurred the wall looks in the background. Next stare at the book through the sheet of cellophane. Everything looks more blurred, but the wall in the background looks disproportionately more blurred. Whenever everything looks less sharp, then the difference between what seems in focus and what seems out of focus becomes more distinct. Focusing is easier.

The paradox here is interesting: a newborn's blurred vision allows objects to appear in best focus over a greater range—but it makes objects beyond that range appear more out of focus.

At first a baby focuses best on objects that are very close to him—eight to twelve inches away.[18] While he is focusing at these close distances, more distant objects fall out of focus quickly, so they rarely attract his gaze.[19] He ignores you until you come close to his face. The baby's ability to focus and his retina develop in synchrony, so he can always focus just well enough to see as clearly as his vision allows.[20] As his ability to focus improves, it enables him not only to see better but to focus on objects that are farther away. Moreover, as his vision improves, misfocused objects appear less unsharp; so while he is looking at something close, distant objects appear sharper in the background. Thus during his first months of life, a baby's visual world not only clarifies, it deepens and expands.

Depth Perception

When a baby is born, his eyes do not work together like an adult's. He lacks the neural ability to keep both his eyes facing the same thing.[21] Only half the time does he even move them simultaneously in the same direction.*[23] And he sees little or nothing from the right side of his left eye and the left side of his right eye.[24]

We studied how much babies see from each eye by observing how far to their side a small blinking light can be yet still attract their attention.[25] The results surprised us. With one-month-olds, the light had to be closer to the center than we tested—less than 15 degrees. That is only three inches to the side from one foot away. To attract their gaze even that far, the light has to be much larger, or moving.[26] In contrast, a tiny, stationary light will attract an adult's gaze when it is 60 degrees away (toward the nose) or 105 degrees away (away from the nose)—that is, 15 degrees behind the adult's head. Figure 6.2 shows the development of the angle over which we found babies can see. Apparently a young baby sees as though he is looking through a tunnel—or rather, through two tunnels, since his eyes range independently over the world.

When the newborn's eyes fixate different things, he may be seeing double, or he may be ignoring one eye and seeing only through the other.[27] In either case, three-dimensional, stereoscopic vision is impossible; for stereoscopic vision comes from combining the similar but *slightly* different images from the two eyes.[28] To determine when stereoscopic vision develops, researchers have used mirrors and various optical trickery to create moving images within the baby's eyes that will look different to him, and hence induce him to move his eyes differently, when he is seeing the images stereoscopically and when he is not. The baby's reactions to these illusions show that stereoscopic vision develops at four to five months of age.[29]

If you close one eye, you lack stereoscopic vision, yet still you perceive depth. Parallel lines converge; distance shrinks things and

---

*The newborn moves his eyes more synchronously in near darkness than in the light, as though the energy of light cannot be contained wholly within the neuronal channels of his immature visual system, so that it floods into the channels controlling his eye movements.[22]

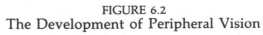

FIGURE 6.2
The Development of Peripheral Vision

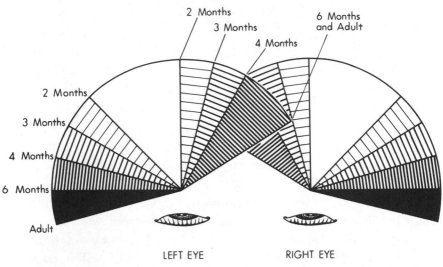

smooths them; one object blocks your view of another; objects block light, creating shadows; and distance raises objects higher toward the horizon.[30] However, using optical illusions, Albert Yonas and Carl Granrud at the University of Minnesota found that babies do not understand any of these cues until they are six to seven months old.[31] For instance, Yonas[32] put an eye patch on five- and six-month-olds, then showed them a window frame angled outward. The babies reached for the nearer edge. Then he showed the babies a photograph of the window frame—a photograph that seemed startlingly realistic to adults wearing an eye patch (see the photograph on page 117). Six-month-old babies reached for the "nearer" edge too. They understood the perspective of the photograph. But five-month-olds reached for the "farther" edge as often as they reached for the "nearer." The perspective of the photograph meant nothing to them.

Since five-month-olds do not understand perspective, or any of those other cues to depth we mentioned earlier, it is hardly likely that a newborn does. But one adult cue a newborn probably can understand is the parallax created by motion. Shut one eye, extend your arm, stare at your thumb, and move your head to the left: the wall beyond appears to move toward the left, while the fold of your elbow appears to move toward the right. These appearances of

Testing a baby's perception of depth. Both sides of this "window" are equally far away; the right side looks farther away to us because it is drawn following the laws of perspective. But this five-month-old does not understand perspective; he reaches toward the right side as often as he reaches toward the left. Photographed in the laboratory of Albert Yonas at the University of Minnesota.

movement provide a very strong clue to depth, the clue that Yonas's five-month-olds were using when they reached for the closer side of the real window frame while one of their eyes was patched. At the University of Exeter, Alan Slater, David Rose, and Victoria Morison found that babies less than nine days old looked at complex objects in preference to life-sized photographs of the objects. These babies were probably seeing depth through the parallax of motion, since they were too young to see stereoscopically or through any of the other means that Yonas and Granrud studied.[33]

However, in other circumstances a newborn can also see depth in a way that adults do not, through changes in the sharpness of what he sees caused by his poor ability to accommodate. Andras Robert discovered this in an elegant study at Queen's University in Kingston, Ontario.[34] Robert showed children only a few days old an approaching and receding checkerboard. While the checkerboard was approaching—and not while it was receding—the babies breathed faster, sucked faster, and wriggled as if they were trying to move away or duck. Clearly they could tell when the checkerboard was coming at them from when it was stationary or moving away. To verify that they were not seeing stereoscopically, he covered one eye and found they reacted the same way. There were only three likely ways the babies could have known when the checkerboard was approaching: (1) because the parallax of motion caused the background to move increasingly far as the baby moved his head; and/or (2) because the checkerboard loomed larger; and/or (3) since the newborn's lens is usually accommodated to close distances, and accommodates to new distances slowly, as the checkerboard approached it came into finer focus.[35]

Now, we just saw that newborns see depth through the parallax of motion. To test the other two possibilities, Robert showed the babies movies—which eliminate parallax of motion since the screen itself stands still—of all the nine possible permutations of size and clarity: movies of the checkerboard looming larger but going out of focus, of the checkerboard staying the same size but coming into focus, and so on. By watching when the babies sucked, Robert found that newborns use both cues. He found that in the newborn's world, an increase in either size or sharpness indicates that an object is approaching. A decrease in size or sharpness indicates that an object is moving away.

In sum, a newborn baby sees depth to some extent, but not as we do. He sees it not through differences in position, shading, texture, and other static elements, but through movements and changes, through visual flux—through commotion and co-motion, as it were. He lies in his crib staring at one of its spindles. It forms an attractive line. He moves his head slightly and sees the clutter behind it—the wall—move with him. Through this he senses that the clutter is behind the line. Then his mother appears amidst the clutter. At first she merely adds to the clutter, but suddenly he catches sight of the burgundy trim that runs up the edge of her white bathrobe. The contrast forms a compelling sight. He stares at it. The dark stripe grows wider, and the edge where the white touches it grows sharper. He stops sucking and his eyes brighten: he sees that something is coming near!

The Immature Cortex

We can understand more about the baby's visual world by looking at the newborn's brain. The highest part of the brain dedicated to vision is the visual cortex. In babies as in adults, it fills most of the back of the head; but for the first month after birth, this area is very immature, less mature than the portions of the cortex that handle most of the other senses. If you look at it through a microscope, you will see that the various types of cell composing it are not segregated by type, as they are in adults; they are intermixed. Most of the cells have not yet become coated with myelin, a white, fatty substance that speeds neural transmission. And the hairlike ends of the cells—dendrites—that will branch far out to interconnect the cells branch out little as yet. They are very short, and each dendrite stays within only one or two layers of the cortex, instead of meandering through all six layers as they will a few months later.[36] Because consciousness involves the cortex, we suspect that this immaturity leaves the newborn less conscious of what he sees than he is of what he feels, tastes, or smells.

The newborn's immature cortex also leaves him unable to coordinate the muscles moving his eyes with the image he sees; so although a newborn is fascinated by movement, he cannot follow a moving object continuously. If you lean sideways while he is staring at your hair, his eyes will remain fixed where they were for a moment, then they will jump ahead of you. He can follow a moving object only by chasing back and forth after it with his eyes. This he can do if the object moves slowly[37]—but in adults, and we think in newborns, while the eyes are jerking from one fixed position to another, the image blanks out.[38] Adults have learned that moving objects have trajectories, so we can still perceive movement from a series of still images, like those forming a movie. However, as we shall see in chapter 10, it takes months for babies to show the most rudimentary understanding of trajectory. Thus when a newborn watches your face as it is moving, he sees it as jumping from spot to spot. He frequently loses sight of it too, especially if you are moving up and down.[39] He sees your face and starts. Suddenly it disappears—then it reappears when it returns to his purview. He starts again. He sees movements like a pictofilm, a montage of still photographs that come and go. Not until a baby is two to three months old can his eyes follow an object smoothly, and even then the object must move slowly.[40] This is the earliest that he sees movements continuously, as a flow.

The newborn's immature cortex also limits his vision in a more profound way, but a subtle and bizarre one that is difficult to describe in a sentence or two. To understand it, let us look at Helen, an adolescent rhesus monkey whose visual cortex was removed. Nicolas Humphrey studied Helen at Cambridge University for eight years while she recovered enough eyesight, eventually, to run through an obstacle course after a passing fly, and catch it.[41]

Cockroaches too she ran after, and currants. Whenever Humphrey scattered a handful of currants on the floor, Helen scampered about merrily, gobbling them up. But when Humphrey outlined a square around one currant, Helen did not find it. A bit of black tape outside the square she mistook for a currant and went for time and again; but a real currant inside the square, never. Apparently she could not see objects that were inside things. Simply because the currant lay inside the square, to Helen it was not there.

This is how a monkey sees without a visual cortex—and a newborn baby sees similarly. With no cortex to direct his gaze, the baby watches whatever part of an object catches his eye, and does not think to examine other areas. Outlines of things are larger than the elements within, and often contrast more against the background, so they catch his attention to the exclusion of all else. Thus when we observed how newborns and one-month-olds watched an assortment of objects including people, we found that most of the time their eyes stick to one spot on the perimeter. In contrast, two-month-olds range broadly with their eyes.[42] A newborn does not examine the world as a whole; he looks at only small pieces of it—minuscule elements, one at a time.

An adult seeing the world like this would nonetheless picture it entire, for he would be able to fit the pieces together in his memory. But a young baby cannot. We can see what a baby notices by showing him a picture repeatedly until he acts bored, then changing the picture: if he perks up, he noticed the change. This kind of test shows that even newborns will notice subtle differences in objects—if the features are presented by themselves, with no outline surrounding them. But if the objects are outlined, newborns and one-month-olds ignore substantial changes.[43] In our own lab,

FIGURE 6.3
One-Month-Olds See No Differences Among These Faces

SOURCE: Reprinted from Maurer, D., and Barrera, M. 1981. Infants' perception of natural and distorted arrangements of a schematic face. *Child Development* 52:197;© The Society for Research in Child Development, Inc.

one-month-olds saw no differences among the drawings in figure 6.3.[44]

In sum, a newborn does not see scenes as we see them; he sees only elements of scenes, one element at a time—a line here, an angle there, whatever catches his eye because it is large and contrasts sharply against its background. He will study doggedly your hairline or chin, but he will rarely glance at your nose or mouth, or stare into your eyes. Nor will he see you smiling at him. When he is around one month old, he may see your facial features if you are heavily made up so that they contrast strongly with your skin, or if you begin to talk to him so that your lips move.[45] But not until a baby is two to three months old will he see your entire face.

Color Vision

One part of the newborn's visual cortex does function relatively well and develops quickly: the part that is required for seeing color.[46] This seems paradoxical, for the cones in the eye are also needed for seeing color, yet the cones in the newborn's eye are sparse, short, and stumpy, not nearly mature. So arises one of the most intriguing questions about a newborn's vision—and one of the most difficult to answer: does he see in color or black and white?

When you look at a painting, yellows almost always seem brighter than reds, greens, and blues. Yellow and blue brush strokes may measure identically with a light meter—they may reflect equal amounts of light—but an adult who is completely color-blind can tell them apart: the yellow looks to him like a brighter gray. The reason for this is that adults are more sensitive to yellow light.[47]

Differences in sensitivity to different colors—spectral sensitivity—have been measured precisely in adults but have proven to be very difficult to measure at all in infants. This has made it difficult to tell what colors a baby sees. If you first bore a baby

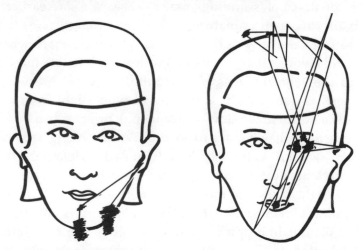

ABOVE: We are peering through a peephole beside a screen, watching a young baby as he watches a drawing of a face. The reflection on his eye shows where he is looking. By training cameras through such a peephole and measuring the reflections, we have been able to study with great precision how babies examine faces. One-month-olds (and we suspect newborns) tend to focus on one or two spots on the hairline or chin (below left), while two-month-olds (below right) scan all the features. The drawings show the movements of one eye of one baby watching a real face for 75 seconds.

with a green square and then show him a red square, he may perk up because he noticed the change of hue—or because the red appears as a darker gray. There is no way to tell unless you know how bright different colors appear to him—that is, unless you know his spectral sensitivity.[48]

So far, the best approach to measuring the baby's spectral sensitivity has been to show him colored light, to note how long it takes him to emit a particular brain wave, then to see how intense other colors must be to take comparably long to evoke comparable waves. Using this method at the Pennsylvania College of Optometry, Anne Moskowitz-Cook tested the spectral sensitivity of twenty-eight baby girls.[49] (She tested only girls because 10 percent of boys are color-blind.) At about four months, the babies' spectral sensitivity was substantially adult, but babies younger than this seemed relatively more sensitive to blue light. Instead of seeing blues as darker than greens, as adults do, they probably see them as more or less the same.

Moskowitz-Cook's findings make sense. We saw earlier that young babies have an immature fovea: like young babies, adults prevented from seeing with the fovea are relatively more sensitive to blue. And a young baby's lens is colorless, so it passes more blue light than the yellowish lens of an adult.[50]

It seems as though light with a lot of blue—light from a clear sky outside a northern window—should look brighter to a newborn and a young baby than it looks to an adult. And a young baby ought to be more aware of extremely blue light—ultraviolet, or "black" light, which adults can hardly see at all. Direct sunlight contains a lot of such light, and it is intense as well, so a newborn finds it overwhelming. He closes his eyes when the sun comes out. The dim, ultraviolet plant light near his crib that we see as dim, he might find brilliant. Whites, too, will often look brighter; for white paints, white papers, and white fabrics commonly contain fluorescent brighteners that work by reflecting ultraviolet light. All in all, there is more brightness in the newborn's world than in ours.

To study the newborn's color vision, it is necessary to obviate this difference. The first studies to do this came out of our own laboratory. We bored babies with an assortment of grays, then showed them a color to see whether they perked up: if they did, they could tell the color was not gray. We found that newborns distinguish yellow, orange, red, green, and turquoise from gray. However, they do *not* distinguish blue, purple, or chartreuse.*[51]

Russell Adams extended this work at Memorial University in Newfoundland by boring newborns with splotches of one color of assorted intensities, then watching whether they perked up to splotches of another color.[52] He found that if the splotches of color are very large, newborns distinguish red from green. However, they do not distinguish yellow from green or from red.

Although newborns distinguish some colors from other colors and from gray, they probably do not see those colors as adults do, even color-blind adults. We as adults have three sets of cones, each of which is more sensitive to one part of the spectrum than to the others. Our sensation of color is the comparison within the visual system of the neuronal energy from these three sets of cones. In adults, color-blindness occurs when one or more sets of cones is abnormal.[53] However, the newborn's inabilities to distinguish colors are unlike those that come from any form of adult color-blindness. This implies that the newborn's failures to distinguish colors come not from the cones but from higher parts of the visual system, possibly including the sensorium itself. Thus although a baby can distinguish red from green as soon as he is born, we cannot say whether red and green look to him as they look to a normal or even a color-blind adult.

After birth, a baby's color vision improves rapidly. By one month he can distinguish blue, purple, and chartreuse from gray, as well as the yellow, orange, red, green, and turquoise he could distinguish at birth; by two months he can distinguish yellow from green; and by three months he can distinguish yellow from red as well.[54] By the time the baby is three to four months old, his color vision is substantially adult.[55]

Now he not only sees colors, he categorizes them like adults

*We also used a second method: we gave babies the choice of looking at a gray square or at a mixture of gray and colored checks, using an assortment of intensities of gray such that at some one intensity, to a color-blind baby, the colors and the gray would match. Normally, a baby will look at checks rather than at a gray square; so if a baby showed no preference at one intensity of gray, then at that intensity, he probably did not see the color. Both of our methods yielded similar results. Moreover, using this second method we found that newborns confuse a medium blue with a medium gray, unlike adults who matched the medium blue with a dark gray: this corroborates Moskowitz-Cook's findings that newborns are more sensitive to blue. Apparently, blue looks to a newborn like bright gray.

as red, blue, green, and yellow.* Mark Bornstein learned this at Princeton by boring 140 four-month-olds with one color, then changing the color slightly while watching to see if the change interested the baby.[57] He changed the color only very slightly, changed it in constant amounts (based on the frequency of the light wave), and went all the way up and down the rainbow. None of the babies could possibly have learned our names or categories for hues, yet they perked up only when the change of color crossed what adults perceived to be a border between different colors. Changing from yellowish orange to reddish orange did not interest them, for example, but changing the same amount from yellowish orange into yellow did. Apparently, a four-month-old sees colors much like an adult.

---

*Most of us learned in school that there are three primary colors: red, green, and blue—or, if we learned about them in art class, either yellow, red, and blue, or yellow, magenta, and cyan. Yet here we say there are four. What is going on?

Sight, like sound, is a psychological phenomenon, not a physical one: it is the brain's response to waves of energy striking receptors of the nervous system. We hear sounds when sonic waves strike the ear; we see sights when light waves strike the eye. Instruments can measure the frequency of light waves, but they cannot measure or define the colors that those frequencies induce within us. Only people can. Since people define colors—all colors—the most basic definition of a primary color is a color that people perceive to be primary: a color that people—all people—perceive to be different from all other colors. To learn what these colors are, psychologists have tested men and women all over the world with paint chips, asking them to put like color with like until the chips are sorted into the smallest possible number of piles. No matter where people live, no matter what language they speak, no matter whether they have words for many colors or few, they always end up with four stacks of chips: yellow, red, green, and blue. In the most basic, psychological sense, these are the primary colors.[56]

These four colors, and all other colors, are induced within the brain by signals from the three sets of cones we mentioned earlier in the text. Each of these sets is particularly sensitive to light waves oscillating near one frequency. Those three frequencies, viewed alone, induce red, green, and blue. Thus red, green, and blue form three primary colors—"additive" primaries, since they work by adding one frequency of light to another.

If we have equal amounts of each of these frequencies, we see white. If we now remove any one of them, we see the sum of the frequencies of the other two: removing the frequencies that induce blue makes us see yellow; removing those that induce green makes us see magenta; and removing those inducing red makes us see cyan, or turquoise. Thus if we start with white light and *remove* colors, we can form every color using yellow, magenta, and cyan. This is what we do when we mix paint, for paint works by removing frequencies from the light that strikes it. For this reason, yellow, magenta, and cyan are also called primaries—"subtractive" primaries. Since most people see magenta as a shade of red and cyan as a shade of blue, the subtractive primaries are often misidentified as yellow, red, and blue.

The Newborn's Visual World

If we could see through the eyes of a newborn baby, we would see a world that resembles our adult world only in the barest outlines. The world would look brighter than ours, with fewer lines and textures. Everything would look blurred and washed out, and objects would be strangely colored. The world would look like a badly misfocused shapshot that has been fading in the sun for so many years that you can barely identify the subject.

However, this is what *we* would perceive; it is not what the baby perceives. A newborn does not know that his vision is not sharp and that the colors he sees are not true. He is simply inundated by light, and so overwhelmed by visual images that they quickly put him to sleep. Moreover, a newborn is a solipsist—he has no understanding that anything apart from himself exists—so to him, the visual images he sees are not images of objects; they are merely images—meaningless sensations. This causes him to see things in ways that we normally do not. If you bore a newborn or a one-month-old with an object, then show him the same object closer or farther away, he studies it afresh as though it were something brand new.[58] To him, a visual image in a new size is a novel sensation, not merely the same object at a different distance. On the other hand, a newborn or a one-month-old does not examine objects as a whole; he examines only parts of their outlines. This makes him see different objects with similar outlines as the same: if you bore him with one face he will remain bored when you show him another, if the overall brightness is the same.[59] This makes him see things startlingly differently from adults. To an adult, ∨ resembles ∠, while ╱ looks very different from ∠. However, to a one-month-old who is bored with ∠, ╱ looks like the same old thing and leaves him bored, but ∨ looks different enough to interest him again.[60] That is in the laboratory. At home, the mother who picks him up and the mother who holds him will not look the same.

One factor more than any other accounts for what a newborn or a one-month-old baby sees: fluctuations of light of varying breadth across his retina. The eye and brain respond to changes in the amount of light striking the retina. These changes can be

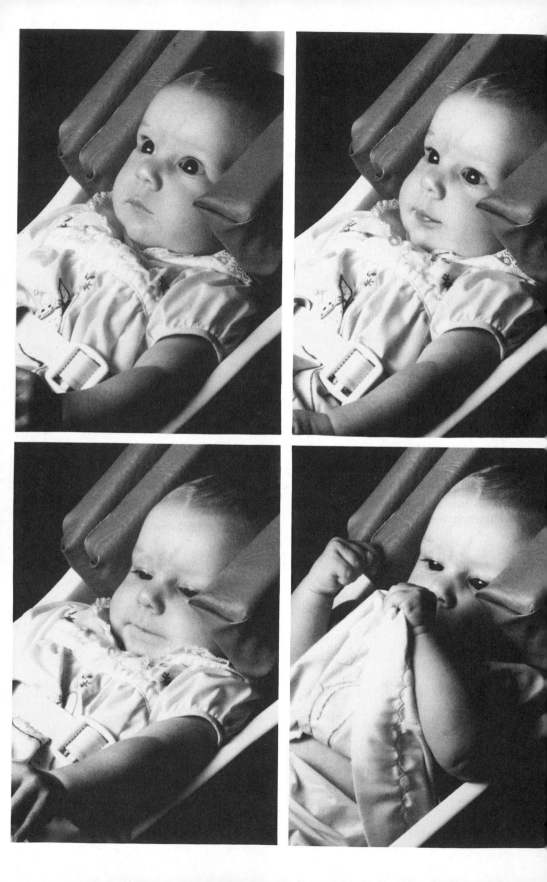

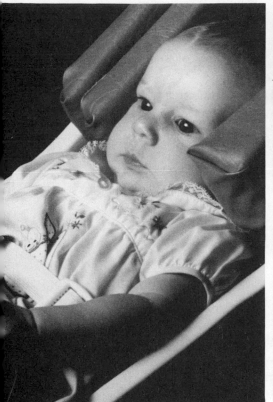
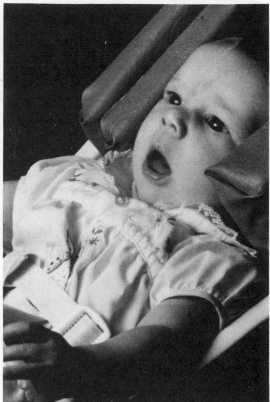
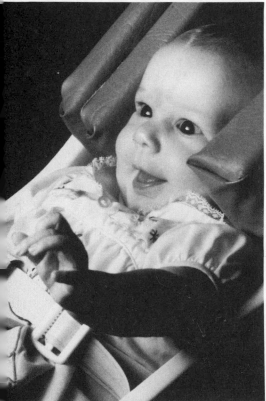

Testing what a three-month-old remembers about what he—or in this case, she—sees. The baby sits before a screen. In the first photo above left, a picture of a face has just appeared. Her eyes widen in surprise and interest. Now we begin to show her the same picture over and over again. Gradually she becomes bored. In photo 7 we change to a picture of another face. Clearly she has noticed the difference.

spread out over large areas of the retina, or restricted to small areas, or any combination thereof: whether we notice a change depends on the area over which the change occurs as much as it depends on the amounts of energy involved. By measuring the luminosity of each part of an image presented to the eye, and analyzing those measurements using a complicated mathematical process called Fourier transformation, it is possible to describe the interaction of the amount of energy with the area over which that energy impinges upon the eye.[61] During the first six weeks of life, Fourier analysis alone can predict with nearly perfect accuracy which of any two objects a baby will prefer to look at.[62] At this time in a baby's life, energy per se is more important than anything that the energy represents. Since mother and father peering down at him represent similar amounts of optical energy, mother and father look the same.

By two to three months, this begins to change. Now a baby's visual cortex begins to control what he sees,[63] so he begins to see shapes somewhat as we see them: an object that begins to move no longer looks as if it is changing its shape.[64] He begins to see shapes inside shapes—to see the features in faces, for example.[65] The mother who picks him up and the mother who holds him begin to look similar. He still does not see colors as we do, nor does he realize that the images he is sensing are objects. On the other hand, he does recognize sights he has experienced before, and he develops preferences that are not based on the amount and distribution of energy alone. He prefers portraits to abstract paintings reflecting comparable energy;[66] and he looks longer at a photograph of his mother or father than at a photograph of a similar-looking stranger.[67] Finally vision has caught up with the other senses: finally he can recognize his parents by sight, and even notice whether they are smiling or frowning.[68]

Around four months the baby can focus at different distances as well as an adult: he will notice you standing across the room, and beam. Now he sees stereoscopically—he will reach more often for the closer end of a toy—and he perceives colors truly. His vision is much sharper than it used to be, and he remembers a lot about what he sees. We shall see in chapter 10 that around this time he also comes to realize that visual images represent objects with a certain amount of stability and durability. Thus now he recognizes that a toy remains the same toy while you pick it up and put it down a few feet away.

Between six and eight months, the baby comes to understand objects much better. Like adults, he even perceives objects with no physical presence—objects that must be inferred, like the square in figure 6.4.[69] Now, too, he understands all the cues that indicate depth. His vision is as sharp as that of many adults without their glasses, so he starts to see textures. Broadly speaking, his vision is becoming adult.

Helping Vision Develop

Normally, babies receive more visual stimulation than they can handle—so much more that most of the time they shut it out by closing their eyes and falling asleep. Special mobiles and other paraphernalia are superfluous for their visual development. Indeed, for the first month of life, the best way to stimulate a baby's visual development is probably to draw the curtains in his nursery during the day and then open them again at night, leaving all of the lights switched off. When our eyes are as accustomed to the dark as a newborn's are, we can see a lot by the light of the stars, and a dim electric lamp is blinding. Brighter light lets us see better by stimulating our cones—but as we have seen, newborn babies see little with their cones. Light beyond the natural light of night overwhelms them instead of helping them to see.

FIGURE 6.4
Babies First See this Square at Six to Eight Months

After the first month or two, babies can handle a lot of light. Then it becomes important that they have things to see. However, they do not need fancy mobiles: a page of a magazine taped to the crib will do quite as well—and be easier to change when the baby becomes bored with it. Ads are usually the best of all, for they have big, bold headlines that are easy for babies to see. Odds and ends you find around the house are also good—a spoon, aluminum foil, or even his shoes.

The baby's visual system develops very fast during the first few months after birth—so fast that by the time he is four months old, it is halfway to adult. During this time, the most important thing a parent can do to ensure proper visual development is to watch out for any abnormalities of the baby's eyes. From birth look for a white pupil, an eye that turns inward consistently, an eye that never moves as far in one direction as the other, or an eyelid that never opens as far as the other. By the end of the first month you should be able to see the baby watch things and follow them as they move. By the time he is four to six months old his eyes should seem well coordinated. If you suspect a problem—or if you have a familial history of serious eye problems—see an ophthalmologist. Abnormalities in a baby's eyes should be attended to soon, much sooner than is necessary for adults.

This is because the nervous system does not form neuronal channels if neurons do not fire; the nervous system loses its ability to form neuronal channels with age; and the visual system in particular begins to lose this ability during the baby's first year of life. If some abnormality in a young baby prevents neurons within his visual system from firing, or distorts those neurons' pattern of firing, the baby's nervous system is likely to become limited in its ability to see. Permanently limited: correcting the abnormality later will not correct the deficiency.*[73]

*The most common early abnormality is one wherein the two eyes do not both look at the same thing at the same time. This is strabismus (or "squint," or "lazy eye"). All babies look strabismic at birth, but by three months a baby's eyes usually converge on the same point most of the time.[70] If they do not, he will see double. To avoid seeing double, he may learn to look through only one eye at a time, alternating between them: then, if his strabismus is not treated, he will lose stereoscopic vision. More likely he will simply ignore one eye: then, if his strabismus is not treated, not only will he lose stereoscopic vision, but after a few years his disused eye will probably go blind.[71]

There are many causes of strabismus. Commonly it is near-sightedness or far-sightedness in one eye. In these cases it can be cured with eyeglasses or contact lenses, plus patching the good eye to force the "lazy" eye to work. Often the cause is a muscular imbalance: then

We have seen this dramatically in our own work with young children who were born with or developed cataracts.[74] A cataract is a clouding of the eye's lens. It cannot be treated, but the lens can be removed and a contact lens worn in its place. With a contact lens replacing the natural lens, the eye cannot change its focus, so it can see sharply at only one distance. However, it can still see. An eye blocked by a dense cataract can see nothing more than light.

We have studied over a hundred babies who have had cataracts removed, testing them at first every few months, then every year, until they are well into school. These tests make clear just how necessary early visual experience is. Babies born with cataracts can still see light, but they cannot see patterns of light; so they may never become able to see fine patterns clearly. The longer the delay until they are treated, the less clearly they become able to see. In the pediatric ophthalmological clinic in which we work, treatment during the first few months of life nearly always leads to virtually normal vision by school age (assuming the child wears his contact lenses). On the other hand, delays in treatment nearly always leave permanent deficits.

Months matter here. When the visual system is first developing, it does not matter what the baby has to look at, as long as he has something more stimulating around him than plain, painted walls. However, if his system is to develop normally, it must be exercised. If a baby's vision is to develop normally, then during the first few months of his life, when he opens his eyes, he must see. One of the most important things a parent can do is to make certain that he can.

---

it can be cured surgically, by snipping out or moving around a bit of muscle. However, whatever the cause, if treatment is delayed until a child is two to three years old, even if his good looks are restored and he retains sight in both eyes, he will likely still lose stereoscopic vision.[72] His eyes will look fine, function fine individually, and both focus on the same thing at the same time; yet the child will never learn perfectly to fuse both images. To save stereoscopic vision, or most of it, the treatment must be undertaken during the child's first year of life.

7

Sounds of Life

A NEWBORN BABY lies sleeping in his crib. The nursery door slams shut. Instantly he opens his eyes wide and flings out his arms like Punch in a puppet show. Clearly he has heard the door slam. Clearly he can hear.

Yet when you talk to him, he hardly appears to hear anything at all. He may stop sucking his hand or he may twitch and start, but he will rarely look at you. He will not even look *toward* you unless you stand far toward the side and talk nonstop for ten or fifteen seconds: then he may turn, but the odds are no better than even.

For just as he sees strangely, a newborn hears strangely too. The world to him is a free-for-all of sounds, a mêlée so chaotic we could make no sense of it at all.

That slamming door, for instance, slams just once, yet the new-born hears it slam repeatedly. Six times or a dozen or more. When you talk to him, he hears your voice reverberating like a train announcer's echoing through a cavernous railroad station. The room may be tiny, but he hears your words echo and re-echo from every wall and surface in it.

Echoes and Resonance

In doing this, the baby is not imagining things: rather he is hearing things that we ignore. When his nursery door slams, it does not stop moving instantly; its panels continue moving from inertia until they bulge outward microscopically into the hall. Then they rebound and bulge inward almost as much. Then outward again, then inward, on and on, bulging less and less each time as the energy dissipates, but continuing nevertheless dozens of times. Each time a panel bulges into the room, it shoves the molecules of air next to it, which in turn shove the molecules next to them, which shove the molecules next in turn, until a wave of shoving approaches the wall. When the door's panels rebound outward, they suck molecules back with them, and they in turn suck back the molecules next to them, and so on until a wave of sucking approaches the wall. One complete cycle of shoving and sucking—of atmospheric pressurization and rarefaction—form one cycle of a sonic wave. When this wave bumps into a wall, the wall reflects it back at perhaps half of its original energy and absorbs the rest and/or transmits it into the next room. Similarly, when you say something, the sonic waves formed by your vocal cords bounce back at you from the wall with roughly half their original power—then they hit another wall and rebound at one-quarter power, then one-eighth power, and so on. These reflections reach you at different times, for sound travels at a constant speed but walls, ceiling, floor, and tabletops are all different distances away. This mass of sonic waves arriving at your ears at different times forms a muddle and confusion that your ears pick up, translate into neural impulses, and pass to the brain. You do not hear any confusion because of how the brain works: like an efficient bureaucracy processing millions of slips of paper, each with an original and six or a dozen carbon copies. Each paper and its copies are sorted, compared with each other and with papers that came through earlier, passed sideways to other interested departments, passed upward to superiors, sorted again, and so on, until eventually they reach the auditory cortex, Vice President for Hearing. The auditory cortex pays assiduous attention to each original sonic wave, so you hear each and every one of these. But the duplicates it ignores—except to notice how thick a file they have built up.[1] A thick file of duplicates does impress the auditory cortex: a sonic wave backed by many reflections of itself sounds more resonant.

The only exceptions to this are reflections arriving at the ear relatively late. The brain will hold open the file for duplicates only one-twentieth of a second after the original sound comes through. Anything coming in later than that—a sound bouncing off a canyon's distant wall—is treated as another original and heard separately, as an echo.

That is why you do not hear all the sounds in a room. But the newborn's brain is not able to do this. Remember our description of his visual cortex: the layers are mixed up, the cells' hairlike dendrites do not branch out far enough to interconnect many cells, and the cells have not become coated with myelin, the grease of neural transmission. The newborn's auditory cortex is comparably immature.[2] Just as his visual cortex does not function properly, so his auditory cortex does not.

This means there is nothing in his brain to sort out original sounds from reflections. A newborn hears nearly every reflection that comes back to him.

Experimental Confirmation

Rachel Clifton and associates[3] confirmed this at the University of Massachusetts using a reflex that has no name, but that might be called the Jack Benny: if you make a prolonged noise near a newborn, he will nearly always turn his head toward it—but he may take several seconds before starting to turn, and then he will turn very slowly, like Jack Benny. The baby is not looking for the source of the sound, since he will turn toward it in the dark with his eyes closed. He simply turns reflexively, just as he turns toward a finger touching his cheek.

Clifton and her colleagues played a tape-recorded rattle seventy-two times through one of two loudspeakers to newborn babies

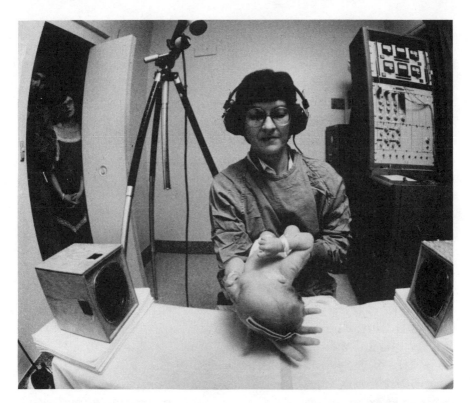

Testing the hearing of a newborn baby: it usually takes him eight seconds, but he consistently turns toward the loudspeaker from which a sound is coming, showing that he has heard it. The experimenter's headphones are to prevent her from hearing the sound, so that she cannot influence the results. Photographed in the laboratory of Darwin Muir at Queen's University in Kingston, Ontario.

still in the hospital.* One loudspeaker was on the babies' right, the other on their left. About half of the time the babies turned their heads, nearly always toward the loudspeaker producing the sound. Next they tested whether the babies heard a reflected sound separately from the original. To do this they created an equally powerful "reflection" from the second loudspeaker: they played the same tape through the second loudspeaker after delaying it electronically by seven-thousandths of a second—equivalent to placing a per-

---

*Psychologists first tried to study babies' hearing with the sorts of scientific stimuli they used to study adults' hearing, like pure tones composed of one frequency only and "white noise" composed of all frequencies equally. But they found that babies do not respond to scientific stimuli: they respond to rattles. Unpopped popcorn in an empty bottle worked best.[4]

fectly reflective wall a few feet away. An adult in that situation could not hear the "reflected" sound at all; all noise seemed to come from the first loudspeaker. But the babies acted as though they heard both and were confused. They rarely turned. When they did turn, they turned after hesitating even more than normal, as though the brain could not decide on the direction; and then they ended up turning as often toward the "reflection" as toward the original sound.[5]

Locating Sounds

A newborn seems to hear more than merely whether the sound is coming from the left or right, for the farther off toward the side it comes from, the farther he turns. But he does not hear this clearly. During the first month, a sound must originate nearly full to the side if he is to locate it: otherwise he will turn toward it no more often than he will turn away.[6] He is also confused by additional sounds coming from in front of him, even when the sounds do not reach him at the same time.[7] Yet it is remarkable that a newborn can place any sound at all, since he hears so many reflections. He ought to live in a sonic bedlam where echoes mix madly with other echoes, and every sound appears to come from every corner of the room.

On the other hand, the "Benny reflex" does exist: if you talk to a newborn from across the room, more often than chance would have it he will turn slowly toward you. Not only does he distinguish your voice from its natural echoes, under some conditions he senses its direction.

Doubtless he distinguishes your voice from its reflections because it is louder, since sonic waves lose much of their energy each time they are reflected off a surface. (In Clifton's experiment the baby could not distinguish the original sound because the "reflected" sound was equal in intensity.) But amidst all those echoes, how can he tell where the original is coming from?

Clifton went on to learn that a baby locates sounds through their higher pitches, which sound louder at one ear than the other. To see how she found this out, we must understand some more about sound and hearing. The predominant rate, or frequency, of the vibration of a sonic wave is the major determinant of a sound's pitch. A man's speaking voice is pitched on average around 130 cycles per second, or 130 Hertz (Hz); a woman's is usually pitched around 260 Hz, one octave higher. But all natural sounds contain higher, harmonic frequencies superimposed upon this fundamental frequency. These audible harmonics commonly extend to 5,000 or 10,000 Hz, and they can go even higher. We hear them not as separate sounds but as overtones superimposed upon the basic sound. They impart to a sound its timbre.[8]

These various frequencies comprising a sound help us to locate its origin. Let us say a baby is crying on your left. His voice reaches your left ear in full gale, but your head acts as a windbreak for your right ear. Waves reaching the right ear have only one-tenth to one-hundredth the intensity. From this difference in intensity your brain calculates the direction of the source—when and if it has frequencies above about 3,000 Hz to work with. It cannot work this way with frequencies that are much lower because lower-frequency waves are long enough to engulf an adult's head and reach the farther ear in full force. Thus we locate high pitches, and only high pitches, through differences in intensity between the ears.

Yet with lower-pitched sounds we still perceive direction. A sonic wave coming from the side arrives at one ear slightly before the other, so we sense it with one ear before the other: the brain times that difference and calculates from it the wave's direction. This it does only with frequencies lower than about 1,500 Hz, because higher-frequency waves are so short that more than one can pass the head at once. When this happens, the brain cannot tell whether a wave passing one ear is the same wave that just passed the other or is a different wave. Thus we locate lower-pitched sounds—and only lower-pitched sounds—through slight differences in the time that the ears hear them.[9]

Those are the two ways that adults locate sounds. Barbara Morrongiello and Rachel Clifton tested whether a newborn locates sounds in both ways that adults do.[10] To find this out, they put the noise of their rattle through an electronic device that could filter out various frequencies, and made tapes containing different selections of the original frequencies. Then they played the tapes to see which frequencies elicited the "Benny reflex" from twenty-four newborns. Frequencies above 3,000 Hz elicited the reflex as often as the complete set of frequencies; frequencies below 1,600 Hz rarely elicited it (although they caused the babies' pulse to slow, showing that the babies heard the sound); and frequencies in between elicited it a middling amount. Clearly, a newborn locates sounds primarily on the basis of the higher frequencies, using the differences in the intensity of the high frequencies reaching his two ears.[11]

Since a newborn's head is so small, there can be a difference in intensity between his ears primarily with very short sonic waves (that is, very high frequencies), for only short waves will not wash over his head. Calculating from the size of his head, he should be able to locate sounds most easily if they contain frequencies of 6,000 Hz and higher, like the higher harmonics in his mother's voice. However, as we just saw in Morrongiello and Clifton's study, 6,000 Hz is not a sharp cutoff: the babies used frequencies below 3,000 Hz too, although less effectively. Since male voices contain overtones between 3,000 Hz and 6,000 Hz (and sometimes higher), a newborn may be able to locate his father's voice too, but not always and not so easily.

This is one reason that a newborn baby often seems to be more responsive to his mother than to his father: he can hear both voices, but he cannot tell where his father's is coming from.

It is difficult to learn exactly when babies stop hearing echoes and become skilled at locating sounds, for the "Benny reflex" functions only for the first month or six weeks after birth. As the auditory cortex matures during the second month after birth, it begins to inhibit the reflex; but not until about four months is the auditory cortex mature enough to control head movements toward a sound. Thus between two and three months the reflex usually is quashed, yet there is nothing to replace it. At that age a baby will rarely turn toward a sound at all.[12] Now when you talk to him from across the room, he will smile and coo, but he is as likely to turn away from you as toward you.

Sometime during the fourth month of life, a baby's auditory cortex becomes sufficiently mature to ignore reflections—to hear only one sound instead of a mass of echoes.[13] Now he can locate sounds in the dark—that is, with no help from his eyes—almost as precisely as an adult can.[14] He turns quickly and accurately toward your voice even if you talk to him with the lights off at night. At the same time, he becomes able to locate low-pitched sounds through the interval between the sensations coming from his two ears.[15] Now, no matter how deeply his father's voice may rumble, he can hear where it is coming from.

Treble Tones

A baby can hear at birth. His aural world would be bedlam to us, yet he can make some sense of it: amidst a mass of echoes, he can sometimes distinguish an echo's source. However, when he hears something—his mother's or his father's voice—he does not hear it as we do. He hears it as thinner and duller.

To see why, we need to examine the ear. The outer ear, the part we see, is merely a horn that gathers sonic waves, concentrates them, and funnels them against the eardrum. The eardrum is a membrane that bulges in and out with the waves, pushing and pulling a lever on the other side. That lever is a bone, the first of a chain of three that takes the weak, air-driven excursions of the eardrum and concentrates them fifteen-fold to thirty-fold onto a smaller drumlike membrane, the oval window of the inner ear. The oval window vibrates in turn against a fluid that fills the inner ear. This fluid carries the waves to an organ, the organ of Corti, where they impinge upon neurons, causing them to fire.[16] The organ of Corti works like a microphone—so like a microphone that physiologists have tape-recorded the electrical signal from it while they talked into a cat's ear, then played back the recording and heard what they had just said.[17]

When a baby is born, a number of anatomical factors weaken his hearing. His outer ear is small, so it collects sound inefficiently. His ear is plugged with a creamy white substance called vernix that can take a week or longer to disappear: this blocks all frequencies to some extent, but especially it blocks high ones. His eardrum is more flaccid than ours, so it does not vibrate as well at high frequencies. The same is true of the main moving part of the organ of Corti, the basilar membrane. And inside the newborn's middle ear is surplus embryonic tissue that has not yet been absorbed by the body and that now damps the vibrations of the three bones—again, especially at higher frequencies.[18] To judge from all this, a newborn should hear middle and low frequencies somewhat less well than we do, while high frequencies he should hear considerably worse than we.

This inference is confirmed by a number of studies. The cleverest of these was done by Kurt Hecox at the University of California, San Diego.[19] Hecox measured the responses of the brain evoked by white noise, a mixture of all audible frequencies in equal amounts—a sound like the hiss between stations on an FM radio. Hecox presented this noise in such short bursts that it sounded like a click, and he presented it repeatedly at a rate of thirty clicks per second. He presented it to newborns still in the hospital and to several adults. For each person he turned the volume up and down until he found the lowest intensity that evoked responses. On average, the quietest noise that evoked responses in the newborn would sound to us roughly four times louder than the quietest sounds that evoked responses in the adult.[20] Apparently, compared to adults, newborns are indeed a touch hard of hearing.

Next Hecox examined newborns' ability to hear different frequencies. To do this he presented the clicks at a moderate intensity, then introduced background noise—the same noise as the clicks but turned on and left on. He turned up this background noise just loud enough to mask the clicks, just loud enough so that the clicks evoked no response. Then he used an electronic device to remove various frequencies from the background noise, to see which were needed to mask the clicks. The fewer frequencies below 4,000 Hz that he included in the background noise, the less the background noise masked the clicks. When he removed all the frequencies below 4,000 Hz, the background noise did not mask the clicks at all. Clearly, although the clicks contained the entire spectrum of sound, the newborns heard only the portion below 4,000 Hz.[21] If we could hear the world through a newborn's ears, it would sound as though the treble were turned down.

Bass Tones

Although the newborn hears most of the low-pitched sounds that we do, he does not hear the resonances we hear that are caused by the accretion of late-arriving, "duplicate" sounds to the original sound. (He hears echoes instead.) And he hears fewer low-pitched sounds in speech or music than we. For we, but not the newborn, routinely hear fundamental frequencies that do not exist.

To understand this, let us return to our discussion of harmonic frequencies. As we said earlier, the fundamental frequency of a sonic wave determines its pitch, and the harmonic frequencies above that determine its timbre. The spacing of these harmonic frequencies roughly equals the fundamental frequency: if the fundamental frequency is 100 Hz, harmonics above that will come more or less every 100 Hz; if the fundamental is 200 Hz, the harmonics will come every 200 Hz; and so on. Organized by musical octaves, they form a distinct pattern, which is illustrated in figure 7.1.

However, nature is not quite so neat as this. When you slam the nursery door, the panels whose vibrations create the sonic wave differ in their rigidity. Stiff parts vibrate faster than flaccid parts, so the stiffer areas create higher-frequency vibrations in the air than the more flaccid areas. Thus any sonic wave is actually many different fundamental frequencies, each of which has its own set of harmonics. When these sets of frequencies are mostly dissimilar, we hear rough noises like the ripping of paper; when they are similar, we hear a more or less musical tone with a more or less distinct pitch. The more similar these sets of frequencies are, the more

FIGURE 7.1

The Harmonic Structure of a 100-Hz Tone

"pure" and "clean" is the tone we hear and the more distinct is its pitch.

This pitch usually comes from the predominant fundamental frequency. However, if the fundamental frequency is missing yet the pattern of higher harmonics is strong, then your brain will infer from the pattern that the fundamental *should* be there, so you will hear its pitch anyway.[22] In this way you hear the pedal tones of an organ through a table radio: the radio emits virtually no vibrations below 100 Hz, yet your brain hears pitches that are normally induced by 32 Hz. You are hearing frequencies that do not exist.

Indeed, a frequency of 32 Hz may not exist even in the hall where the organ is playing. A 32-Hz pipe is nearly eighteen feet long, and expensive. For hundreds of years organ builders have cut corners by eliminating 32-Hz pipes, instead rigging shorter 64-Hz and 96-Hz pipes to play together. Sixty-four and 96 Hz are the first two harmonics above 32 Hz, so 32 Hz is what the audience and organist hear.

Instantaneously and automatically inferring one frequency from a pattern formed by others is an extremely complicated task that is beyond the capability of a young baby's auditory cortex.[23] Robert Bundy, John Colombo, and Jeffrey Singer at the State University of New York (Buffalo and Oswego) confirmed this indirectly.[24] They tested the ability of four-month-old babies to hear a melody— ♪♪♪ —created with notes formed from different combinations of harmonics. To one group they played notes containing the fundamental frequency and the first three harmonics above it; to a second group they played notes containing the fundamental frequency and a random assortment of higher harmonics; and to a third group they played an assortment of the higher harmonics with no fundamental. The first time the melody was played, the babies oriented toward it: their hearts slowed down. By the fifth time, they were used to it. Then Bundy played the same notes in a different order, forming a different melody. One group of babies oriented toward it again, showing that they could hear the difference, and hence the pitch of the notes: this was the group hearing notes that contained the fundamental and the first three harmonics above it. However, the other groups seemed not to hear the change: unless all the lower harmonics were present, including the fundamental, four-month-olds seemed not to hear pitch at all.

This affects how a young baby hears most sounds, for voices, music, and most noises are centered around one pitch. Every sound like these is induced by one predominant fundamental frequency beneath a more or less orderly arrangement of higher frequencies. When we hear such sounds, we hear their pitches not from the fundamental frequency alone but from the harmonic frequencies as well. The harmonics reinforce the fundamental, helping us to hear it and making it sound more resonant. However, when a young baby hears them, the higher harmonics do not reinforce the fundamental. Thus the sounds he hears are thinner and less resonant than the sounds we hear. Since he also hears high frequencies less well, he hears the world as we might hear it through a little radio with both the treble and the bass turned down. His parents' voices sound weaker and thinner, as though he were hearing them through a telephone.

By the time a baby is seven to eight months old, this has changed substantially. A baby this old can hear a missing fundamental,[25] and his ability to hear high frequencies is much better than it was at birth. By adult standards he is still hard of hearing, but the bass and treble are no longer reduced as they were.[26] If we could hear through his ears now, we would think we were hearing a fairly good stereo with the volume somewhat lower than we are used to. His hearing continues to improve thereafter, but it has a long way to go to become adult. He will not hear as well as an adult until he is in school.[27]

The Sounds of Speech

We have said much in these last chapters about the cortex of the newborn's brain and how immature it is. Yet some areas of his cortex, although immature, are relatively precocious—disproportionately large and specialized even before birth. These are the areas that discern short sequences of sound.[28] Because of their precocity, a baby begins life distinguishing the elements of melody and speech.

William Condon and Louis Sander demonstrated this at Boston

University in an astonishing study of sixteen newborn babies, fourteen of whom were less than two days old.[29] Condon and Sander had someone talk to a baby while they filmed the baby's body movements with a high-speed movie camera. Next they analyzed the individual frames of the film and the corresponding parts of the sound track, looking at what happened every thirtieth of a second. They looked at (1) what sound the speaker was producing and (2) what movements the baby was making—whether he was waving an arm, turning his head, or whatever. Most of the sounds lasted more than one-thirtieth of a second, and so did most of the movements, yet the babies rarely moved during a sound. Moreover, if a baby was moving, he usually changed his movements as the sound changed— as an *mmm* changed to an *ah* in *mama,* for instance. In this way all sixteen babies demonstrated that they distinguished the individual elements of speech. Moreover, they distinguished those elements quite as well when the speech came from a tape recorder or when the language was Chinese. However, the babies did not move in synchrony with isolated vowel sounds and taps: they did not distinguish sounds disconnected from language's natural patterns and flow.

Usually these babies did not begin moving as a sound began; rather, if they were already moving when the sound began, they continued to move until it stopped. Sounds seemed to keep them going. Moreover, in a similar study in Tokyo, researchers found that one- to six-day-olds move more vigorously when adults talk louder, but not when white noise, taps, or unpatterned sounds are played louder.[30] Apparently the patterns of speech form a vehicle that carries individual sounds past the muddy ditches of the immature brain and takes them into more precocious areas.* From there

*These areas tend to be in the left side of the brain.

It has become a truism in popular psychology that the left and right sides of the brain—at least the adult's brain—specialize in different things, the left side in linguistic, analytical, and numerical tasks, the right side in musical, synthetic, and geometrical tasks. These differences are nowhere near so clearly defined as they are purported to be, and when one side of the brain is damaged, the other side can learn to take over to some extent; yet in 95 percent of adults, specialization along these lines is unquestionably there.[31]

Psychologists used to think that a baby's brain is not specialized this way, because it is so plastic: if one side is damaged, the child usually grows up nearly normal.[32] But now we know that the sides are specialized at birth. Anatomical differences have been found in the newborn's brain fully comparable to anatomical differences in the adult's,[33] and a number of researchers have found that the two sides already function differently between birth and six months of age.[34] In general, the left hemisphere (right ear) handles speech better, while the right hemisphere (left ear) is better with noises and musical chords. There is some the energy represented by each sound spills out into other areas, continuing for a moment other neuronal events—like those causing a movement—that were about to end.

When a sound is part of a pattern such as speech or music, even a very young baby hears that sound much as we do, not as an isolated noise but as a thread of a fabric, a thread that can be compared to other threads by denier and dye. Thus a baby hears as we do the most minuscule elements of speech, the smallest distinguishable particles of its sound—sounds like the *p* and the *a* of *pa*, and the *b*, the *ee*, and the *t* of *beet*.

These elements of speech are called phonemes. Linguists have devised elaborate ways to distinguish phonemes according to the frequencies they contain. By generating those frequencies electronically through loudspeakers, linguists can synthesize any phoneme for study in the laboratory and vary it as desired. One variation they have studied extensively is the difference between *pa* and *ba*. Hold your hand in front of your mouth and say them. Say them aloud, do not whisper. When you say *ba* you feel an explosion of air against your hand, and simultaneously you hear your vocal cords. When you say *pa* you feel a similar explosion and hear a similar sound from your vocal cords, but there is a short delay in between. That delay is the essential difference between the two sounds.[36]

The delay between the explosion and when the vocal cords start to vibrate is called the voice-onset time. By varying the voice-onset time, not only of *pa* and *ba* but of other phonemes as well, linguists have learned that adults do not hear a change in sound corresponding to each change in voice-onset time. We hear distinct categories. When the delay is less than approximately one-fortieth of a second, we hear *ba*. When the delay is longer than that—no matter how much longer—we hear *pa*.

At Brown University, Peter Eimas and colleagues tested whether babies distinguish these categories as we do.[37] They studied one- and four-month-olds; but since their study found no difference between these ages (nor have many similar studies), and since the linguistic areas of the brain develop little anatomically

suggestion that initially this specialization is greater in girls than in boys. By six months, the left hemisphere, but apparently not the right, also recognizes a correspondence between speech and the lip movements producing it.[35]

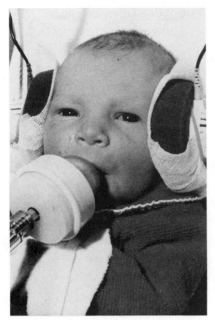

Learning what a newborn hears. This two-day-old has learned that if he sucks hard, he will hear something interesting: the sound *pa pa pa pa pa*. As he becomes bored, he sucks less hard—but before he loses interest completely, the sound changes to *ba ba ba ba ba*. If the baby begins to suck hard again, he has probably heard the difference. Photographed at the laboratory of Josiane Bertoncini and Jacques Mehler at the *Centre d'Etude des Processus Cognitifs et du Langage* in Paris.

between birth and one month,[38] their results should apply to newborns as well.

To learn how babies hear differences in voice-onset time, Eimas and his colleagues gave them a pacifier, a pacifier wired to record how often an infant sucked on it. Whenever an infant sucked, *pa pa pa pa pa* . . . sounded through a loudspeaker. The faster he sucked, the louder it sounded. The baby learned quickly that sucking caused the sound to appear, and he sucked faster to hear it. But eventually he tired of the sound and sucked slower. Then the experimenters changed the voice-onset time. When they lengthened it by one-fiftieth of a second, the experimenters still heard *pa,* and so apparently did the baby, for he continued to suck slowly. But when they reduced the voice-onset time by one-fiftieth of a second, then the experimenters heard the *pa* shift to *ba*—and then, too, the baby sucked faster. He heard it differently as well.

Babies hear more than just phonemes in this adult way: they hear whole syllables too. *Pit* and *pat* contain different phonemes, yet they sound fairly similar to us. The same with *tip* and *tap*. On the other hand, *pit* and *tip* or *pat* and *tap* contain similar phonemes, yet they sound dissimilar. From another study like Eimas's[39] we know

that one-month-olds categorize these syllables in the same paradoxical, adult way.

Of course, one-month-old babies might have learned to categorize sounds this way by hearing their parents talk. But Lynn
Streeter from Bell Laboratories found in a similar study[40] that Ken-
yan two-month-olds make distinctions in voice-onset time that
their parents do not make when speaking in their local language,
Kikuyu.*

Dozens of studies similar to these point to one conclusion:
babies naturally sort phonemes into the same categories that languages commonly use.[42] Moreover, even the youngest babies do
much of this better than adults; for since no language uses all
possible phonemes, learning to speak a language requires not only
learning which phonemic distinctions matter in that language, and
sharpening them, but also learning to ignore all those that do not
matter. As soon as babies start to speak, they begin to lose some
ability to hear distinctions not used by their parents.[43] After eight
to ten years of ignoring distinctions, a child loses the ability to hear
some of them at all. Virtually no amount of practice will enable him
to regain this ability as an adult. That is why, no matter how well
we learn to speak a second language as adults, we almost never have
a perfect accent: we cannot hear as well as babies when we are
pronouncing something wrong.

Of all the researchers who have demonstrated this, Sandra
Trehub at the University of Toronto makes the clearest case—not
through her work, which is excellent, but through a story she tells
about one of her *faux pas.* Trehub designed a study to learn whether
one- to four-month-olds can distinguish as well as their English-
speaking parents a certain pair of sounds used in Czech. To obtain
these sounds, she ordered a tape-recording of two phonemes from
a linguistics laboratory. The tape arrived. Trehub played it but
heard no difference between the phonemes. She played it again, and
yet again, but no matter how often she listened to it, she could not
hear a difference. Eventually she telephoned the lab in a huff to
complain that someone had recorded the same phoneme twice.

*Although some categorizations we make depend on experience for their development
and/or maintenance, the categorization of voice-onset time seems built into the auditory
system. Adults will categorize voice-onset time this way in the lab even if the language they
speak does not make use of the distinction. Chinchillas and monkeys do too.[41]

"No," she was told. "Two phonemes are there." She was firmly convinced that she was wasting her time, but she went ahead with the study anyway.[44] Sure enough, the English-speaking parents, when forced to say which sound was which, were right only slightly better than chance. But their babies had no difficulty telling them apart at all.

The Sound of Speech

Not only does a baby hear the sounds of language—phonemes and syllables—but he hears the *sound* of language as well—timbre,[45] intensity,[46] duration,[47] and, to some extent, pitch.[48] A newborn will turn toward a rattle, but not toward a flutelike pure tone; he will start when a sound is made louder; he will twitch more when a sound is longer than when it is shorter; and low-pitched tones soothe him more than high-pitched tones.

Stripped of linguistic meaning, these elements of sound form the elements of music. If we deal with them in isolation as music, we find that a young baby seems to hear them much as we do. Even newborns are more likely to respond to a sound with overtones than to a tone composed of only the fundamental frequency.[49] By two to three months of age—as young as they have been tested—babies hear patterns of notes in simple melodic and rhythmical groups as adults do. Like adults, they hear a simple melody as unchanged when it is transposed into a different key, but as different when its notes are played in a different order, or when its rhythm is altered.[50] And they can be taught easily to coo on the pitch (more or less) that an adult sings to them.[51] There is even some suggestion that babies are better at matching a pitch than older children are; it may be that learning to ignore the pitches of voices in order to concentrate on the meaning of what they are saying interferes with this ability.

Under some circumstances even a newborn hears these aspects of language and music nearly as well as an adult does. As a result, even a one- to two-month-old (the youngest age tested) can hear differences in intonation and tone of voice. "Eat!" sounds different to him from "Eat?"[52] Indeed, a baby just three days old can distinguish one voice from another. Anthony Decasper and William Fifer showed this in a fascinating study at the University of North Carolina.[53] They taught ten babies how to change the "stations" on a "radio": a baby could choose to hear through headphones either his mother or a stranger reading Dr. Seuss. Normally with a pacifier, a newborn sucks hard for a few seconds, then rests for a few seconds before sucking again. But Decasper and Fifer wired their pacifier in such a way that by resting longer than his norm, a baby could switch on the stranger, or by starting sooner he could switch on his mother (or vice versa). These babies were all less than seventy-two hours old and had spent nearly all those hours in a general nursery cared for by nurses. None had spent longer than twelve hours in all with his mother. Yet after fifteen minutes of learning how the "radio" worked, eight of the ten spent most of the time listening to their mothers. Apparently, not only can a newborn distinguish his mother's voice from another woman's, after only a few days of life he prefers to hear it. Amidst all the novelty barraging his sensations, he clings to whatever he can recognize.

His mother's voice, incidentally, he came to recognize in the womb: the newborn shows no comparable preference for his father's voice, although he can tell two men's voices apart.[54]

A baby also comes to recognize very quickly the sound of his own voice. At Brown University, Martin Simner[55] found this by comparing how long three-day-olds cried while hearing the following sounds:

- Normally quiet hospital noise
- White noise as loud as a newborn's crying
- A poor imitation of a baby's crying created by a linguist's electronic speech synthesizer
- The tape-recorded crying of a five-and-a-half-month-old
- The tape-recorded crying of another newborn
- The tape-recorded crying of the baby himself

Simner found that the babies cried little during the quieter hospital noise. They cried equally little during the loud white noise. But the rest of the noises did set many of them to crying, and the babies cried more when they heard crying lower on our list—that is, they cried more when they heard crying more like their own.[56]

A newborn not only recognizes his own voice, he listens for it too. If some electronic device delays the sound of his voice on the way to his ears, he produces truncated cries.[57] He acts as though he were disconcerted, like an adult talking through the delayed sounds of a transatlantic telephone call. This may explain why, as physicians commonly note, deaf infants cry very little.

Baby Talk

In sum, a baby begins his life a little hard of hearing, and during his first month his world is full of echoes. Yet through all those echoes he discerns subtle distinctions in the sound of the human voice. Gradually he comes to know those distinctions and to become more aware of those he hears more often. These he pays more attention to in turn, clinging to them as islets of familiarity in a sea of sound—variably smelling, variably tasting, and variably feeling sound. The recognition makes him smile—his first true smiles, as we shall see in chapter 11. By becoming aware of these distinctions, he begins to learn his native language. Then, once he begins to say his first words, he becomes less able to hear some of the distinctions that he does not need but that he could hear shortly after he was born (although he will be able to learn to hear some of them again through his late childhood or early adolescence).[58]

While a baby is learning to speak, one thing in his aural environment is more important than any other: hearing speech, especially "baby talk." One of the curious phenomena of human existence is that adults in all cultures seem to reserve a special form of speech for talking to babies. This speech is simpler, slower, clearer, higher in pitch, more variable in pitch and intensity, more regular in tempo, more regularly broken by pauses, and repetitive—almost like singsong. *"Hel*lo *ba*by, *how* are *you* to*day? Ar*en't *you* a *pret*ty *ba*by? *Oh* you *are* a *pret*ty *ba*by!" The most macho of men use this speech naturally when talking to babies, especially young babies.[59] Its exaggerated rhythms grab the baby's attention; its pauses help the baby to hear its components; and its slower speed helps a young baby to sort out the important sounds from the echoes. All in all, it falls easier on his ear than the sounds of adult conversation. By the time he is four months old, if not before, a baby definitely prefers hearing baby talk to hearing adult speech.[60] Before then, even if he does not show a preference, he hears baby talk more clearly and learns more from it.[61] In a very real sense, baby talk is what he understands.

8

Activities of the Day

IF ANY CREATURE on earth is incapable of fending for itself, it is a newborn baby. Cute a baby surely is, yet as an independent organism, he is woefully incompetent. All he appears able to do is sleep and suck, and flail his arms and legs uselessly in the air.

But surprise! If you hold a newborn upright with his feet touching a tabletop, and support his weight, he will walk across it. And, like a puppy, if you put him in water, he will swim.[1]

Neurologists and psychologists have documented scores of hidden abilities like these. We have seen several of them in this book. A newborn will turn slowly toward a sound, for instance, or toward something touching his cheek; and he will open his mouth if you press his palm.

Many of these movements look deliberate. However, deliberateness implies purpose, and purpose requires knowledge based on experience: not necessarily the knowledge that moving an arm or a leg will remove a blanket, but at least the knowledge that moving *may* have *some* kind of effect. A newborn baby has had little chance to learn that he can cause anything to happen, so he does not move purposefully. Rather, he moves reflexively, just as your leg moves reflexively when a physician taps your knee. These movements come from very low levels of the brain, and they are important insofar as they are the neural building blocks of the coordinated movements that develop later. But this is an importance of which the baby is unaware. From the newborn's perspective, the activities of the day are not the actions of his arms and legs, they are the feelings within him that those actions induce—primarily the sensations of movement, touch, and balance. These are our topics in this chapter.

Movement Without Intent

We can see how involuntary are a newborn's movements by trying to teach a newborn to move on cue. The simplest way to do this is repeatedly to induce a movement immediately after sounding a bell, until sounding the bell alone triggers the movement. There is no logical reason for the bell ever to trigger the movement: the nervous system illogically infers the generalization, "all ringing bells presage food (or whatever)." (This is an unprovable broadjump from single instances, a classical fallacy.) However, the nervous system learns not by logic but by association, and this is one of the simplest circumstances in which an association can form. Adults will learn quickly to associate the bell with the reflex, as will dogs, cats, pigeons, goldfish, and every other species with a nervous system that has ever been brought into a lab.[2] But a newborn baby finds this almost impossible: he just barely learns.

In Prague's Institute for the Care of Mother and Child, Hanuš Papoušek taught babies to turn toward a bottle at the sound of a bell.[3] A bell (or buzzer) sounded, then ten seconds later, if the baby had not turned, a nurse stroked his cheek to induce him to turn, or turned his head for him if stroking his cheek proved ineffective. As a reward for turning, he was allowed to draw on the bottle for one minute; then the procedure began again. After ten repetitions, the baby had imbibed a normal meal, so the lesson was continued the next day. It took four-month-olds less than three days to learn to turn their head at the sound of the bell. It took three-month-olds hardly more than four days. But it took newborns two and a half weeks: they started on day three of life, and were typically three weeks old by the time they learned. (This is also the time a baby first shows that he anticipates a feeding by sucking before the nipple enters his mouth.) Considering the difficulty that a newborn has in this rudimentary kind of association, it is not likely that he has made the more complicated networks of association that are prerequisites for even the simplest forms of voluntary behavior.

This becomes even clearer in a study at Brown University.[4] Lewis Lipsitt and Herbert Kaye sounded a tone, then gave newborn babies a whiff of vinegar. The vinegar made the babies wiggle and hold their breath—clearly they did not like it—but the babies never learned to respond merely to the tone.

"But," you might well say, "a newborn does learn things. He learns to draw milk when nursing, for instance." This is true: if a newborn is rewarded for performing some action, he does become more likely to perform the action again. However, the circumstances under which a newborn learns are very limited, as we shall see in chapter 10. And, more to the point, a newborn can become more likely to do something without intentions entering into it at all.

Think of the nervous system as a slough of energy that is channeled into organized networks by neurochemical floodgates. A reward shifts some of these gates into a different position, so the flow of energy is likely to change. *But changing the flow of energy does not require a reward.* The flow can be changed by chance neural events comparable to individual gusts of wind, or by changes in energy applied to the nervous system by stimuli from outside, changes comparable to the approach or recession of a gale. Moreover, this change in flow tends to maintain itself with a certain inertia and to alter the topology so that a similar flow becomes easier in the future. Thus the mere occurrence of a movement raises the odds that the movement will be repeated. This is why, in adults, a nervous tap of the foot is more likely to be followed by a second tap of the foot than by a wave of an arm, a gnashing of teeth, or a wiggle of an ear. Some "nervous" taps of the foot are certainly voluntary—hints to a spouse that it is time to be off, for instance—but we have all found ourselves moving restlessly and rhythmically, unconsciously and unintentionally. When this happens, we are acting like a newborn baby who waves his arm, then waves it again for no reason but that he had just waved it before. (We shall see in chapter 10 that this kind of repetition is the primary means through which the baby learns about the world during his first six months of life.)

Awareness of Movement

After we finish moving—or while we are moving—usually we, as adults, are conscious of our motions. Even when we are not conscious of them, they are still controlled, so some portion of our brain is aware of them. A newborn's movements and actions are far less controlled than ours—they are almost completely undirected—yet even so they are not *completely* uncontrolled. If you hold a key in front of him, for instance, and catch his eye with it, he will not be able to reach out and grab the key, yet he is likely to extend his arm toward it, and often he will open his hand.[5] Even when the newborn flails his arms, he does not just fling them into motion with a jerk, letting them go and fall where they may, like brachial ballistic missiles. Rather, he moves his arms continuously, remaining in moment-to-moment control of their motion. Indeed, it is difficult to induce him to loose his control: once he grasps your finger or starts to kick, he continues doing it for some time.[6] His movements look like those of a sleepwalker who does not know where he is heading and who would be incapable of getting there if he did know, but who acts deliberately in his attempt.

The human body has no one single sensory system through which the nervous system monitors movements and activity. Rather, the nervous system perceives activity through the combination and interactions of four sensory systems: the visual system, which allows us to see what the body is doing; the proprioceptive system, which allows us to feel muscular contractions and the position of the joints; the sense of touch, which allows us to feel things that we contact as we move; and the sense of balance, through which we feel changes in the head's acceleration and position.[7] To some extent, each of these systems is functioning in the newborn, but in various ways each of them is also deficient.

The Sense of Touch

The sense of touch begins to function before any other sensory system. As we mentioned in chapter 2, a fetus aborted during the third month of gestation will respond reflexively to the touch of a hair around its mouth.

Like other sensations, a sensation of touch begins when a jolt of energy shoves ions through the membranes sheathing a nerve ending. The skin has a vast number of nerve endings of various shapes and structures, and these different shapes and structures, plus differing structures of the adjacent tissue, cause them to differ in how sensitive they are to different kinds of energy impinging upon skin: some are set off most easily by heat, while others are set off most easily by cold; some are set off by light pressure, while others require heavy pressure. Once a nerve ending does fire, it sets off a chain reaction within a tree of nerves that ends inside the brain. Within the brain, the lower portions sense the heat or cold or pressure, and act upon it reflexively, while the upper portions are responsible for deliberate actions and conscious perceptions.[8]

A newborn's skin is thinner than an adult's,[9] so it should insulate less well the nerve endings within it. These nerve endings are mature and are more numerous (although smaller) than those in the adult.[10] Also, the portion of the brain's cortex that processes touch, the somatosensory cortex, is more developed at birth than any other portion of the cortex.[11] Thus it looks as though the newborn should be more or less as sensitive to touch as an adult. (Especially on the right side of the body, for most babies are also more sensitive there than on the left, especially if they have been lying with their heads turned toward the right, as they commonly do. This may either presage or be the cause of right-handedness.[12]) It is difficult to tell just how sensitive the baby is to specific temperatures and pressures, but it is possible to examine his overall sensitivity by stimulating him in a way that sets off easily every kind of nerve ending, regardless of its structure: an electrical current.

At the Nebraska Psychiatric Institute, Ron Ellis and Robert Ellingson tickled two- to three-day-old babies on the palm with weak electrical current.[13] The currents were very weak—so weak

that adults could barely feel them—and hence too weak to be painful. (Remember from chapter 3 that babies feel less pain than
adults.) Adults tickled this way could feel a current only one-third
the strength of the weakest current that would elicit a "just visible"
reflexive twitch of the thumb or fingers. This weakest current that
adults could feel was also similar to the weakest current that elicited
a measurable electrical response higher up the stimulated nerve, on
the wrist. Thus the response higher up the nerve indicated the
weakest current that adults could feel. In newborns, the weakest
current to induce a twitch was two milliamps, just as it was in
adults. But in the newborns, the weakest current measurable on the
wrist—and hence, presumably, the weakest current that the babies
could feel—was roughly three times higher than it was in adults,
roughly comparable to the minimum current that caused a twitch.
Apparently, in the newborn and in the adult it takes the same
minim of energy at the skin to induce the same minim of reflex, yet
the newborn will not feel anything until it is three times as strong
as what an adult would feel. If you tickle a newborn very lightly,
he may not feel a thing.

Among newborns, girls tend to be more sensitive to touch than
boys. On average, girls only a few hours old will react to a weaker
puff of air against the belly; girls will squirm and cry sooner after
they are uncovered; and girls will react to a weaker electrical current
applied to a big toe.[14] (On the other hand, boys only a few hours
old are stronger: they lift their head better and kick and grip more
forcefully.[15] Again, this is *on average:* any one boy may differ from
any other boy, or any one girl may differ from any other, far more
than the average boy differs from the average girl.)

Although the newborn is perhaps one-third as sensitive to
touch as the adult, he is infinitely less discriminating. With his sense
of touch as with every other of his senses, the newborn's synesthesia makes a kaleidoscope of reality. Harvard's Peter Wolff showed
this with four colleagues in another study that used electrical stimulation.[16] Wolff and his colleagues measured the somatosensorily
evoked response—the electroencephalogram in response to touch
(see chapter 4). They found that turning on noise while applying a
momentary current to the wrist of three- to four-day-olds strength-
ens later components of the brain's response to the current. This did
not happen when they tried the same thing with adults. In other

words, within the baby's brain, the noise added to the touch. The sensation of one reinforced the other.

The Sense of Proprioception

Very similar to the sense of touch is the sense of proprioception, or kinesthesia—the sense of the body's own position and of its muscular contractions. This is what enables us to touch our lips with our eyes closed—which a baby can do the first day he is born. In essence this is an internal sense of touch. It comes from nerve endings in muscles and joints that work much like the network of nerve endings in the skin, except that their locations cause them to be triggered by the energy of muscular contractions and movement.[17] Like the sense of touch, this sense is highly functional in the newborn—but also like the sense of touch, it mixes with, and hence becomes confused by, other sensory systems. Thus when his eyes are closed, the newborn can feel the position of his arms accurately enough to bring his fingers directly to his mouth, *yet after a few days*—after he has had some experience seeing his arms and fingers—*then he becomes unable to do this.*[18] His sense of sight interferes with his sense of proprioception. In this way he is like an adult learning to dance who trips over his own feet for watching them.

The Sense of Balance

The last two ways we perceive movement are through our senses of balance and sight. As the visual system is responsible for the sense of sight, so the vestibular system is responsible for the sense of balance. The main organ of the vestibular system is the inner ear. This contains several fluid-filled tubes lined with hairs connected to nerve cells. The fluid inside these tubes behaves like the passengers in a bus: when you first begin to move forward, the fluid lurches backward; then it settles down; and finally, when you slow down, it lurches forward. As it lurches backward and forward, it shoves against the hairs, which trigger the neurons attached to them. These tubes are oriented in different directions, so they detect movements in different directions—or, more precisely, they detect changes in acceleration.[19]

Although the sense of balance is manifestly distinct from the sense of sight, the two senses are very closely allied. They continually support each other, and occasionally trip each other, like two topers tottering down the street. You can see this by standing on one foot: it is much easier to retain your balance when your eyes are open (and can see vertical and horizontal lines like the walls and the horizon) than when they are closed. Now back on two feet, try closing your eyes and pirouetting a few times. After you open them, the world not only feels as if it is swaying, it *looks* as if it is swaying; for spinning confused your vestibular system, which in turn confused your eyes. Your eyes can similarly confuse your vestibular system with similar results. You have experienced this if you have ever seen an Imax movie—a film projected with the audience close to a screen that is several stories high. These films seem inevitably to include footage shot from a light airplane flying low over the countryside. The vestibular effect is not quite so pronounced as the real thing, but it can be strong enough to warrant avoiding the theater immediately after dinner.

Of all the sensory systems, the vestibular system is the first to mature. The organs of balance in the inner ear are mature in shape and are partially innervated before eight weeks of gestation. By six months of gestation they are not only mature in shape, they are also mature in size and are completely innervated—the only organs in the body to become adult during gestation.[20] They have had a lot of exercise too, since the fetus is continually tumbled about in the womb. So the newborn feels the motion when he is carried, pushed in his stroller, rocked, or turned over; and just as with adults, unwonted motion can make him sick.

We can see this in a study by Margaret Lawrence and Carl Feind, who whirled sixty-four newborns (from three hours to ten days old) on a table-sized merry-go-round that rotated at about the speed of a record player.[21] Adults riding a merry-go-round show a peculiar sort of eye movement: as the body and head rotate forward, the eyes rotate backward to maintain a constant fixation; then the

eyes dart ahead quickly. The cause of this is vestibular as well as
ocular, since an adult's eyes will show this motion even while they
are blindfolded. (Indeed, an adult's eyes are more likely to show it
while they are blindfolded.) Lawrence and Feind found that the
newborns' eyes showed this nystagmus too, so we know that the
babies sensed their movement. And they flushed, belched, and
voided just as adults do under comparable circumstances.

Although the newborn's vestibular system is precocious, the
connections of his vestibular system to his other sensory systems
are not. If you move a newborn, for instance, he will move his eyes
as we just described, but he will not move them so smartly as an
adult will under similar circumstances.[22] This is not merely because
he cannot move his eyes as quickly as an adult: if he is stationary
while you twirl things around him, so that only his visual system
is involved, his eyes move similarly, yet much faster.[23] A newborn
being moved does not move his eyes quickly in part because the
connections between his vestibular and visual systems are not fully
formed.

As adults, we rarely notice how much our visual and vestibular
systems interact. Nor do we notice how much our vestibular system
interacts with our proprioceptive system just to keep us balanced on
two feet. What we commonly think of as the "sense of balance" is
not really the sense of balance alone; it is an integrated mixture of
balance, sight, and proprioception. Since the newborn's vestibular
system is ill connected to his other sensory systems, his integrated
"sense of balance" is not nearly so advanced as his vestibular system
on its own. It is difficult to put numbers on this, but we can gain
some feeling for what the newborn feels from a series of studies by
François Jouen, of the *Laboratoire de Psychobiologie de l'Enfant,* in Paris.[24]

Jouen studied babies between one and seven months old. He set
them in an infant seat inside a cubical crate one meter to a side. On
top of the baby's head he placed a little helmet that worked like an
electronic plumb bob to measure how vertically the baby held his
head while Jouen tilted the seat and/or some black-and-white
striped "wallpaper" inside the crate. Now, whenever an adult is
tilted—while he is balancing on the deck of a heeling sailboat, for
instance—he will try to keep his head aligned with the pull of
gravity (or rather, with the strongest G-forces, which usually
amounts to the same thing). But Jouen's babies did not. When he

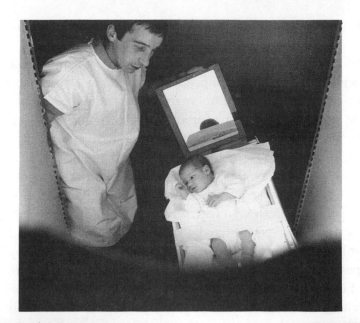

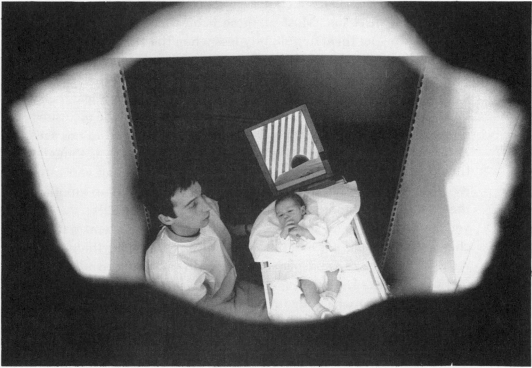

Testing the sense of balance of a three-day-old baby. We are looking through a hole cut into the back wall of a small cubicle. In the photo above, that wall is plain white; in the photo below it is covered with black-and-white stripes: we can see this in the mirror that is mounted behind the baby's head. A newborn has very little control over his head, so that whenever he is tilted, his head flops toward the side. Nevertheless, when he has something vertical to look at—the stripes in the photo below—his head flops a little less. This is work of François Jouen of the *Laboratoire de Psychobiologie de l'Enfant* of Paris, photographed in his laboratory in Rouen.

tilted them twenty-five degrees, he found that some of the younger ones just let their heads flop sideways, and most of the others kept them more or less in line with their bodies—that is, at about twenty-five degrees from plumb. (This was when the crate provided nothing to look at. When Jouen put a red, woolen pom-pom in front of them, both groups of babies held their heads a little higher, as though the sight of the pom-pom was energizing—which it was, quite literally, as we know from chapter 3.) None of them had the adult's righting reflex. In fact, when Jouen later kept babies upright but gave them some angled stripes to look at, he found that the older babies angled their heads fifteen degrees in sympathy with the stripes, as though they expected that such almost-vertical lines must indicate verticality. Finally Jouen tried tilting the babies while offering them stripes to look at, stripes that were slanted twenty-five degrees in the same direction as the baby or twenty-five degrees in the other direction. Most of these babies let their heads flop, although they let them flop slightly less when the stripes slanted in the direction opposite the baby. But when the stripes slanted with the baby, a few babies who were especially mature kept their heads aligned with their bodies and the stripes: these babies also held their heads vertically, like adults, when the stripes slanted in the opposite direction. In short, Jouen found that very young babies do not act as though they care or know which way is up. They act as though they do not even know that there is anything special about verticality. And once they do discover verticality, then for some months thereafter, more important to them than feeling verticality is *seeing* verticality. Although the newborn's vestibular system senses changes of acceleration like the adult's, it does not contribute to a sense of balance as we experience it. If you pick him up with his feet over his head, he does not feel upside down.

We suspect that a baby first develops adult feelings of balance during his second six months of life, after he has learned to creep or crawl, for that is when all of the various reflexes combining the vestibular and visual systems begin to look adult. Only then will a baby reach out and spread his fingers as he is lowered toward a surface.[25]

This leaves us with an interesting paradox. Adults' sensations rarely spill from one sensory system into another, as the newborn's do. But a signal exception to this lies with our sensations of balance and sight, which work together so closely that if we close our eyes and pirouette, after opening them again, the world looks as if it is moving. In contrast, the newborn's sensations spill about throughout his brain from one system to another, because his brain lacks the adult's deep network of neural channels; and one set of these channels that is not mature is the set that links the vestibular and visual systems. So the one place where adults are signally synesthetic, the newborn baby is not.

Crawling

Creeping and crawling are instrumental in the development of adult feelings of balance. We can see this in a fascinating pair of studies by the team of Bennett Bertenthal of the University of Virginia, and Joseph Campos and Karen Barrett of the University of Denver.[26] These researchers tested the reaction of babies placed upon a glass-topped table called a visual cliff. Spanning the center of this table like a bridge, directly above the glass, ran a plank of wood. A baby started each test lying upon this board. Looking down on one side of it, he saw a checkered floor more than a yard away; on the other side, he saw a very much higher checkered "floor" formed by a sheet of plywood just one-quarter of an inch beneath the glass. Across the deep side he saw his mother enticing him to cross.

Eleven days after the babies had first begun to crawl, about two-thirds of them did cross the deep side to their mother and cross blithely, as though either they did not mind falling or they lacked the sense of downwardness required to become worried about a fall. But a month later—forty-one days after they had first crawled—most babies would not venture over the deep side. During this month, they had learned something of downwardness and falling.

This understanding did not come merely from living an additional month, for babies of similar age performed differently, depending on how long they had been crawling. (The babies included six-and-a-half-month-olds, seven-and-a-half-month-olds and eight-and-a-half-month-olds—about sixteen of each age—and among the babies of each age group, those who had crawled more were more timorous.) This understanding came from crawling; or more specifically, it came *through* crawling, from the babies' experience of moving about in the world under their own steam.*

There is an obvious explanation for this: babies fall down more often once they have begun to crawl. But that explanation itself falls down in the face of a second study of six-month-olds performed in the same laboratory, on the same visual cliff. In this study, the researchers enabled babies to walk around before they had learned to crawl. They did this by providing each baby with a rolling "walker" that supported him in a sling like a breeches buoy: the baby's feet touched the ground but the walker took his weight, so he could wheel himself about. After a baby had had forty hours of experience using this walker, the researchers lowered him onto the deep side of the visual cliff, while recording his heart rate electronically. While being lowered onto the cliff, other babies that age who could not crawl and who had had no experience with the walker showed a momentary slowing of the heart, which typifies an "orienting reaction," a reaction of interest and attraction. But those babies with experience in the walker showed a *quickening* of the heart, which typifies a negatory "avoidance reaction."[28] Apparently, a baby can develop adult notions of downwardness *without falling*, merely by moving about on his own. Falling may well speed the process. Indeed, the greatest quickening of the heart came from those babies given walkers who had also begun to crawl a little by the time they were tested (see figure 8.1). But we have just seen that locomotion by itself is sufficient to teach an appreciation of height. So although falling may commonly be involved in learning to appreciate height, it is not necessary.[29]

A baby's creeping and crawling teach him about downwardness as a by-product of teaching him about directionality in general. Before a baby begins to creep and crawl, he has no control over where he goes, so he has no impetus to learn about how to get from point A to point B. Not only has he not learned this, he has not even learned that point A and point B exist at specific, fixed places. Instead he thinks of all objects' locations in terms of himself, as

---

*When a baby cannot move himself about, this understanding may be delayed. Campos observed a baby whose movements were restricted by a cast long past the normal age of crawling. This baby did not show an avoidance reaction when placed upon the visual cliff until six weeks after his cast was removed.[27]

FIGURE 8.1
How Experience "Walking" and Crawling
Affects Babies' Reactions to the Visual Cliff

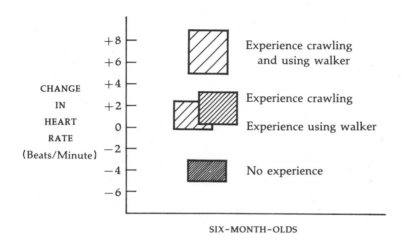

SIX-MONTH-OLDS

NOTE: A slowing of the heart (negative values) typifies an "orienting reaction" directed *toward* a stimulus of interest. A quickening of the heart (positive values) typifies a negatory "avoidance reaction."

though he were at least the Greenwich of the universe, if not its center. This is difficult to understand, but it is easy to see by playing peek-a-boo with a baby who cannot yet creep or crawl. If you stand to the right of him while you play, he will turn toward you. Do this repeatedly until he learns to anticipate your reappearance. Now pick him up, turn him halfway around, put him back down, and play peek-a-boo again, standing at the same place. Since you have just rotated him 180 degrees, you are now on his left, yet still he turns toward his right. For he has learned not that you are in a particular location in relation to the room; *he has learned that you are toward his right.* To a baby, directionality exists only in reference to himself—until he learns to creep and crawl.[30]

When the baby first starts to creep and crawl, he has no concept of space or directionality; so you may find him toddling fearlessly off the edge of the bed or sitting in a corner, crying in frustration because the wall is blocking his way. But creeping and crawling both allow and force him to learn that objects have fixed positions. This learning is not instantaneous. For a long time he will make silly errors, especially if there is not much furniture in his playroom or if you often pick him up and move him instead of letting him turn himself around.[31] But gradually he does come to understand the layout of things. He becomes able to turn toward you in the correct place after he is moved. And now he begins to fear falling down; for now he perceives that there is such a thing as a direction "down."

Stimulation and Growth

Since a newborn baby has no comprehension of directionality, his universe is a fluid place that continually swirls and whirls about him. Within this universe, the only constancy lies with sensations that he causes to happen repeatedly himself—the sensations of his own movements. These sensations loom like an island in the middle of the sea. They loom far larger within his world than do the sensations of our own movements within ours. Imagine yourself at a very loud, unpleasant concert—perhaps chaperoning a school dance where a rock band is trying to blast down the walls of the gym with a megawatt amplifier. The sound drowns you, cacophonies breaking over your head like hurricane-driven surf. The racket makes it impossible to think about anything else, or even to daydream, yet the music has no meaning and repels your attention. In this situation, you are far more aware than usual of the sensations of your body's positions and of its movements. Your bottom aches; your legs feel cramped; the top of your head itches; your left arm feels numb; and twiddling your thumbs becomes a fascinating tactile sensation. This is the kind of awareness that a newborn has continually. But with you, the situation is relatively unusual, and the circumstances are uncomfortable, so the net effect is unpleasant. With the newborn, this kind of concentrated awareness of his bodily sensations is all he has ever known. With him it is neither unpleasant nor pleasant, it is merely normal.

That is how the young baby feels his day, not as a sequence of activities but as sensations of movement, touch, and balance. He has little or no volition and has little control over what he does. Indeed, to a large extent, what he does controls him.

Energy washes over the baby's body and sensory systems like rain. It washes over our adult bodies too. As adults, we channel this energy through neural irrigation ditches, and put it to efficient use reflecting, cogitating, making connections with neuronal representations of past experience. Thus the initial deluge represents a relatively small part of our total neural experience. But the newborn does not have this network of channels, so the initial deluge is a relatively greater part of his neural experience. Indeed, this sensory deluge is so great a part of his experience that over the eons his physiological systems have evolved in ways that assume it to be there. Thus when a baby is insulated from sensory stimulation, he will take as much nourishment as any other baby, but he will not grow normally. With an insufficient influx of energy, his nervous system will not stimulate the normal production of hormones. Physical and mental retardation are the result.[32]

This has been seen in innumerable orphanages, although the cause is usually identified incorrectly. Let us look at two foundling homes in Tehran, for instance. The observations come from a paper by Wayne Dennis, a psychologist at Brooklyn College who studied babies in the two homes in 1959 while taking a sabbatical year at the American University in Beirut.[33] Although the paper is not rigorously scientific, it is illustrative nonetheless.

The first foundling home took in nearly all of its babies during the first month of life. It was severely understaffed. The younger babies lay on their backs alone in their cribs, except while their diapers were being changed or, every other day, while they were bathed. They were even given bottles in bed, with the bottle supported by a pillow. After weaning they were commonly fed in bed. They were never placed prone, or propped up, or given toys. Once a baby could pull himself up to sitting, he was placed, while awake, upon a piece of linoleum on the floor. In two rooms, some of the children who could sit were seated in a row on a bench with a bar across the front to prevent their falling. Aside from two such benches and the frames for the cribs, the rooms had no children's furniture or play equipment of any kind. In this home the children were "exceedingly retarded in their motor development."

After a few months of this, some of these retarded children—probably the more retarded—were transferred to a second home. In this home attendants turned the babies over from time to time and often propped them up in their cribs. They also provided numerous toys, and put those who could sit up in play pens during the day. They held them in their arms to feed them. Without exception, those babies weighed much less than normal upon their arrival, but they attained normal weight within a few months.

The general phenomenon illustrated here is that when babies are not fondled, they do not develop properly either physically or mentally. It is not that they do not eat—they will take quite as much nourishment as other babies—it is simply that they fail to thrive on the normal amount of nourishment. Since the absence of fondling usually comes from an absence of parental love, many people believe that the cause of this failure to thrive is emotional, caused by an unfulfilled, innate necessity for love. However, the cause is far more mechanical than this, for premature babies grow faster when they are merely massaged regularly but quite impersonally by the gloved hands of an unseen technician.[34] Neither is this failure to thrive peculiarly human. Baby rats separated from their mothers also eat normally yet fail to thrive—unless their separation is vitiated by frequent, heavy stroking like the grooming they normally receive from their mothers.[35] Indeed, rat pups resemble human babies so closely in their need for stimulation that researchers have been able to switch back and forth between studying rats and studying babies, to work out some of the physiological mechanisms involved. The requisites seem to be merely that the baby receive a sufficiency of physical stimulation and muscular exercise of the multivarious sorts that an active baby normally receives. This stimulation usually comes through the aegis of love, but for the first few weeks at least, it need not.

Just as a deficiency of stimulation and exercise retards development, so additional stimulation and exercise may promote development. Many African and Caribbean peoples believe this, just as we North Americans believe that babies require coddling.[36] Among many of these peoples, sound child-rearing practice involves stretching and exercising their babies to an extent that would bring charges of abuse from an American or Canadian social worker. After a mother bathes her baby, often while he is still wet, she may suspend him by first one arm and then the other, shaking him up and down until she hears the joints crack; then she may do the same thing holding him by the ankles. Next she may hold his head on both sides and lift it upward, stretching the neck.

It is by no means clear whether these practices are abusive or beneficial (or both, in some combination). Janet Kilbride and Michael Robbins of the University of Missouri and Philip Kilbride of Bryn Mawr College studied babies of the Baganda tribe in Uganda.[37] On a standard test of motor development, the Bagandan babies scored distinctly higher than North American babies usually score—higher than North American black babies during the first year and higher than North American white babies during the first two years (older Bagandan babies were not tested). There are many possible reasons for the Bagandans' precocity (or for North Americans' retardation?). One may be genetic. In at least one African tribe, the Gusii in Kenya, newborns behave surprisingly maturely considering the unfavorable conditions surrounding their gestation and birth: parasites, maternal anemia and malnutrition, and filth.[38] But other reasons may be environmental. Of these, the most striking is that a Bagandan baby spends his days not in a crib but sitting on his mother's back, so that a Bagandan baby gets much more sensory stimulation and muscular exercise. It is quite possible that exercising a baby more than the North American norm may promote his neuromuscular growth.[39]

Certainly *less* physical stimulation than the norm will retard his growth, both physically and mentally. This is a particular problem with babies who are born small enough to be kept for weeks or months in a hospital's nursery. For these babies need to grow as much as they can, yet nurses do not have the time to handle them as often as they need to be handled for this to happen. Parents of one of these babies should not be put off by the tubes and other hospital paraphernalia, or by the baby's unresponsiveness (or the hospital's unwillingness): they should visit him several times a day if possible, and sit by him for ten to twenty minutes each time, stroking and handling him inside the incubator. In this way they will promote his development.

Movements Bring Stability

All in all, the newborn has a good sense of his own movement through his senses of touch and proprioception and, to a limited extent, his sense of balance. However, he lacks an understanding of normality. He has no notion of the normality of the world, from which we infer position and direction, nor does he understand the normality of his body's physiological state, deviations from which we feel as pain. The newborn lives in a kaleidoscopic world in which every movement is intertwined with everything else that he hears, sees, and smells. From his perspective, activity is merely one more kind of sensory stimulation—stimulation that he feels on its own as well as intermixed with the smell of his mother's voice, the sound of her smile, and other synesthetic admixtures.

These make a confused and confusing mélange. Yet from the baby's point of view, *more activity is likely to be less confusing than less activity.* Remember that in his world, the only constant phenomena are his sensations of his own bodily movements. While he moves and is moved, the world whirls about him unintelligibly and randomly; *yet simultaneously, he feels himself move,* and these feelings of his own movement he knows. Indeed, they are the most stable thing he knows. This paradox brings us to the heart of the newborn's world—a looking-glass world, as we shall see in the next chapter. A world in which the quicker he and the world about him whirl and move, the slower these movements seem to become.

9

Inside
the Looking Glass

THE NEWBORN'S INVERTED CONSCIOUSNESS

So FAR in this book we have intermixed in our discussion two different levels of the baby's experience: his sensations and his conscious awareness of these sensations, which are his perceptions. We have concentrated on his sensations, for these are the easier to discover, and discovering them is prerequisite to discovering the others. Yet what we would really like to know is what the baby perceives—what he is aware of consciously.

Now we are ready to concentrate on his consciousness. This will be rather a difficult exercise, involving the intellectual equivalent of standing on our head. Also, for longer than we like, it will seem far removed from babies. We shall begin with Einstein's special theory of relativity and continue in an abstruse and unconventional direction, reasoning as much like theoretical physicists as psychologists. In doing this we ask your patience and indulgence. The result will be a glimpse of a world so different from our own that we can scarcely imagine it—a world that slows down when you pick the baby up out of his crib to rock him, then speeds up when you lay him back down. A world in which movement stands still, and stillness moves. A world in which Lewis Carroll would be at home.

Clues from Einstein

All of us have grown up thinking that distances and times are absolute, and that speed is derived from them. We think that no matter whether we measure in miles or in kilometers, the actual distance to grandmother's house remains constant; we think that as we drive there, the clock ticks off hour after hour evenly; and we define our speed in terms of miles per hour or kilometers per hour— distance divided by time. This comes straight out of Newtonian physics, and at human rates of speed, it is a useful way of dealing with the world. However, Einstein demonstrated that, conceptually, this is backward. He showed that physics makes more sense if we take speed to be the logically prior phenomenon, and distances and times to be merely descriptors of speed.* Although Einstein was thinking about and describing the world of physics, yet each of us is part of the world of physics and functions according to physical laws. For this reason, much of the thought he applied to the rest of the world can also be applied to us—and to the baby.

Einstein's reasoning is based on limitations inherent in the

---

*This statement may seem strange, since Einstein's work is concerned almost exclusively with measurements of time and distance. Nonetheless, the primacy of velocity pervades Einstein's work on relativity from the first paragraphs of the first paper in 1905.[1] Einstein presumes the existence of velocity with his second postulate, "Light in empty space always propagates with a definite velocity V. [. . . *Sich das Licht im leeren Raume stets mit einer bestimmten . . . Geschwindigkeit* V *fortpflanze.*]" By saying this, Einstein is saying, "I assume that there is such a thing as velocity; I assume that there is some velocity that is constant; and I assume that this constant velocity is the velocity of light." When he does later define time, he defines it ultimately in terms of velocity; for he defines time in terms of simultaneity, which he has previously defined in terms of the velocity of light. Moreover, unlike the velocity of light, he does not postulate any distance or time to be constant, or even to exist on its own apart from an observer. Instead he proves that time and distance are *not* constant; that they are defined by an observer in proportion to the relative velocities of the observer and the observed. Thus nowhere does he say of velocity that it is a *product* of distance and time. Rather he states of distance and time that we employ them only "If we want to *describe* a motion . . ." (italics added). Einstein says in full, *"Wollen wir die Bewegung eines materiellen Punktes beschreiben, so geben wir die Werte seiner Koordinaten in Funktion der Zeit."* The difference is subtle, and it has no bearing on everyday problems of physics, yet it is fundamental to relativity.[2]

conveyance of information. Information cannot be conveyed to man more quickly than light can travel, so the speed of light is a natural limitation of man's knowledge of the universe. Man cannot define distances and times with any degree of precision except through the medium of light (or other forms of electromagnetic energy). Hence, as far as man can ever understand his universe, the speed of light is an omnipresent, natural factor—*the* natural unit (and, Einstein assumes, a constant unit) of velocity. Physicists call this unit C.*

Of course, we usually think of the speed of light not as C but as 186,000 miles or 300,000 kilometers per second. For we think of speed as distance over time. But we think of speed as distance over time merely because the speeds we usually deal with are such minute fractions of C that it is awkward to measure them directly. At the speeds we deal with, it is easier to describe speed indirectly by counting off lengths and periods.

To understand this, let us imagine we are walking across a park. Our pace is sprightly: we know this because, although we are concentrating on the path before us, we are also aware that trees seem to be moving past us with alacrity. Thus we are aware of our speed—aware of it directly, without the aid of distance and time. What we do not know is the amount of our speed: we have no idea that we are walking at one-two hundred millionth the speed of light, or 0.000000005 C. Moreover, we have no convenient way of ascertaining this. On the other hand, we can *describe* our speed precisely. We just count off the number of times a stick can be laid end to end between two trees; then we count the swings of a pendulum as we walk between the two trees. The result describes our speed

---

*Einstein does not develop his argument explicitly in these terms, yet they reflect its substance. In his first article on relativity (Zur Elektrodynamik), immediately after he says that we can describe a motion using distance and time, he states, "Now we must keep in mind that a mathematical description like this only has a physical meaning if one first becomes clear about what will be understood here by 'time.'" He then continues by discussing "judgments of simultaneous events": "We have to take into consideration that all our judgments in which time plays a role are always judgments about *simultaneous events* [Einstein's italics]." If two events occur at different places, we can judge their simultaneity only if we establish *"by definition* [Einstein's italics] that the 'time' required by light to travel from A to B equals the 'time' it requires to travel from B to A. . . . "* Einstein does not state the reason for using light in this definition, but he implies it very clearly: when we judge simultaneity, our finest judgments are based on observations made through the medium of light ("or other forms of electromagnetic energy" we might add, considering today's technology). Einstein next adds, "We deem [*festsetzen*] in agreement with experience, that the quantity [defining simultaneous events] be a universal constant (the speed of light in empty space)."

in stick lengths per pendulum swing. This kind of description proves so handy in day-to-day living that people from many countries have assembled as international committees and determined that everybody should use sticks and pendulums of a common, specified size, which they have named the meter and the second.* But stick lengths and pendulum swings in principle they remain— not the elements of velocity, but arbitrary, convenient, *descriptors* of velocity.

However, distance and time are not always convenient descriptors. They can be convenient only when both an observer and the object he is measuring are moving slowly in relation to each other. When the speed of either approaches C, time and distance start to seem plastic and hence lose their utility. This is the basis of half the world's science fiction, wherein Joe flies off in a rocket ship at half the speed of light and returns one month later—by his reckoning— to find that fifty years have elapsed on earth and his girl friend has become a wizened hag. People think of this phenomenon as occurring only at velocities approaching the speed of light, because we think of this phenomenon only in the context of physics. Indeed, so did Einstein. Yet the mathematics that imply this are not limited to physics.† They apply to any universe‡ in which an observer might find or imagine himself, including universes with a slower speed of transference of information—that is, universes with a lesser C.

Finally, let us point out something that is so obvious that it escapes most people's notice: laws of physics are not laws that nature obeys. They are perceptions—perceptions of men and women about the things we sense. Although the real world presumably exists outside our consciousness and functions as these laws predict, yet within our consciousness—within our minds—reality and our perceptions are the same.

---

*Our basic unit of distance is the meter, defined officially as the length equal to 1,650,763.73 wavelengths in vacuum of the radiation corresponding to the transition between the levels 2p10 and 5d5 of the krypton-86 atom. (An inch is defined as 0.0254 meter.) Our basic unit of time is the second, defined as the duration of 9,192,631,770 periods of the radiation corresponding to the transition between the two hyperfine levels of the ground state of the atom of cesium 133.[3]

†Indeed, the mathematics do not directly involve physics at all. They deal only with the transference of measurements between different systems of coordinates.

‡More specifically, to any universe whose dimensions can be represented by coordinates.

C and Consciousness

Now we are ready to go back into the world of the newborn. Recall from chapter 4 that consciousness arises in the neuronal interconnections between the brain's midbrain and cortex, and from interconnections within the cortex. In these interconnections arise our conscious awareness. Insofar as these neuronal interconnections provide this awareness, they function within the brain as an observer.*

Since this observer is part of the baby's brain, he has no direct contact with anything outside the baby's body. As the baby's body develops, neurons become stranded together in such a way that they do come to provide a plenty of information about the external world; but at first our observer does not realize this, for since he has never had direct contact with this world, he does not realize that the world exists. All he is aware of are his immediate surroundings formed by his supply of blood, his bath of bodily fluids, and the continual movements of neurochemical energy impinging upon him from neurons nearby. To him, this is the universe.

Within this observer's universe, the quickest transference of information comes through the movement of neurochemical energy. Thus the fastest movement that the observer can know of is a movement occurring at the maximum velocity of neurochemical energy. In other words, to *him,* within the restricted universe that he perceives, the maximum velocity of neurochemical energy is C, just as to us, within the larger universe that we perceive, the speed of light is C. To avoid confusion, let us call these two units $C_{[NEURON]}$ and $C_{[LIGHT]}$.

Now we can mentally kick our feet up over our heads. For not

---

*At this level of explanation, it is not necesary to know or speculate on what about these interconnections actually forms conscious perceptions; we need only assume that perceptions arise through the matter and energy that form them. Whatever else may or may not be involved—God, life force, or subatomic particle—at that point we have the functional equivalent of a physical observer.

It is worth noting that since the observer is part of the brain, he is probably engaged in some of the activity that he is observing. He is like the American army officer assigned to a dependent state's army as a military observer: he reports on what he sees, yet he also has a hand in forming the events he reports on.

only does the observer function within a universe whose C is $C_{[\text{NEURON}]}$, he himself is moving at speeds approaching* $C_{[\text{NEURON}]}$. For he himself consists of moving neurochemical energy. Thus we can understand how the newborn perceives his sensations—we can understand what he is conscious of—by understanding the situation of an observer moving near his universe's C.

The Universe Near C

To an observer moving near his universe's C—including the observer within the baby—time and distance cease to define velocity in any meaningful way. We can understand this without mathematics by imagining an example within the universe we know, in which information comes to us with light. Imagine yourself riding Pegasus at close to the speed of light. You twist halfway around in the saddle and hold out a watch in each hand, one toward Pegasus's head and the other toward his tail. Hold them a fair distance apart, yet close enough together to let you keep an eye on both of them at once. Figure 9.1 shows what is happening from the perspective of somebody riding abreast of you a very long distance away. You are moving toward the light emanating from watch A as that light is moving toward you; but you are moving away from the light emanating from watch B. So you see watch A tick 3:00 before you see

FIGURE 9.1
How Time Becomes Plastic Near the Speed of Light

*Neurochemical energy moves at very different rates along different neuronal pathways, and along the same neuronal pathway at different stages of maturation. Thus it is unlikely that more than a small proportion of the neurons forming the observer function *at* $C_{[\text{NEURON}]}$. Most function merely near it.

watch B tick 3:00. You will take longer to see any other movement of watch B as well, so watch B will appear to run slower.

Something equally peculiar happens if you hold rulers in your hands instead of watches (see figure 9.2). Rays of light emanating from both rulers are traveling toward you. But you are also moving in the direction of ruler A at nearly the speed of light, so you intercept the rays of light emanating from ruler A before they have gone halfway toward ruler B. On the other hand, rays from ruler B must travel more than halfway toward A to reach you. Thus within your eye, the rays of light coming from ruler A are spread over a larger angle (α) than those coming from ruler B (β). Since these angles define the rulers' sizes to the eye, ruler A looks longer than ruler B.

Since watches and rulers are so inconsistent, you cannot describe your speed meaningfully to yourself in terms of distance and time. Moreover, since Pegasus is flying at a constant speed, you do not observe your own movement, just as you do not observe your own movement while you are cruising in a jetliner. Instead you observe that the rest of the world appears to move.

Of course, you as an adult identify this moving world as composed of trees and fields. You remember that trees and fields usually are stationary and are too substantial to move, so you deduce that they are still stationary and that you yourself are moving. This is an elementary deduction that you make at very low levels of your visual system. But if you had never seen nor heard about trees and

FIGURE 9.2
How Distance Becomes Plastic Near the Speed of Light

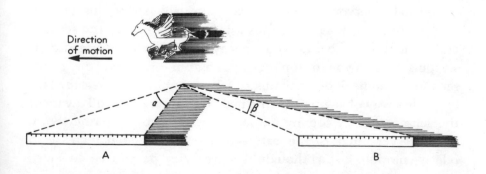

fields—if you were newly born—then you would not deduce this. Instead you would accept your direct observation, that the trees and fields are moving. Then too—if you were newly born—if you overtook another flying object, like a helicopter, you would think that the helicopter is moving slower than the trees and field; for since both of you would be moving in the same direction, you would take longer to pass the helicopter than you would take to pass the trees. Moreover, if you overtook a jetliner also moving in your direction, then you would think the jetliner is moving even slower than the helicopter, because you would take still longer to pass the jetliner.

This is the world that the newborn lives in. It is a looking-glass world compared to ours—a looking-glass world in which movements that we perceive to be slow, he perceives to be fast, and vice versa. That is why he seems to act so often in looking-glass ways—like being soothed by vigorous rocking. As adults, we can enjoy rocking only when it is very gentle indeed: we may submit to being rocked as vigorously as we rock babies, but only occasionally at an amusement park, and even then not immediately after lunch. But then, we have learned that the world is stable, and our nervous system has become used to this stability; the newborn is used to being thrown about within the womb. Moreover, in the universe of the newborn's perceptions, C is $C_{[\text{NEURON}]}$. Since the sensory signals caused by the rocking travel through the newborn's brain at speeds relatively high compared to $C_{[\text{NEURON}]}$, the difference between their speed and the neuronal observer's speed is relatively little; so when the baby is rocked, the observer—that is, the baby—will perceive that the world slows down, for the same reason that a baby riding Pegasus would perceive the movement of a jetliner to be slow. In short, the rocked baby enjoys a sudden calm.

Nevertheless, the rocking is actually adding a lot of sensory energy to his nervous system, so that eventually parts of his nervous system shut down. Thus he falls asleep.[4] This reduces the sensory energy he receives, because now his eyes are closed and because his sleeping induces you to stop rocking him. But remember from chapter 4 that the newborn remains conscious while he is asleep. This is another way of saying that the neuronal observer is still aware of the sensory energy coming in. So as you stop rocking a newborn, the observer—that is, the baby—perceives a sudden increase in relative motion, just as though he were flying past a tree. In short, as you stop rocking him, he perceives the world as beginning to move faster.

Movement Makes His World Slow Down

This difference in C between the newborn's world and ours explains many other peculiarities in a young baby's behavior. For instance, we saw in chapter 6 that a newborn will look longer at an object if it is moving slowly than if it is stationary. As adults, we see nothing remarkable in this, for we know from everyday experience that movement catches the eye. But we have had decades of practice in using our eyes. A newborn has had no experience whatsoever, and is so ill-prepared for vision that even ordinary room lighting can easily overwhelm him, causing him to close his eyes and fall asleep.[5] Nor can a newborn even watch a moving object properly: until he is two or three months old, he is usually unable to move his eyes smoothly along with the object; he must broad-jump with his eyes, catching up to the object from place to place and often losing sight of it. Under these circumstances, it seems curious that he should prefer to watch a moving object than a stationary one.

We can understand what is happening here by distinguishing three factors: (1) the coordination of sight with the muscular movements that position the eye, (2) the changes in light that the baby senses, and (3) the awareness of those sensations of change—that is, the baby's conscious perceptions. Changing the eye's position smoothly and continuously requires more extensive neural coordination than the newborn's immature nervous system is capable of, so the newborn can rarely follow a moving object.[6] However, he can sense the changes in light that represent movements—provided those movements do not reach $C_{[NEURON]}$. These sensations he can *perceive* more readily when they are moving fast enough to approach $C_{[NEURON]}$; for since the observer within the newborn's brain is functioning at a very high velocity relative to $C_{[NEURON]}$, sensory signals moving through the brain at comparably quick velocities appear to the observer to be moving slowly, while sensory signals that are nearly stationary appear to be moving fast. Thus up to a point, the more quickly an object moves, the more slowly the baby will perceive that it moves, and hence the more easily he can attend to it.

The fastest movement that a newborn can be conscious of is slower than the fastest that an adult, or even a two-month-old, can be conscious of. For a newborn's nervous system is deficient in substances and structures (for example, myelin and synaptic contacts) that speed neural transmission.[7] This leaves his $C_{[NEURON]}$ slower (compared to $C_{[LIGHT]}$) than our $C_{[NEURON]}$, or than the $C_{[NEURON]}$ of a two-month-old. Thus the newborn cannot perceive sensations moving as quickly (compared to $C_{[LIGHT]}$) as adults or even two-month-olds.[8] To us, a hummingbird's wings flap so quickly that they exceed our adult $C_{[NEURON]}$, and so are invisible. To a newborn, many movements that we are aware of—a blink or a twitch—are as invisible as a hummingbird's wings.

In sum, if we could put ourselves inside the newborn's head, the world would look like clips of movies taken from the cutting-room floor and played back sometimes in slow motion, at other times speeded up. To summarize, let us look first at objects that are stationary and then at objects that are moving, and see how we and the newborn perceive them:

Stationary Objects.   Neither a baby nor an adult can sense anything that is *completely* stationary, for sensory neurons fire only to change. That is why we stop feeling a bandage shortly after tying it on. Yet as adults, we rarely encounter an object with only one sensory system, and our brain readily associates one set of sensations with another in our memory. So if the brain finds itself missing a sensation, it simply ignores the fact and functions as though it were there. This allows us to perceive things without direct cause. During a television program, for instance, we perceive that the hero is falling from some great height, when actually we see him merely disappear from an image in which he was surrounded by a window-frame, then reappear lying on the ground. We have made the neuronal associations to perceive things in the absence of sensation, but a young baby has not.* As a result, we can often perceive a perfectly still object even though our senses fail to notice it, but a young baby cannot. As soon as an object stops moving in relation to him, within his mind it disappears.

---

*For example, young babies do not anticipate where a moving object will reappear from behind a barrier (see chapter 10); nor do they react to an illusory figure (see chapter 6).

Moving Objects.   In adults, as in the newborn, the neuronal observer can be aware of moving sensory signals only if the movement
is slower than $C_{[NEURON]}$. But as adults, we can also perceive movements faster than we can sense, just as we can perceive movements
slower than we can sense. We can also slow down some sensations
of movement by tracking fast-moving images with our eyes. As a
result, $C_{[NEURON]}$ does not always limit our perception of speed. For the
same reasons, neither does it always define our perception of speed.
Our associations define speed instead. We have learned to associate
basset hounds with sluggishness and joggers with rapidity, so we
can look out the window and think, "Gee, either that jogger is
incredibly slow, or that basset hound alongside him is mighty
quick."

In contrast, a young baby has virtually no associations. A newborn's neuronal observer perceives the speed of moving and changing sensory signals solely in his own lights, in relation to his own
speed—which approaches his universe's C. Under these circumstances, sensory energy that to us might seem to be nearly stationary would seem to the observer in the newborn to fly by at an
enormous rate, while sensory energy that to us might seem to move
moderately quickly would seem to him to be moving at nearly his
own speed, and hence very slowly. In this way, the newborn's
conscious perceptions form a looking-glass world compared to our
own, a world where our fast may be his slow, and vice versa. And
when a sensation moves across his brain more quickly than $C_{[NEURON]}$,
his perception of it, like his sensation of it, disappears.

Touching Reality

So far we have dealt with the baby's direct perception of velocity,
since this is appropriate to an observer moving at a rate approaching
C. Of course, the baby does gradually learn about the rest of the
world: the observer does begin to move into our adult universe
where C is $C_{[LIGHT]}$ rather than $C_{[NEURON]}$. We shall deal with this process
at length in the next chapter, but let us consider the beginning of
this change here.

Throughout gestation, as the fetus touches himself and the umbilical cord and the womb, neurons from the skin transmit neurochemical energy to the brain in a pattern that virtually maps the skin. This map provides measuring sticks of length or distance— measuring sticks that are juxtaposed with the neuronal signals forming sensations. Also juxtaposed with these neuronal signals are neurophysiological cycles, physiological pendulums that form measuring sticks of time: that is, clocks.[9] All these measuring sticks are imprecise and plastic, of course; yet still, their juxtaposition with sensory signals enables the neuronal observer to begin to associate movements with distance and time. Thus the observer—that is, the older fetus—forms the beginning of an awareness of the relationship of movement to distance and time.

Now the baby is born and senses the world. Insofar as the stimuli inducing these sensations move within a certain range of speeds, the neuronal observer within the baby is also aware of them, is also conscious of them. Some of these stimuli are small enough to be compared to his body, so the observer can not only perceive their movement, he can also perceive something of their length. Other stimuli occur rapidly enough to be compared to neurophysiological cycles, so the observer can perceive not only their movement but also something of their periodicity, of their duration. These additional learned perceptions—distance and duration—add salience to a stimulus. The effect is comparable to experiences that we as adults have continually at a more advanced level of learning. We watch someone remove a paper from beneath a stone paperweight, for instance. We are conscious of this, but we consider it no further—until we learn that the stone is an axehead chipped from flint 8,000 years ago and found in the steppes of Russia. This new information makes us associate the stone with cavemen and archaeologists, bringing it into a larger mental landscape than it lay in as a mere paperweight. Suddenly we become much more aware of it.

In this way the newborn is especially aware of movements that he can perceive not just as movement but also as occurring over a certain distance compared to parts of his body, and through a certain duration compared to some of his neurophysiological cycles. If you approach him from the other side of the room, he will be aware of your approach, but he will not think much of it, just as you will be thoughtlessly aware of your approach toward a car half a mile away on the highway. But as you come within his body's length, suddenly you become not just a movement but a movement spanning a certain distance. This makes you seem much more salient: you loom into his awareness. He reacts as you would if you drove around a bend to discover that the car you were following from a quarter-mile back is now only fifty feet ahead: he starts, quiets down, and begins to watch you intently. If you next pick up a toy and dangle it before him, he becomes aware of you still more strongly. For now he can see a motion occurring not only over a recognizable distance, but also through a recognizable span of time.[10]

Paradoxes Resolved

At the beginning of this chapter we said that reading it would involve the intellectual equivalent of standing on our head. Now that we have done this, the question reasonably arises, is our reasoning correct? Surely this looking-glass world sounds absurd; and one of the basic dicta of logic holds that if the conclusion is absurd, something is awry.

But to say that the newborn's world sounds absurd is merely to say that the newborn's perceptions are radically different from ours. And this is just what we should expect; for the newborn or young baby *is* radically different from an adult, or even from an older baby. Throughout this book we have mentioned innumerable ways in which the young baby differs. Some of these ways may not be obvious, yet most of them require no subtle ingenuity to discover. Just watch two babies sleep: a one-year-old is relaxed, while the one-month-old next to him keeps his muscles as taut as an amateur actor paralyzed with stage fright. The more you think about these differences, the less absurd our description of the newborn's world will seem. So let us review some of them, examining each sensory system in turn. We will see that what once were curiosities and paradoxes now make sense.

Sight. A few pages ago we saw that a newborn prefers to watch moving objects because their movement slows them down within his consciousness. This is why a young baby recognizes objects and their properties better when they are moving than when they are still;[11] and why he uses motion to perceive depth (see chapter 6). And it is another reason (besides the salience of being within his body's length) that he may be fascinated by an object if you hold it close up, yet if you hold it beyond arm's length, he will rarely look at it—even if you hold up a larger version of this object, a version large enough to create a similarly sized image within his eye.[12] Remember that the image of an object moves on the eye not just when the object moves, but also when the head moves. You know from riding in a train that when you are moving, everything else appears to move, and distant objects appear to move slower than nearby objects, in most instances irrespective of the size of the images within the eye. The newborn senses this slower movement of distant objects, and in his looking-glass world, he perceives it as quicker. Thus it is no wonder that he prefers to examine closer objects. Not only are they more salient since he can measure them against his body, but they seem to him to move less fast.

Hearing. One of the most surprising things about a young baby is his adeptness with the sounds of language and music—his ability to hear distinctions among sounds that adults cannot hear, his ability to recognize the sounds of a story read to him in the womb, his propensity to move in synchrony with the rhythm of language, and so on. But this is less surprising when you consider that the rhythms and cycles of language consist of movements of energy over time. These rhythms and cycles have numerous periods that are similar to periods of his neurophysiological cycling. Thus the sounds of language occur for the baby through time. This gives language an extra salience, so that he is more conscious of language than he is of other, less periodic sounds.

Balance. Babies enjoy being rocked much more vigorously than adults can tolerate. More than this, shortly after a baby becomes able to—at about four months—he rocks himself, spending a considerable amount of the day nodding his head and upper body like an Orthodox Jew at prayer.[13] This is not comparable to rocking in a rocking chair; it is far quicker—faster than anything that adults experience as pleasurable. But through the baby's eyes, the movement of rocking slows down the world to enforce a perceptual calm, and the periodicity creates a fresh, interesting dimension: time.

Touch. More than they do almost anything else, babies suck. They suck before meals, after meals, between meals—at any and all times of the day and night. As we discussed in chapter 5, they probably find pleasurable the sensation of pressure around the mouth, much as we do. But sucking is not merely squeezing with the lips and tongue; it is squeezing with them rhythmically, metrically—beating time with them.[14] Or from the newborn's perspective, *creating* time, to enhance the pleasurable sensations.

Taste and Smell. Once a baby learns to nurse, he attacks the breast or bottle with a continuous, single-minded intensity that he will never apply to the spoon or glass. Indeed, to a baby, food that does not come through a nipple is as much a toy as sustenance. The pleasures of sucking clearly create some of this difference; but to a baby, food also has more taste when it comes through a nipple. For sucking it through a nipple is a rhythmical activity, so tasting it is a rhythmical phenomenon that creates time and hence increases his consciousness of the flavor.

The world of the newborn certainly differs surprisingly from our own, but we should expect it to differ surprisingly. The newborn started life as a fertilized egg, which bore no resemblance to anything human. From that he developed into a fishlike embryo. His metamorphosis from embryo into a walking, talking, human being requires quite as many changes as the metamorphosis of a caterpillar into a butterfly, or a tadpole into a frog. Birth is an important event in this metamorphosis, but that is only what it is: one event. The newborn has numerous quantitative and *qualitative* changes yet to undergo.

One of the first and most important of these qualitative changes is stepping through the looking glass—removing himself from his looking-glass world and taking himself into ours. This is the first course of his mental development, and the subject of our next chapter.

10

Through
the Looking Glass

THE EMERGENCE OF THE MIND

TIME AND AGAIN throughout this book we have seen that a newborn can learn things, often complicated things. For instance, we saw that a baby only a few days old can learn to vary his sucking in order to hear a story that he had learned to recognize while he was still in the womb. On the other hand, we saw in chapters 5 and 8 that a newborn baby is generally *not* able to learn the very simplest associations: he does not even learn to associate the breast with food. This is most curious: the seemingly easy task he finds impossible; the seemingly difficult one he can do.

In this chapter we shall try to understand this paradox—to understand how and what a newborn learns, and why he cannot learn other things. We shall see that what he does learn steers him into the passage through his looking glass into reality. We shall follow him as he sidles into this passage, then eventually—it takes nearly a year—we shall watch his mind, as we know it, emerge.

What the Newborn Can Learn

To begin, let us summarize the kinds of things that a newborn baby can and cannot learn to do.

The newborn can learn:
- to recognize something that he has just encountered.[1]
- to repeat an action for which he was just rewarded.[2]

The newborn has difficulty learning (because his memory is short):
- to recognize something that he encountered a few minutes earlier.[3]
- to repeat an action for which he was rewarded a few minutes earlier.[4]

The newborn cannot learn:
- that the presence of an object or an event indicates he will be rewarded for doing something.[5]
- to associate one object or event with another, unless a part of his body is involved.[6]

The newborn can learn to recognize something that he has encountered before: he jumps the first time you slam a door, but not the third. He also learns to repeat an action for which he was just rewarded: he sucks better in the middle of feeding, after he has tasted a bit of milk. However, his memory is very short. A newborn takes several days to learn to draw milk because he can hardly remember from one minute to the next what he just did; and those three-day-olds who recognized a story read to them in the womb had heard it on average sixty-eight times. Normally a baby will not recognize his name until he is more than one month old.[7] For the newborn, more complicated forms of learning are virtually impossible. A newborn cannot learn to suck *only* when a light is switched on, or *only* when someone is holding him. Neither can he learn that being held in a certain way presages food, or even that it accompanies food.

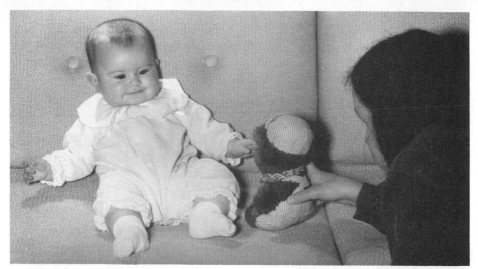

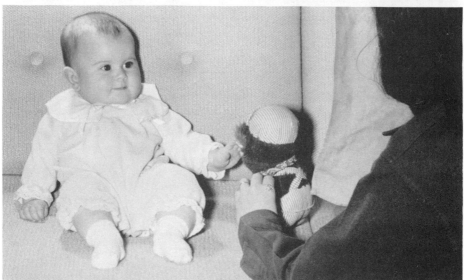

To a young baby, out of sight is literally out of mind. Top photo shows a six-month-old girl delighted with a toy. In center photo the baby sees Daphne bring up a towel, which Daphne is about to drape over the toy. The instant Daphne does this (left photo), the baby loses interest. The toy seems no longer to be there.

The Permanence of Objects

To understand these abilities and inabilities, we need first to examine a baby's understanding of objects. As adults, we understand that objects have an element of permanence. When you look up from this book, you know that the book does not disappear. When you look back down at it again, you know that you are looking at the same book once more. This understanding is the foundation of everything we know about the world. But from observations of the Swiss biologist/psychologist Jean Piaget, we can see that babies are not born with this understanding.[8] It takes most of the first year to develop:

From birth to one month of age the baby shows no sign whatsoever that he understands the permanence of objects. Out of sight seems to be literally out of mind.

Between one and four months the baby stares for a moment at the point where an object disappears from his sight, as though he is intrigued by its disappearance. This is the earliest evidence of his thinking about an object while it is out of sight. But he thinks about it only for a moment: the object disappears from his mind almost immediately.

Between four and eight months the baby appears to begin to understand. He will pull a toy from your pocket when it is only partly visible. He will look toward the floor after he drops a toy. If a toy train runs into a tunnel, he will watch the tunnel's exit for the train to reappear. He enjoys playing peek-a-boo. But this understanding is very limited. If you drape a handkerchief over a toy that he is holding, thereby hiding it entirely from his eyes, he will not remove the handkerchief, even if the toy is making a noise. If the handkerchief falls off, he appears surprised to find himself holding the toy.

Between eight and twelve months the baby appears to understand that objects are permanent. If you hide a toy beneath a handkerchief, he will retrieve the toy. If you play a conjuring trick by replacing the hidden toy with another, or making it vanish, he acts surprised.

This understanding does not happen suddenly; it develops gradually. At first the baby may retrieve a toy from beneath a handkerchief, but not from behind a board; a little later he may retrieve it from behind a board, but not from within an up-ended cup; then he may retrieve it from within a cup, but not from within a box. According to a study by Carl Dunst, Penelope Brooks, and Pamela Doxsey,[9] the abilities to find a toy inside a cup and box come one and two and one-half months later, respectively, than the ability to find it beneath a handkerchief. This may be because the baby has had more experience with subjacency and postjacency than he has had with interiority; or it may be because he finds subjacency and postjacency inherently simpler and more straightforward than interiority.[10] We suspect both. In any case, he comes to understand subjacency and postjacency first. As his understanding develops, more and more things around him, more and more often, stop materializing and dematerializing, and stay put. But for everything to stay put takes time.

Memory and Objects

Understanding that objects are permanent requires a certain amount of memory. For a baby cannot generalize that all objects are permanent until he understands that a number of individual objects are permanent; and after any individual object disappears from his sight, he can think of it as still existing only insofar as it remains within his memory. Moreover, in the baby's consciousness—from the perspective of the "observer" within the baby's brain—the memory of an object is the object itself.* Thus the baby's memory

*In the baby's consciousness, an *imagined* object is also the object itself. Sensory organs send neural signals into the brain. The brain processes these, and in so doing the baby senses an object's presence. Some of these processings of the brain, interacting with the midbrain, form the baby's consciousness. As we saw in chapter 4, this consciousness can occur whether or not it is being fed by sensory systems. In adults, when consciousness is largely not being fed by sensory systems, we call it dreaming or daydreaming. The material being processed while we are dreaming or daydreaming—the material we are conscious of—is predominantly past sensations infused with some small proportion of signals from sensory systems. We have had to learn that when consciousness is severed from the sensate world, the stuff of which we are conscious is unreal. Babies do not know this. When a toddler awakens from a nightmare, no amount of explanation will convince him that the monster he just dreamed is not still lurking in the closet waiting to eat him.

provides a window on his understanding of the world: by observing the limitations of his memory, we can gain an idea of how much he does and does not understand.

The kind of memory involved in recalling objects is cued recollection—recollection aided by recognition. You are driving to a friend's summer cottage. You drove there once before, but a year ago, so that you have forgotten where to turn after leaving the main highway. Nevertheless, you manage to "feel" your way there: you recognize a house here, a barn there, and these recognitions act as cues to help you recollect each successive turning of the route before you get to it. In just this way, if you hide a ball beneath a cloth, the cloth provides a context or clue helping the baby to recollect that he was just looking at a ball.

Cued recollection is very weak even by the end of the first year. Leslie Brody showed this in his doctoral dissertation at Harvard.[11] Brody sat eight- and twelve-month-olds on their mothers' lap and showed them a pair of clowns. The nose of one clown was a red light bulb; the nose of the other, a yellow light bulb. One nose or the other glowed awhile. After it dimmed, if the baby reached forward and touched it, a door opened and twirling puppets appeared, accompanied by music and flashing lights. With this puppet show as a reward, Brody had little difficulty teaching babies of each age to touch whichever nose had been illuminated—provided they were allowed to touch the nose *immediately* after the light had gone out. But if they were forced to wait a mere three seconds, the eight-month-olds—but not the twelve-month-olds—could no longer remember which nose had been illuminated: they reached toward the wrong clown as often as they reached toward the right one.

Although a baby's recollection is weak between eight and twelve months of life, it does work much like an adult's: a baby remembers what he does longer than he remembers what he sees. Hide a toy beneath a handkerchief while he is watching you, and let him retrieve it. Then—while he is watching you—hide it beneath a sheet of paper. Unless you let him look for it *immediately,* he will search for it not where he saw you put it but where he found it the first time: beneath the handkerchief. (A baby is especially likely to make this mistake if the two hiding places are nearby and look similar, if you hide the object and let him find it several times at the first hiding place, and if you prevent him from searching for it for at least one second after you hide it.[12])

The Newborn's Confusion

Now we are in a position again to imagine ourselves as a newborn baby facing the world—or rather, as the newborn's consciousness, the "observer" within his brain facing not the world but neurochemical events emanating from sensory systems—neurochemical events that the baby will eventually come to understand as the world.

As we have seen, a baby is conscious twenty-four hours a day as soon as he is born; so he must also have been conscious for some time before he was born. Since consciousness is the interaction of particular levels of the brain, consciousness arose gradually as the fetus's brain developed—gradually, like a prolonged awakening from sleep, but devoid of the disorganized thoughts and half thoughts that accompany an adult's awakening.

Initially, the fetus/baby is conscious of a confused profusion of sounds, feelings, tastes and—after birth—of sights. Initially, few of these sounds, feelings, tastes, and sights hold any meaning to the baby. They are as senseless as the patterns of a kaleidoscope. However, many of the patterns occur and recur repeatedly, like a kaleidoscope of time. Each repetition engenders a similar set of neurochemical events; and neurochemical events, repeated and repeated, gradually change the neurochemical topography of the brain. This changed topography is recognition. It occurs initially in sensorial levels of the brain; but eventually, manifold waves of neurochemical energy lapping around at these lower levels combine into larger waves of sufficient force to climb to the level of the observer—that is, to obtrude themselves into conscious attention. When this happens often, or when the concorporated energy is sufficiently forceful, the neurochemical topography at this level is changed as well. This is conscious learning. In the first stages of this process—the sensory stages—the baby may learn something yet be unaware that he has learned it. He is like the amnesiac who cannot remember ever using a computer, yet can sit down in front of one and program it.[13] But eventually, after the baby has encountered something often enough, he becomes conscious of his recognition and feels a wave of familiarity when he encounters the thing again.

As we have seen, a normal newborn is not good at learning. He *can* learn to recognize things, but only after many encounters with them. Then he will forget them almost instantly. He finds learning difficult because his brain is chaotic. Neurochemical activity suffuses from one sensory system to all others, creating synesthetic confusion—a neurophysiological maelstrom in which ripples caused by individual events are all but lost. Because of this confusion, a baby born with only a minim of brain can actually cope with some things better than a normal newborn can. For example, Frances Graham and three colleagues studied a pinheaded, "anencephalic" baby at the University of Wisconsin until the baby died during its seventh week of life.[14] This baby had only one-ninth the normal newborn's brain, and seemed to be blind and to be always asleep. When Graham presented linguistic sounds, the baby's heart slowed, showing—strongly—the interested, attentive, orienting reaction we encountered in chapter 8. Then the baby learned to recognize the sounds well enough to become habituated to them. (This was not just fatigue: he perked up again upon hearing different sounds.) He did this even when he was only nineteen days old. Yet a normal baby even a month older than this rarely shows any orienting reaction: except under unusual circumstances, the normal baby younger than two months exhibits only the wary, racing-heart, "avoidance reaction."[15] His world is too confused to make most kinds of change a positive experience.

This confusion is not complete. If the newborn encounters something salient enough often enough, he can come to recognize it. Thus he can learn. An extension of this is his learning to repeat an action for which he was just rewarded; for a reward is a stimulus of especially salient import. However, his confusion does make it difficult for him to pick out an individual object or event. To pick out two individual objects or events, and to perceive a relationship between the two—a relationship that forms a third event in itself—this, for a newborn, is virtually impossible. He cannot learn that if a round object appears and he sucks, then he will draw milk.

Synesthesia Simplifies

Often in this book we have described the newborn as living in a world of synesthetic confusion. The sight of his mother's voice, the sound of her face, the smell of her warmth—all these intermixed make a muddle of reality. Yet the newborn does not know that there are such things as people, and that people have faces and voices with characteristic qualities. He does not know that there is a constant in his life called Mother. Indeed, he does not yet know that any constants exist—or that anything exists outside himself. The observer is cognizant of sensory impressions but of nothing else: the source of those impressions he has not yet deduced. Thus the synesthetic confusion of those sensory signals does not confuse him as it would confuse us: since he does not know that voices do not have odors—or that voices even exist apart from himself—he is not confused when he smells a voice. His consciousness changes like a kaleidoscope, but all he has ever known is this kaleidoscope: he does not realize that the kaleidoscope is a distortion of something else.

Indeed, in the newborn's naive state, his synesthesia simultaneously confuses his world and simplifies it. It causes him to perceive the world not as an ordered set of discrete objects but as a single, multivarious set of sensations—a mélange of sensations affecting every part of his body. The elements of this mélange are confused—the beads within the kaleidoscope are unrecognizable—yet the newborn has no notion that it contains individual beads. The newborn is not conscious of innumerable, discrete, unchanging objects. The newborn is conscious of only one thing at a time. His is a monodic universe instead of our polyphonic one—a monodic universe whose melody modulates through markedly disparate keys and tempos.

We can see this in a fascinating study by Andrew Meltzoff and Richard Borton of the University of Washington.[16] Meltzoff and Borton made two peculiarly shaped pacifiers. In one, a smooth sphere replaced the nipple; in the other, a knobby sphere replaced it. Then they put one of those pacifiers in a baby's mouth without letting him see it, and held it there for ninety seconds. Finally, they showed the baby both pacifiers. They did this with thirty-two one-month-olds. After the babies had sucked on the knobby pacifier, they looked longer at it; after they had sucked on the smooth pacifier, they looked longer at *it*. Clearly, the one-month-olds made a connection between what they felt and what they saw. In a one-*year*-old, this would be evidence that the child could abstract the nature of the pacifier from one sensory system and apply it to another—that he could deal with objects as discrete and permanent with predictable properties. However, a one-month-old does not understand that objects are permanent. A one-month-old cannot feel an object, identify it, transform it into a visual image, then recognize that visual image. When a one-month-old connects what he feels with what he sees, he is doing it directly, synesthetically. When he feels something knobby in his mouth, he sees knobbiness, and hears and tastes and smells knobbiness; and when he sees something knobby, he feels knobbiness, and also hears and tastes and smells it. With a knobby pacifier inside his mouth, the baby finds that the universe is somewhat knobbier than it was—knobbier all over. Looking at the pacifier does not change this: the universe remains just as knobby as it was when the baby held the pacifier in his mouth.

The newborn's world is so integrated, he does not always distinguish even between his actions and his sensations. This accounts for curious findings by Annie Vinter of the *Instituto Scientifico Stella Maris* in Pisa, and by Sandra Jacobson of Harvard. Vinter found that four-day-olds appear to imitate someone who is sticking his tongue in and out (not just holding it stuck out) or opening and closing his hand—a seeming impossibility, since four-day-olds have no notion of what faces or hands are, either their own or anybody else's. And Jacobson found that six-week-olds will "imitate" objects just as though the objects were facial expressions.[17] Jacobson, like Vinter, found that a baby was more likely to stick out his tongue if she had stuck out her tongue at the baby than if she had stood still—the baby seemed to be imitating her—but she also found that the baby was almost as likely to stick out his tongue after she had swung a ball on a string toward and away from his mouth.

None of this is imitation as we know it. Rather, the baby sees something advancing and receding—and because of his synesthesia, he *feels* it advancing and receding as well, in a mélange of sensations that affects every part of his body. As part of this mélange, the baby feels movement in his tongue. This feeling of movement provides proprioceptive feedback to the reflexes that move his tongue, so that his tongue moves forward. Thus the baby's synesthesia makes him appear to imitate an adult by sticking out his tongue. When this occurs in his mother's arms rather than in the lab, his mother may playfully stick out her tongue in response—which will cause him to see and feel something advancing again, so that once again he will complete the reflexive circuitry within his body by sticking out his tongue. Thus the "imitation" is prolonged, and the baby learns to play a kind of game.

Yet the baby is not conscious of this game. Although he senses the movement that forms it, he does not distinguish two players. Moreover, the six-week-old still lives in the looking-glass world of his birth, where stasis and kinesis become interchanged in consciousness. The baby "plays" because he is sensing movements, but within his consciousness, these movements slow to form a pendular status quo.

Circular Reactions

Sometime in his life, the baby must cross through the looking glass into the world. To do this he does not have to shed his synesthesia—like the Russian mnemonist we described in chapter 4, some people retain it through adulthood—but normally the baby does lose nearly all of it. And if he should be among the few who retain it, he must still learn to perceive the world accurately. He must still cross through the looking glass.

When the baby is first born, nearly all of his actions are accidental or reflexive. Nevertheless, as we have seen, if the baby is rewarded for doing something, then he is likely to do it again. The newborn finds that his finger is in his mouth, for instance. He finds this pleasurable, and becomes alert to his enjoyment, his attention fixed upon it. When his finger slips out of his mouth, he keeps his hand close in front of his face, as though groping for his mouth—which, eventually, his finger finds again. He does this time and again until he learns to put his finger into his mouth: by one month he has learned to suck his thumb.[18]

Once the baby has developed a new skill, he practices it. A one-month-old will spend ten minutes at a time bringing his thumb up to and into his mouth.[19] Repeating an action seems to feel good to a baby, much as it does to an adult who is learning to play tennis and has just maintained a lengthy volley.

We know from studies in the laboratory that a newborn is capable of learning to repeat his accidental actions, if those actions are rewarded. But a laboratory is one thing; home is quite another. In the lab, an experimenter can arrange things so that accidents are rewarded frequently; at home, few accidental movements reap rewards frequently enough for the newborn to learn to repeat them. As a result, babies normally learn to repeat only reflexes. Thus for the first few months, nearly everything a baby can do originated as a reflex.

But by the time a baby has become three to four months old, his brain has matured markedly and he has had much more experience of the world. He learns quicker, he remembers what he has learned for several days,[20] and he has grown blasé about the games of his youth. He is ready for more sophisticated stimulation: shaking a rattle, or kicking a mobile and watching it swing. Of course, when he first sees a rattle or a mobile, he does not know what it does. But once he accidentally bumps into it, he learns. That is, he learns to associate a certain kind of shaking with the rattle and a certain kind of kicking with the mobile. This association is simple and direct, a beeline in the brain: when he kicks in a certain way, he notices the mobile; when he notices the mobile (because he or you just shook it), he kicks. The reaction is circular, and stops only when he becomes distracted by a more powerful stimulus, or when he habituates to the reaction—that is, becomes bored.[21]

A four-month-old has a large repertory of circular reactions like this. He can finger a teddy bear to feel the fuzz; he can drop a pie tin to hear it clatter; he can pull your glasses off to see you make a face. Clearly he knows that a teddy bear differs from a pie tin, and that a pie tin differs from your face. Nevertheless, we saw earlier that the four-month-old does not realize objects are permanent. How can this be?

The answer is, everything the four-month-old has learned to do is merely an accident or a reflex repeated by rote. These actions are no longer accidental or reflexive, of course, but they are stereotypical. He has as little understanding as the rube who negotiates the big city by following exactly the circuitous route he has always taken before. He knows objects only by what he has done with them before. As a consequence, the four-month-old cannot cope with altered conditions. If he has found a block on his right, and you put it there again, then turn him around so that now it is on his left, he will still look for it on his right.[22]

Nevertheless, stereotypical actions like these build a baby's mind. By repeating an action the baby extends and deepens the neuronal patterns of his brain, both the neuronal patterns that cause an action and the neuronal patterns that result from it. Soon these patterns become interleaved in rudimentary networks, allowing and causing him to make one action work in several circumstances and with several objects. Thus the first time he is put on the breast, he sucks on it merely because he finds the nipple in his mouth; a week later he has learned to suck on the breast, and to suck differently on the breast than on his finger; then by a month he has learned to suck only on the breast or a bottle when he is hungry, and to reject a pacifier.

Around eight months, the baby's neuronal networks become sufficiently developed to link two actions together. Now for the first time he pushes aside a net to kick the mobile, or pulls a cushion toward him to reach a ball on top of it, or crawls around a chair to retrieve a toy. This represents a breakthrough not just in his abilities, but also in his capability to learn. For no longer is his learning restricted to repeating accidents and reflexes. Now he can purposefully combine old skills to make new ones: he pulls the cushion to fetch the toy not accidentally but with intent.[23]

Until he became able to compound actions, every action was paired with an object as intimately and inseparably as the two faces of a coin. But now, by combining various actions with various objects, the baby splits object and action apart. For the first time objects exist by themselves. *For the first time objects exist.* By this time too, the baby's memory is significantly improved; for the neuronal patterns forming his memory have been developing alongside the neuronal patterns forming his skills. Hence not only do objects exist, they exist from one day to the next. The world begins to seem permanent, a fixed place of address.

The Emerging Mind

This perception brings the baby from the newborn's looking-glass world into our own. From the perspective of the "observer" within the baby's brain, this perception is the realization that something exists outside the brain. It is the "observer's" realization that the universe is formed not of neuronal activity alone but of objects and events *represented* by that neuronal activity. At the beginning of his life, the baby perceived the universe as motion centered about himself: now he begins to perceive the universe as a set of discrete and durable objects that can be stationary and can move, and can move close to other objects or far from them, and can move while other objects move or after other objects move. In short, the baby begins to perceive space and time like adults.

This is not quite an emergence of butterfly from chrysalis, yet it is quite a change nonetheless. It enables the baby to learn to do numerous things that he could never learn to do before—things that provide the foundation for adult life and learning. For instance, now that the baby can distinguish between others and himself, he becomes able truly to imitate other people's actions, not merely to give the appearance of imitating them by being caught up in a circular reaction.[24] Now too the baby can begin to imitate adults' expressions, gestures, and movements, even when the imitation involves doing something new.[25] Thus for the first time he becomes able to learn from other people. And although he was able to learn things even while still in the womb—he could learn to recognize the sound of his mother's voice, for instance—yet his learning was always limited to recognizing things: he could *recollect* nothing. If an object disappeared from sight, it disappeared from the universe; and since he confounded the universe with himself, an object disappearing from the universe disappeared from his mind as well. But now objects are permanent. Now he recollects his mother after she leaves the room, and cries for her.[26]

Now, because the baby can string together actions to make something happen, he understands much more the notions of cause, effect, and agency: he understands that he can cause something to happen through the agency of his mother by going to her and pushing on her hand.[27] He also begins to anticipate other people's actions.[28] He may cry, for instance, when his mother dons her coat, anticipating that she will leave; or he may call for his father when he hears the car in the driveway. And the more he learns about objects, the more he learns about space. No longer is his body the center of the universe. No longer does a chair revolve about him as he crawls: now he crawls around the chair.[29]

But still, an eight-month-old perceives that an object continues to exist while it is out of his sight only if he sees it disappear. Understanding that *all* objects *always* exist is much more difficult: it is one thing to understand that if your ball rolls under the couch, you can retrieve it; it is quite another to recollect out of the blue that you own a ball. This is why an eight-month-old is more likely to cry for his mother after she leaves his room at night than when he awakens later while she is no longer there. A full understanding of objects' permanence does not come before the middle of the second year.[30]

Now Language Can Blossom

Because the eight-month-old is able to recollect things, and because he understands that objects can be permanent, he is finally able to begin to learn his mother tongue.[31]

He begins to learn this much as he began to learn about the world: by coming to recognize things within the context of some activity. In the morning as his sister goes off to school, his mother holds him in her arms, waves her hand, and speaks to him in baby talk: "Bye-bye, Susie. Say 'bye-bye' to Susie, dear." The eight-month-old learns to recognize *bye-bye* and to understand from it that he should wave his hand.

Recalling *bye-bye*—speaking it—comes later. Speaking also begins within a context of some action or movement. Initially he will say "Bye-bye" only while he is in his mother's arms seeing Susie go off to school, and while he says it he will wave his hand.[32]

Until he is eighteen months old, a baby learns new words very slowly; but then his vocabulary soars. Lorraine McCune-Nicolich of Rutgers tape-recorded half-hour play sessions of five baby girls during their second year of life.[33] She recorded them monthly, and found wide variation in the number of words each girl used, quite as you would expect. However, each girl's vocabulary increased radically around eighteen months. During the half-hour observations, Shanti, for instance, used only ten different words at fourteen months and eleven words at fifteen months, but between sixteen and nineteen months she used over thirty; then between twenty and twenty-four months she used sixty to seventy.

This is the time a baby begins to walk around the house asking "Wat's 'iss? Wat's 'iss?" For around eighteen months, a baby finally begins to understand words not as sounds allied with actions but as objects in their own right—objects that represent other objects and actions. To an eighteen-month-old, "Bye-bye" no longer means waving your arm as Susie leaves: "Bye-bye" means "leaving." Now that the baby understands that objects exist, he becomes able to pretend in play—to put a doll to sleep, or to be mommy reading the newspaper;[34] and just as he plays at cooking by piling pots together, now he begins to play at talking by stringing words together: "Mama bye-bye!" "Mama bye-bye?" "Papa bye-bye!" "Papa bye-bye?" Adults respond to those combinations that make sense to them. Thus by the time he is two years old, the baby learns to form rudimentary sentences.[35] He makes innumerable errors, of course—often comical ones, like calling an orange "ball." But, like calling an orange "ball," his errors tend to be understandable. They are sensible errors—errors like those which adults commonly make while learning a foreign language.

Indeed, the errors of a two-year-old indicate just how well formed his mind is, for by calling an orange "ball," he shows that he fits objects into categories. Sorting the universe into categories is one of the most important things a baby must learn how to do. We saw earlier that the one-month-old categorizes the sounds of language much like adults, and that the four-month-old categorizes colors; but a young baby seems able to categorize little else. On the other hand, at about eight months—as soon as he becomes able to recollect objects—a baby becomes able to categorize a large part of what he sees and hears. Show him a giraffe, then a tiger, then an elephant, then a deer, then a sheep, then a lion, then a bear, then an antelope, then a dog, then a horse: by now he is thoroughly bored. If you next show him a cow, he will stay bored. He has had enough of animals. But if you show him a bridegroom in a monkey suit, he will perk up. Many studies have tested babies this way with happy faces, fearful faces, men, women, fruit, furniture, *M*'s, *O*'s, and a host of other things. All find that between eight and twelve months, a baby lumps together items from these categories much as adults do.[36] Now, one chair resembles another chair, and one dog another; they do not look entirely different. An eight- to twelve-month-old can even lump together objects by their quantity, provided there are no more than four: he has a rudiment of the understanding of number.[37] With all of these new abilities, a baby during his second year of life begins to function more like an adult than like a newborn.

Fostering Development

We, as adults, distinguish between body and mind. Body and mind influence one another, yet they seem separate, distinct. The mind, like the body, has a life of its own.

But this is not true of the newborn. As we have seen, when a baby is first born, he understands no universe outside himself, and his universe is a universe of movement—his own movement. The movements of his arms and his legs and his mouth and his hands all combine with whatever movements occur nearby to become adsorbed to his cognition as his own. In a universe like this, thought, as distinct from body, cannot exist. Hence, in a newborn, the mind as we think of it does not exist.

The baby's mind is first conceived eight months after his body is born, fertilized by the perception that objects exist. Nine to ten months of additional experience brings him to understand that not only do objects exist, but all objects exist all of the time, and their existence is independent of himself. This understanding delivers his mind.

Until then the baby lives a life as different from ours as the life of a tadpole is from a frog, or the life of a caterpillar is from a butterfly. It is a looking-glass life, a life where nothing makes sense because there is no sense, no capacity for thought. Reflex and accident rule.

Yet from these reflexes and accidents develop the stereotyped skills of the four-month-old; and from the sterotyped skills of the four-month-old develop the understanding of objects that leads ultimately to the mind. As different as the newborn is, he is, nevertheless, father to the man.

We can see this by following individual babies as they grow into school age. School-aged children differ from one another in their mental ability—some are smarter than others—and these differences generally persist through later life. A relatively bright first-grader usually becomes a relatively bright adult.[38] Many psychologists, including ourselves, have tested how quickly babies learned when they were less than six months old—that is, how quickly they habituated to something they saw or heard—and then tested the same children again five or six years later, after they reached school age. Generally, young babies who are quicker than their peers remain quicker than their peers.[39] Because this difference is evident at school age, it is likely to continue through maturity as well. Although a young baby has no mind as we know it, his capacity for learning will endow his mind once it develops.

However, this does not mean that intelligence arrives with genes and is fixed for life in some kind of neuronal formaldehyde. Intelligence is like an image on photographic film: it is the embodiment of certain material capacities, but it lies dormant until it is developed by the environment, and different environments develop it to different extents—extents so varied that they can easily obliterate differences in the basic material. A baby who is *extremely* slow to learn is indeed likely to remain retarded no matter what the rest of his life is like (although a stimulating familial life will leave him less retarded than a boring institutional one). However, a baby who learns but moderately slowly may end up with a Ph.D. if he grows up in a sufficiently stimulating family, while a "brilliant" baby may become molded into an adult dolt by inadequate nutrition, uninterested parents, and television as his primary mental fare.[40]

The optimal environment for a baby is just stimulating enough to challenge his ability to cope with it, but not stimulating enough to overwhelm him. Such an environment changes continuously as the baby learns and matures. To conclude this chapter, let us describe the kinds of things that provide it.

When a baby is first born, almost all of his actions are reflexive or accidental. His first task in learning about the world is to learn to repeat these reflexes or accidents, to turn them into a kind of habit. Nearly any kind of stimulation will facilitate this, unless the stimulation is so great that the baby falls asleep. (Although the newborn is conscious while he is sleeping, he cannot see while his eyes are closed, and visual learning is very important.) Ideally this stimulation will be varied, with differently shaped toys to put in his mouth, to feel and to examine. A variety of toys stimulating his reflexes will broaden the context in which his reflexes function, thus widening his abilities.

Beginning at about one month of age, a baby becomes able not only to habituate to things (which he could do even before birth), but to remember things that he has habituated to, and to associate one action with another. These abilities help him to discover the constants and continuities of his environment. The more stable his environment is, the more quickly he will do this, provided that amid the constancy is sufficient variety to stimulate him. Better that he not be put down on whatever blanket or rug is handy: better that he spend most of his time in and on one set of furnishings—one crib, one infant seat, one car seat, and one baby carrier. But better too that he not be left lying in his crib staring at the wall. Let objects appear, move, and disappear within a steady framework.

A one-month-old begins also to associate one action with another and to realize that one action can be contingent upon another. Repeatedly *making* one action contingent upon another can further this understanding: always dressing him in a yellow bib before feeding him, for instance. Rewards help teach contigency too: tickling him after he kicks his foot, or cooing at him after he grabs something. Rewards can be used to broaden his reflexes and to encourage him to repeat accidents. They can also encourage more complicated activities, like looking and listening simultaneously, or grasping something while sucking on it. Remember that in the newborn's world, the merest movement or change can be stimulating, so rewards need not be complex. A music box need only start *or stop* playing after the baby turns his head to look at it.

Between one and four months, imitating the baby helps him to consolidate his skills by inducing him to continue a behavior or repeat an action. If he coos at you, or sticks out his tongue, then you coo back or stick out yours, he is likely to continue. Although he is not really imitating you, he gets as much practice as if he were. Also, a young baby will learn more if you turn up the heat and take off his clothes. He will be able to move more, feel more, and see more of his body. (Babies born in summer develop faster than babies born in winter.[41])

At around four months of age, the baby's interest shifts to things beyond him in the world, and he wants more stimulation. Take him with you in a baby carrier when you go places, and prop him up once you get there: he will stay awake and look around (then fall asleep after he has had enough). Now he begins to show interest in a mobile and in what he can make it do—particularly in what he can make it do: a mobile hanging motionless above his head he will habituate to rapidly. Try tying a string to his ankle such that moving his leg shakes the mobile. (Do this only while you are watching him!) He will soon learn to shake it, and will shake it gleefully over and over again.

To vary things, sometimes tie the baby's wrist to the string instead, and hang different objects on the mobile every few days. The more varied the contingencies he learns how to deal with, the more capable he becomes.

A four-month-old will also "imitate" you when you cough or coo at him, or do something he knows how to do; so you can induce him to practice his new skills by modeling them. Moreover, remember that at this age the baby's "imitation" is really a circular reaction. Since a circular reaction can begin anywhere, the tail can wag the dog: if you tie a string from a mobile to the baby's arm, you can induce him to shake the mobile by waving your arm—or you can induce him to wave his arm by shaking the mobile.

At around six months, the baby is on the verge of understanding that objects exist. Playing hiding games should hasten this understanding. So should games that involve rolling toys through tunnels, and encountering situations where he must do something else to achieve a goal, like pull a string to retrieve a toy. After the breakthrough at around eight months, these games need to become more difficult and more complex, to maintain their challenge.

These kinds of activity will provide an optimal environment for the emergence of a baby's mind. However, it is important to realize that they are examples rather than a prescription, and that by and large they are things that interested, loving parents do naturally. Moreover, judging from the families we have seen, the converses of those two statements hold as well: interested, loving parents will probably provide an optimal environment naturally, and prescriptions of one or another ideology of child-rearing are no more likely to work.

This, we think, is just as well. For psychology can make reliable predictions only about *groups* of babies, not about individual ones. When psychologists measure how well a baby learns, they do the equivalent of drawing a ruler on a blackboard, then measuring against it a stretched rubber band: our yardsticks are imprecise, and babies have better days and worse. Infant "IQ" tests are useful for comparing two groups of babies because the errors tend to be random, so that they cancel themselves out, leaving the average accurate. But unless the baby has a severe problem, the tests are not reliable enough to predict how an individual will turn out.[42]

Nor can a child's later ability be predicted by anything else in his infancy. The beginning of creeping or crawling or walking or talking—none of these shows any relationship to later intelligence.[43] Certainly parents should not worry if their baby seems to be developing slower than their neighbor's child: he may well overtake him at school. All in all, the most helpful approach parents can take is to relax, be interested in their baby, love him, and do as love and interest call.

11

Learning to Love

WE HAVE SEEN that a newborn baby may feel comfortable or uncomfortable at times, but that he is born without emotions as we know them; that he is does not feel happy or sad; and that he feels very little pleasure or pain. Yet looking at a baby, it is difficult to believe this. When a baby cries, he looks miserable, and when he smiles, he glows.

In this chapter we shall explore why it is that babies smile and cry, and why they laugh as well. We shall see that their smiles and cries mean different things at different ages, for smiling and crying develop in a process that is inextricably bound up with their learning to understand objects. And we shall see that with smiling and crying develop love, anger, attachment, fear, and the foundations of all other emotions.

Smiling

If you gently stroke or rock a newborn baby, or blow on his skin, or coo at him in a high-pitched voice, the odds are high that he will stretch his mouth into a slight smile. However, if you look carefully,

During the first month of life, a baby almost never smiles except while he is asleep, like this one-month-old. These smiles are fleeting and do not involve the eyes: they do not indicate pleasure but are merely reflexive twitches of the muscles of the mouth. Contrast this to the social smile of the three-month-old on page 129 (last photo).

you will see that his smile does not include his eyes. It looks nothing like the broad, sociable grin of a two-month-old: it looks more like a grimace or a muscular spasm.

Many people believe that a newborn's smile is actually a grimace caused by gas; but it is not. Robert Emde and Kenneth Koenig of the University of Colorado carefully observed thirty newborns shortly before, during, and for twenty minutes after a feeding.[1] They found no relationship between when the babies smiled and when they burped, spit up, or passed gas.

Most of a newborn's smiles are muscular spasms caused by the random, neural spasms that characterize his active sleep. Observing twenty newborns for three and one-half hours, Emde and Koenig found that each baby smiled three times an hour on average, 95 percent of the time during active sleep.[2] Moreover, in another study comparing prematurely born newborns to full-term newborns, Emde, Robert McCartney, and Robert Harmon found that the earlier a baby is born, the more often he smiles.[3] Among the forty babies they studied, those born prematurely smiled on average three times more often than those born at term. Apparently, a newborn's smile is not only a muscular spasm, it is a sign of immaturity.

Yet Emde and Koenig did see a few smiles while babies were not asleep—a total of twelve while the babies were drowsy, and one in a hiatus during a bout of crying. These tell a different story. Remember that, although a sudden influx of energy will start a newborn crying, an excess of energy accumulating slowly will put him to sleep (thereby reducing the amount of energy entering his nervous system). If his nervous system contains excess energy, but not quite enough to close it down into sleep, that energy will spill into various pathways, stimulating reflexes. The baby will twitch, jerk, and flail about. Most of these movements involve his limbs and diaphragm, but often they involve his mouth: sometimes they make it frown, sometimes they make it smile.[4] Those movements are like the dancing weight atop a pressure cooker: they indicate a superfluity of energy, and simultaneously they provide the means to dissipate some of that energy.

This is what a newborn is doing when he smiles in response to your cooing or stroking. He is contracting muscles in an indiscriminate, reflexive reaction that indicates and controls a sudden influx of energy into his nervous system. In a few minutes he will probably be asleep.

Or rather, *she* will probably be asleep. Judith Feldman, Nathan Brody, and Stephen Miller, respectively at Columbia, Wesleyan, and the New School for Social Research, found that a newborn girl is more likely to smile or otherwise move the mouth than is a newborn boy, while a boy is more likely to move an arm or leg.[5] This is a broad, general tendency that shows up in many ways at birth and forms a congenital substructure that will be built up by learning and experience into some of the differences between the sexes we see in adults. Partly because newborn girls smile and frown more, and are less active, and partly because parents expect different things of girls and boys, parents tend to behave differently toward

newborn girls than boys. The nature of this difference varies radically from one society to another. In middle-class white America,
for instance, mothers coo at and talk to girls more than to boys;
while just across town, lower-class black mothers coo at and talk to
boys more than to girls.[6] Since the two sexes differ congenitally to
a certain extent, and since parents behave differently toward the
sexes beginning at birth, differences between boys and girls begin
to develop immediately. At any age in any task, the difference
between any two boys or between any two girls may far exceed the
difference between the average boy and the average girl; yet at any
age, in many ways, males and females, *on average,* differ.

After the baby is a few weeks old, his smiling reflexes are better
developed, so he begins to crinkle his eyes while he smiles and to
pull his mouth back farther than he did before.[7] Now too, gentle
stimulation becomes less likely to put the baby to sleep and is more
likely to induce subtler energy-controlling reflexes like smiling and
frowning. So the baby smiles more while he is awake than he used
to.[8] But he still smiles mostly just before he goes to sleep. While he
is smiling he looks glassy-eyed, almost intoxicated.

During the second month, almost any influx of energy while
the baby is awake becomes likely to cause him to smile. He smiles
at anything he sees, anything he hears or anything he feels, especially if it is moving or changing—a puppet, a mobile, a jack-in-the-
box, his mother's voice, a silent stranger, an upside-down monster
(or a rightside-up one), a hand stroking his forehead, or merely
fingers wiggling before his eyes.[9] The more he sees, feels, or hears,
the more he smiles. He will smile for minutes on end, quite undis-
criminating in his seeming delight. But *seeming* delight is what this
is; for anything that makes him smile is just as likely to make him
frown, and he will readily trill between a smile and a frown.[10]

At this time, a baby still has not formed emotions as we know
them. Emotions are the interplay of common physiological reactions
with current sensations and previous experience. You feel your feet
slip, so your heart races from a release of adrenaline. This reaction
you feel as either terror or exhilaration, depending on whether you
are expecting fun because you are rappelling down the side of a
mountain or are expecting disaster because you are falling into a
crevasse (see chapter 3). Without your expectations, which are
gained by experience, you would feel your racing heart merely as

a racing heart: you would not feel any emotion. This is the baby's situation. The one-month-old is only just beginning to recognize things that occurred beyond the immediate past. He does not yet have the store of experience needed to transform physiological reactions into emotional experiences.[11]

First Feelings

On the other hand, a one-month-old and even a newborn has the *rudiments* of feelings. Sweet tastes and odors give the newborn pleasure. So do moderate pressures about his mouth and the successful repetition of an action. He feels discomfort from intense lights and sounds, bitter flavors and smells, cold, pinpricks, circumcision, and other vigorous forms of stimulation.[12] He also shows the basic, physiological reactions that underlie emotions. In adults, these reactions are various, variegated, and vague—no specific reaction leads to a specific emotion or group of emotions[13]—yet the reactions wind themselves around a common core: the pulse. The pulse can slacken slightly, or it can quicken. If there is no change in muscular activity (even tiny movements can speed the pulse), then the physiological reactions intertwined among those slackenings and quickenings become the substructure of positive and negative feelings.[14] (If there is muscular activity, as there would be in our mountain-climbing example, the feelings can go either way.) These physiological reactions are less well formed in babies, but they do show themselves even in newborns as the orienting and avoidance reactions that we discussed in chapters 8 and 10.

Particularly they show themselves in avoidance reactions. Most of the time a newborn baby sleeps, and reacts little to stimulation; but when he does react to something, he almost always reacts negatively—even to his mother's stroking and cuddling. While he is quiet and alert, few stimuli occasioned by others are gentle enough to elicit a positive, orienting reaction. A flutist playing long tones in another room when everything else is silent; or switching on a night light while the baby is staring at the ceiling—slight events like these are what it takes.[15] Thus most of the time a newborn baby finds the world neither agreeable nor disagreeable; and although he sometimes finds it pleasant, usually when the world obtrudes itself upon him, it is too rough for him to enjoy.

The Social Smile

By the end of his second month all this is changing fast. A baby can handle much more stimulation now, so numerous aspects of his environment that once overwhelmed him, putting him to sleep, now interest him. Avoidance reactions become far less common; orienting reactions take their place, and become more pronounced.[16] Now his breathing slows along with his heart, and he turns to look at things. He orients toward anything and everything, including horrendous noises loud enough to repel the most deafened aficionado of rock music, and sights which he will later find fearsome: the deep side of the visual cliff, a stranger moving quickly toward him, an object looming toward his face.[17] After two months, life begins to seem more pleasant, and he tries continually to soak it up.

Moreover, when he was first born the baby could recognize things only if he had encountered them *immediately* before, or innumerable times; but now he can recognize them after just a few encounters and a delay. Thus the world around him has become familiar, and is becoming associated with various of his experiences. These memories and associations combine with his newly strengthened physiological responses to create emotions. No longer does the baby feel merely vaguely positive or negative: now he feels pleasure and gall.

Now, too, his smiles and his frowns become more adult. As adults, we often smile and frown purposefully, yet we often smile and frown reflexively too. When we do, it is for much the same reason the baby does: to regulate neuronal energy within the brain. You are on a holiday in Paris taking a tour of the *Opéra.* In the midst of the grandeur, you find yourself standing beside somebody who looks vaguely familiar. Within your brain, energy swirls through neuronal networks, dredging up memories of people you once knew. With your attention focused like this, your heart slows slightly. Suddenly you place him: he was in the class behind you in high school. With this recognition, a mass of energy swirling about suddenly becomes channeled from disparate neuronal networks into networks connected specifically with him. This sudden channeling creates a wave that overflows the normal pathways into the brain's equivalent of a storm sewer—neuronal channels that carry it away, to be dissipated in harmless reflexes. This overflowing combines with your slowed heart and your sensation of recognition to create a feeling of pleasure, while the "storm sewer" channels energy into a reflexive smile, and possibly, if there is a lot of energy, into reflexive movements of the diaphragm, to form laughter. Suddenly, although you never had much to do with him earlier, you find yourself breaking into a grin.

That is much like what happens when a two-month-old smiles. When a baby becomes two months old, he becomes able to recognize commonalities among peoples' faces. He does not yet know what a face is—he does not know that it is a part of a person—but given a little time, he recognizes a face when he sees one.[18] This recognition brings pleasure to his heart and a genuine smile to his face.[19] For the first time in his life, the baby acts like a *mensch.*

Yet still he is not smiling at people per se. He is quite as likely to smile at an Indian war mask, or at a grotesque drawing of a face with six eyes or no mouth and nose. If an object is roughly circular with two *or more* eyelike spots, and if he sees it from the front, he is as likely to smile at it as he is to smile at a person—especially if it is moving.[20]

Laughter, Humor, and Fear

Perhaps two months after this, when he is around four months old, the baby's neuronal pathways and storm sewers are developed enough to cause him not just to smile but to laugh. Now he will likely laugh if you sing "I'm gonna get you" with your hands poised to grab him, then suddenly grab him by the belly. He may even laugh if you just kiss his belly. What matters is that the stimulus be sudden and strong enough that its energy is not dissipated gradually; that he both recognize the stimulus and recognize it as benign; and that he have to work at recognizing it. (If you repeat "I'm gonna get you" a few times, he comes to recognize it too well to laugh: he smiles instead.) Alan Sroufe and Jane Wunsch found this in a study of ten baby boys at the University of Minnesota.[21] Sroufe and Wunsch tested those boys in their homes between four and twelve months of age, to see what would make them laugh. They had the mothers try popping their lips, saying "Boom, boom boom," whispering to them, talking in a squeaky voice, neighing like a horse, blowing in their hair, playing peek-a-boo, wearing a mask—thirty-three things in all. At one or another age, babies found each of these funny, but the four-month-olds laughed only at strong, sudden stimulation. They were oblivious to games and comical sounds.

That is because a four-month-old's laughter is still without humor. Humor comes with the juxtaposition of the expected with the unexpected, the familiar with the strange. A four-month-old has few expectations, so there is small ground for humor. Sroufe and Wunsch found that only toward the end of the first year would babies laugh at the unexpected—at Mom sucking a baby bottle or walking like the comedian Stanley Laurel. Moreover, when the four-month-old's expectations are breached, he feels not tickled but cautiously interested.[22] If he does not recognize a stimulus (and if the stimulus is not so strong that it overwhelms him and makes him cry), his heart slows slightly. He knits his brow, perhaps pulls back a little, and stares at it intently. There is no humor here. His laughter is merely a reflex at the level of the knee jerk, the kind of laughter elicited from adults by tickling.

Similarly, when the four-month-old encounters something strange, his cautiousness does not reflect fear. Fear feeds on itself: if you show an older baby something he fears, then show it to him again, he will react more strongly the second time.[23] But a four-month-old reacts *less* strongly the second time he sees something than the first. Neither does the four-month-old show the face of fear, a face that is the same in every culture the world over.[24] His cautiousness reflects merely an unsettled feeling, the same unsettled feeling that we adults sometimes feel in the face of the unknown.

This changes at around eight months. Now the baby begins to understand that objects exist, and to appreciate cause, effect, and agency.[25] Now he becomes able to react to aspects of our world much as we react ourselves. He has learned that a box is a solid object, so that he is surprised when a clown springs from a jack-in-the-box. With this surprise flows either humor or fear, depending on the circumstances—that is, depending on who shows him the box. When his mother shows it to him, his heart slows slightly as he orients himself toward the closed box and examines it. When the clown pops out, this unexpected event combines with his orienting to create feelings of delight. Alternatively, if a stranger approaches him, the eight-month-old feels anxious. His heart races slightly. Now when the clown springs out of the closed box, the surprise whips his anxiety into fear and terror. In both cases, the neuronal energy forming the baby's perception of the clown splashes into the neuronal energy forming his perception of the box. When the context is familiar, pathways are established that bring this splash of energy to his mouth and diaphragm, making him laugh. When the context is unfamiliar—or when he has already been frightened, so that the context is negative—the energy comes out in a cry. Any number of things can cause fear now, even things that only weeks before aroused his interest: Santa Claus, the shot of a cap gun, mechanical toys, even grandmother if she has been away for a while, so that the baby does not recognize her easily.[26]

As we age, we experience more and we recognize more, so we require ever more sophisticated surprises to tickle our wit or to terrify us. But the mechanism and the feelings remain the same. A jack-in-the-box to an eight-month-old is the equivalent of a prat-fall or a horror film to an eight-year-old, or a *bon mot* or dark alley to a middle-aged adult.

Frustration and Rage

As the baby is learning to feel pleasure and to fear things, he is also learning to feel displeasure and is developing a sense of malignancy, a sense of rage and anger.

When a baby is first born, he often cries as if he is in distress. Several investigators have analyzed the frequencies of the sonic waves forming his cries, and have discovered that some cries start more explosively and contain more high-frequency energy than others. Those are the ones that sound like cries of distress.[27] However, we have seen that a newborn baby does not feel hunger, and is fairly insensitive to pain. He may sound as if he is being starved or crucified, but he does not feel that way. Rather, he feels stressed by excess stimulation—overstimulated, like a farmer visiting New York City. When he first awakens, light overwhelms his dark-adapted eyes, so that he cries. Toward the end of the day, the accumulated energy from what he has seen and heard overwhelms him, so that he cries. The more overwhelmed he is, the more energy he dissipates through the movement and tension of the muscles that make him cry. Stronger muscular movements and tension create more explosive and higher-pitched cries, which sound to adults like cries of distress or pain. These cries of distress do reflect distress, but only a generalized distress, the distress of overstimulation.[28] They do not reflect any specific hurt or specific emotion. Negative emotions, like positive emotions, the baby must learn.

By the time a baby is two to three months old, he has repeated actions often enough, and remembers them well enough, so that when he is in the midst of an action, he expects to complete it. If he is stopped, his heart is still racing from his activity and the neural pathways forming the activity are loaded with neuronal energy. Since this energy no longer has a specific place to go, it overflows into reflexive pathways that cause the baby to kick, flail his arms, and cry. This surplus energy also combines with the sensations caused by his racing heart, to engender feelings of frustration and rage.[29]

At this point the baby's frustration and rage are not formed around or directed toward specific objects, for the baby does not yet distinguish objects from himself. His upset is amorphous spleen. "I am gall. I am heartburn" is what the baby might say, if he could quote Gerard Manley Hopkins. But like everything else in the baby's world, his gall matures radically when he becomes seven to eight months old. Now, when you take away his teething biscuit, he reacts not just with distress but with anger.[30] Now, too, he begins much better to understand cause, effect, agency, and objects: now he feels furious when the *intention* of an action is thwarted, and directs his fury at the cause.[31] If you grab his bottle before he manages to throw it to the ground, he will stomp his foot and slap your hand, or push you away and pout.

More Complex Emotions

After eight months, as the baby learns, his emotions continue to develop. Around twelve months he understands cause and effect well enough to look at the cookie jar, think about raiding it, and to smile at the *thought*.[32] Now, too, he has learned enough of the world to be affected by what his mother does: he follows her gaze to see what she is looking at; he becomes fearful if she acts fearful; he is reassured if she acts blithely unafraid.[33] At around eighteen months he perfects his understanding of objects and of their relationship to himself. This understanding is reflected in shame and pride: the baby blushes and looks embarrassed if he breaks something, and smiles after he solves a difficult problem—smiling the more broadly as the problem was more difficult to solve.[34] Now, too, he understands that other people are much like himself, and perceive the world like himself, with emotions like his own. Now if his sister is crying, he understands some of what she is feeling and how to cure it: he toddles over to give her a cookie or a hug.[35]

Emotional Attachments

At the same time that a baby is developing emotions, he is developing emotional attachments to other people. The first precursors of this occur at two to three months, but the baby does not form any attachments per se until he is approximately eight months old, when he begins to understand that there is a world other than himself.

When a baby becomes two to three months old, he begins to prefer interacting with his mother more than with a stranger. He smiles and coos more at her than at others. This is not because his mother feeds him: he will usually prefer his mother to a stranger even if he has been fed all his life by a nurse.[36] Yet this has nothing to do with maternity per se. The two-month-old has no idea that there is such a thing as Mother, or that *anything* exists other than himself. He prefers to interact with his mother merely because she has played with him more than strangers have, so she forms sensations that he has encountered before and learned to recognize. She looks and feels and smells familiar. Moreover, because she has played with her baby more than others have, she has become more sensitive to his abilities, reflexes, and rhythms. She has learned when he wants excitement and when he wants calm. When she plays with him, she gets into his swing of things better, stimulating him, waiting for him to react, then stimulating him again when he is ready. She dances with him, as it were.[37] From our adult perspective, it looks as though the baby prefers his mother to other people; and in a sense he does. But from the baby's perspective, his mother is not a special person, nor even a person—nor an object, for that matter: he simply feels comfortable around her because he is encountering a particular set of familiar sensations and because he is being stimulated appropriately. This is why the baby seems comparably attached to his father, even when the father has little to do with him except to play with him a little after he comes home from work: their short but frequent play is enough to develop and maintain a mutual familiarity.[38]

After several months of being stimulated by his mother—or by anyone else who plays with him frequently—a baby does begin to develop a real preference. For gradually he associates the pleasure from his play with the particular sets of sights, sounds, and feelings that his mother creates within him. Yet still the baby has no real attachment to his mother, for he does not yet realize that there is anything else apart from himself to be attached to. Real attachment cannot develop before seven to eight months, for the baby must understand that things exist before he can form attachments to them, and he must be able to recollect things that are not in front of him to be able to maintain those attachments from one moment to the next.[39]

As soon as the baby does come to appreciate the existence of other things, he begins to develop attachments. A study in

Guatemala shows this clearly. Researchers there tested a dozen nine-month-old babies and a dozen twelve-month-olds.[40] They tested the babies' understanding of objects and observed the babies' playing in a strange room after their mothers had left them alone with a stranger. Of course, more of the older babies had a better understanding of objects. But those babies of *either* age who understood objects better also played less after their mother's departure. These babies had become sufficiently attached to their mothers that they became uncomfortable when separated from them.

Attachment is formed from two factors: the pleasure that the baby has come to associate with certain sensations—sensations that he now recognizes as individuals—and insecurity. On the one hand, the baby has learned that certain of these other beings portend pleasure; on the other, he has come to realize that there is a vast world out there beyond him, an unknown, various, and changing world, a sea in which one of the few islands of stability is the object we call his mother. To keep his bearings while he explores this world, he keeps one eye on her. In a strange room, he crawls but a few feet before turning back to look at her. He defines all of his movements there in relation to her. When his mother leaves him in a strange place, he becomes anxious. If a stranger approaches him in her absence, he cries with fear. Thus pleasure in his mother's presence and insecurity in her absence form a carrot and stick that drive the eight-month-old toward love.[41]

Styles of Attachment

Among any group of eight-month-olds, some appear to be more attached to their mothers than others. The baby we have been describing so far is an archetype. Real babies vary enormously from one to the other, and many differ from the archetype substantially.

To see how a variety of babies develop feelings of attachment, we need somehow to measure their attachment. The most useful gauge was devised by Mary Ainsworth at Johns Hopkins University.[42] With various colleagues, Ainsworth carefully observed babies in their homes for many hours at a time, then observed the same babies in a laboratory procedure designed to elicit certain behaviors that proved to be telling in the home. In the laboratory procedure, a baby's mother brings him into a strange room and puts him down to play; then a stranger enters; next the mother leaves; and finally the mother returns. Movie or television cameras record all this, so that various of the baby's reactions can be noted and scored. Since the situation is strange, of course the baby does not behave as he usually behaves. Nevertheless, the baby's behavior in this situation stems from his temperament and his relationship to his mother, just like his behavior at home; so babies who behave alike in this strange situation tend to behave alike at home. Thus we can use babies' behavior at home to describe their emotional attachment in a natural environment, and use their behavior in the laboratory to examine individual aspects of their attachment in a more controlled situation. We shall not do this study by study, for the studies are too numerous. However, since the studies are highly consistent, we can summarize them as a body.

Toward the end of the first year, every baby is attached to his mother (and to other people who are around him much of the time: babies commonly become attached to a number of people).[43] A baby shows this attachment in many ways: by crying when his mother leaves the room, for instance, or following her as she leaves; then by running to her when she returns and snuggling up to her. Underneath these various behaviors lie two underlying factors: how secure the baby feels and how much he enjoys physical contact with his mother.[44] Babies who feel secure generally enjoy physical contact with her; babies who do not feel secure may also enjoy it, or they may not. All in all, one-year-olds show three modes of attachment: secure, anxious, or unsocial.[45]

Secure Attachment.   If the mother is talking with a visitor at home while the baby is playing on the floor and then leaves the room, the baby does not cry or protest, but the odds are even that he will follow her out the door. When she returns, nearly half the time he will greet her by smiling, laughing, bouncing, jiggling, waving, reaching for her, or crawling or walking toward her. When his mother picks him up, she does this at the baby's instigation between one-fifth to one-quarter of the time. Whether he initiated it or not, most of the time he acts delighted. He smiles at her, laughs, kisses her, hugs her, clings to her, sinks into her body, fingers her face or

body, or buries his face against her. He will almost never cry, stiffen
his body, squirm or push himself away, hit her or bite her. When
she puts him down, he will probably smile and seem content. About
one-quarter of the time he will not want to be put down: then he
will cry and try to clamber back up. If his mother tells him to do
something, or not to do something, the odds are very high that he
will obey. He makes his wants reasonably clear with gestures, facial
expressions, and vocalizations. He will cry as often as other babies,
but he will usually stop crying sooner. He rarely acts angry and
generally seems to be happy. When his mother takes him to a
strange place, his heart pounds, but soon he recovers his equanimity
and explores his surroundings. As he explores, he is absorbed in
what he is doing: his heart slows frequently in orienting reactions.
He will turn around frequently to look at his mother. When his
mother is nearby, he will usually not be afraid of a stranger but will
explore the person just as he explored the room. If he finds something to play with, he may turn toward his mother and smile or
bring it to her. If his mother leaves this strange room, his heart races
and he may or may not be visibly upset. If he is upset, then upon
her return he will go to her, hug her, snuggle up to her, and try to
stay by her awhile. If he was not upset, still he will go to her,
although this time he will bring her a toy and try to play with her.
In either case, soon he settles down to playing as contentedly as he
played before. All in all, he seems to enjoy his mother's company
and is easily reassured by her when he is upset.

Anxious Attachment. If his mother is talking with a visitor while
the baby is playing on the floor and then leaves the room, this baby
is twice as likely to cry as a securely attached baby, although still,
two times out of three, he will not cry. Neither will he follow her
out the door as a securely attached baby often will. When she
returns, he will greet her warmly less often, and he is almost as
likely to break into tears as into a smile. When his mother picks him
up, she rarely does this at the baby's instigation, and the baby is
only half as likely as a securely attached baby to react positively.
Indeed, he is as likely to react negatively as positively: he may cry,
stiffen, squirm, push away, hit and bite. A baby who hollers when
he is picked up is likely to holler just as loudly when he is put back
down and to try to clamber back up. If his mother tells him to do
something, the odds are hardly even that he will obey. When his

mother takes him to a strange place, he does not settle down to play, but moves about restlessly. If his mother leaves, he is very distressed. When she returns, he may tearfully gesture for her to come to him, but when she does, he continues to cry. Alternatively, he may go to her to be picked up and held—yet then, while she is holding him, he will squirm, push, and kick, trying to be put down. Either way, if his mother tries to distract him with a toy, he will push it away. He seems to be seeking comfort from his mother, but is unable to receive it.

Unsocial Attachment. At home, this baby reacts to his mother's comings and goings much like a securely attached baby, although he is somewhat more likely to cry when she leaves and somewhat less likely to greet her when she returns. However, when his mother picks him up, he rarely smiles, laughs, hugs or kisses her, or acts playfully rambunctious. One time in five he will actively object to being picked up, which is three to four times more often than a securely attached baby will object. On the other hand, when his mother puts him back down, he is almost as likely to object as he is to act content. Like the anxiously attached baby, if his mother tells him to do something, the odds are even that he will disobey. The baby frequently acts angry. For no apparent reason he will throw his toys against a wall, or walk over to his mother and hit her. In a strange place this baby appears unflappable, even if his mother leaves him alone with a stranger. When she returns, either he will avoid her or he will start toward her but then turn away and begin to play; and if she picks him up, he will act just as he does at home—rarely positively, more often negatively. Yet as soon as she returns, his heart begins to race, and it continues racing for a long time thereafter. And all the while he is ignoring his mother, he does not play; or if he does play, his heart races. He is working very hard to act as though his mother is not there. In short, he seems attached to his mother but mistrustful of her.

In the United States, one-half to two-thirds of one-year-old babies are securely attached to their mothers, approximately one-fifth are anxiously attached, and approximately one-quarter are unsocially attached.[46] In other countries, where parents value different things and rear children differently, these proportions vary markedly. In northern Germany, for instance, parents who grew up before World War II (and hence before Germany became American-

ized) thought that babies should be relatively independent creatures
and not require the constant attention that Americans deem natural.
The securely attached child who is the American ideal seemed
spoiled to even a sensitive psychologist like Kurt Lewin. Northern
Germans reared their children to foster independence instead—not
to act upset when left alone and not to demand attention. Thus they
reared more unsocially attached babies.[47] In the United States, securely attached babies tend to become more sociable and successful
than others; in other countries, with other values, this may not be
the case.

What Causes These Differences?

These differences in the one-year-old come from interactions of the
mother with the baby—interactions, beginning at birth, of the
mother's personality with the temperament of her child. Babies
have different temperaments at birth; and of course, mothers have
different sensibilities. Insofar as babies differ from one another,
they tend to develop differently, and they instigate different reactions toward them from their mothers. And insofar as mothers differ
from one another, they react differently as well. By the time a child
is one year old, the entanglement of personalities and reactions has
become a Gordian knot.[48] *very complex*

During the baby's first month of life, his temperament is em-
bodied in his reflexes—in how often he cries, how quickly he stops
crying, whether he flails or cuddles while he is being held. These
reflexes all reflect physiological mechanisms which he has inherited
from his parents, plus prenatal influences of his parents' lifestyle.
They vary markedly from baby to baby, just as the genes and
lifestyle of parents vary markedly. With various colleagues, Daniel
Freedman of the University of Chicago has examined newborns of
a number of races using standard behavioral tests.[49] In his first
study, he examined twenty-four Chinese-American babies and
twenty-four European-American babies, all while they were still in
hospital. The parents came from similar socioeconomic classes, and
all of them received similar medical care. The typical European-

American newborn got excited more easily, slipped back and forth more readily between content and discontent, and reddened more often in face and body. In contrast, the typical Chinese-American newborn was less excitable. Once he had begun to cry, he stopped sooner. And he would lie placidly on his back with a cloth draped over his face, unlike the European-American baby, who "immediately struggled to remove the cloth by swiping with his hands and turning his face. . . ."

Not only do groups of babies differ from one another in temperament; individual babies differ even more. Anyone who has been around a "colicky" baby knows this: a "colicky" baby—usually a one-month-old—may cry more than five or six hours a day, many times longer than any group's norm. (Note the quotation marks around *colicky*. There is no evidence that these babies are actually suffering colic; the diagnosis is merely a guess applied by default when a baby cries a lot with no apparent cause. A typical "colicky" baby may be just receiving more sensory stimulation than he can handle.[50]) Most mothers believe babies differ in more subtle ways as well, and several studies have confirmed this. For instance, Anneliese Korner and a number of colleagues at Stanford recorded the movements and crying of several dozen babies during the first three days after birth; then four to eight years later, they used an electronic transmitter to record the same children's movements throughout a day.[51] They found that babies who cry and move more the first day tend to cry and move more the second and third days as well—and still to be more active after they reach school age.

The more quiet, alert, and responsive a baby is, the more responsive his parents are likely to be—and the more responsive the parents are, the more likely the baby is to be quiet, alert, and responsive. This is a circular reaction that begins at birth and does not necessarily end. Moreover, other circular reactions may circle about this one, and about one another, like an intricate nest of Ptolemaic epicycles. For instance, the less experience a mother has had around babies, the less likely she is to be appropriately responsive—or the more likely, depending on whether she reacts with less or greater alacrity than is wanted, and upon whether her culture's child-rearing practices stress involvement, like the Japanese, or detachment, like the Dutch. Similarly, a mother may have more time to respond to her baby if she has a supportive family with a comfortable income than if she is a single parent who needs to go back to work.*

We can see this in a number of studies that use Ainsworth's strange situation as a measure of attachment. For instance, one study found that newborns who had been rated by nurses as less alert and less active tended at one year to be unsocially attached, while those whom nurses had found easiest to care for tended to become securely attached.[53] This shows congenital differences in temperament. On the other hand, mothers who respond more quickly to their one-month-olds' crying have babies who cry as much as others do at one month—but who cry less than others at three months.[54] Mothers cause this latter difference, not babies. Attachment is clearly a two-way street—and because it is a two-way street, babies can become attached differently to their mothers and their fathers. In one study, approximately the same number of babies were attached securely to their fathers as to their mothers, but one-third were attached more securely to one parent than to the other.[55] (Note that this does not mean that attachments to one person are made at the cost of attachments to another. Attachments are not formed by a congenital glue held in limited supply: they are welded by the heat of interactions. Babies can become attached to many people as strongly as they become attached to one.[56])

Of course, this is from the adult's perspective. The baby's perspective is quite different. When a baby is first born, he mostly absorbs stimulation from the world about him and reacts reflexively to the amount of stimulation he receives, crying and sleeping when it is too much, vegetating when it is too little, and coming to grips with it, and learning, when it is the right amount. If the baby's mother is responsive and appropriately stimulating, during his first

*Differences among babies' temperaments are so striking that psychologists and psychiatrists have spent much time devising the means to classify and describe them. The set of categories used most often are "easy," "difficult," and "slow to warm up," terms formulated by psychiatrists Stella Chess and Alexander Thomas on the basis of their New York Longitudinal Study, which has followed 133 children for a span of thirty years. This classification has gained wide currency, and it may be appropriate for older babies, but we do not know whether it describes the newborn well, for the classification is based on information gleaned long after birth when the baby's congenital temperament has been modified through interaction with his parents. In any case, the classification tells as much about the psychologist (or the mother who makes the observations that the psychologist works with) as it tells about the baby; for temperament, like beauty, is largely in the eye of the beholder. What a middle-class, white American deems to be pleasant, sociable behavior, a Japanese might deem to be difficult; and the baby whom a middle-class, white American considers "slow to warm up" might seem "easy" to a northern German.[52]

six or seven months he comes to recognize a certain set of smells, sights, and sounds, and to associate them with pleasantness and the relief of discomfort. Then, at around seven or eight months, he realizes that this set of smells, sights, and sounds is in fact something else, an object whose presence portends pleasantness and that usually appears in the presence of discomfort, thereby relieving it. If his mother is insufficiently responsive or stimulating, he still comes to recognize her, so that he still links himself to her as to an anchor; yet he does not come to believe that her presence normally portends pleasantness or that she usually appears when he is distressed. He becomes one of those one-year-olds who wants contact with his mother yet feels insecure about her—one who is anxiously attached. In contrast, if his mother is *overly* responsive and stimulating—no matter whether she talks and plays with him incessantly, or he wants less stimulation than other babies—then she will overwhelm her child. Her child will certainly come to recognize her, and link himself to her, yet he will come to realize that her presence often *causes* distress. The same will happen if she is inconsistent, perhaps because she attends to him often, but when it is convenient for her, not when he wants attention. By the time he is one year old, he feels insecure around her and is chary of contacting her: he becomes unsocially attached.[57]

Caveats

To conclude this chapter, let us point out that there is a serious problem with the terms securely attached, anxiously attached, and unsocially attached. We are using them because the English language offers nothing better, but they come inappropriately laden with the peculiar values of twentieth-century, English-speaking North America. Feelings of security we consider to be good; anxiety and unsociality we think of as bad. This is fine in a protective and wealthy society like ours. However, in most eras, and in most societies, it has not been. If your house were in the jungle, you would not want a child who felt secure enough to play by himself and crawl off on his own. If you had a dozen children with no servants or electrical appliances, you would want a baby to be sufficiently unsocial not to want often to be in your arms.

Nevertheless, within our time and place, the securely attached infant does have an advantage over the others. He is the baby we admire. As a result, he gets more attention than the others, so that he develops better social skills, and he learns more.[58]

This is our ideal baby. Yet ironically, a mother who is eager to mold her baby into such a child is likely to be unsuccessful. For trying to force a child's behavior into a preconceived mold is likely to overstimulate him, leading him to avoid contact. On the other hand, the opposite—ignoring a baby's crying to avoid rewarding it—is likely to make him feel insecure. During the first years of life the most effective approach is to attend to his needs immediately, to give him attention when he wants attention, and to back off when he is cranky from overstimulation.

12

Metamorphosis

BEFORE the twentieth century, a baby's mind and emotions were deemed to be formed through the aegis of God. Their development was a mystery that few but philosophers thought about; and few philosophers thought about it either, for babies were assumed to be homunculi, with homuncular emotions and minds, and one can hardly expect a homunculus to provide insight into the affairs of adult man. One read homilies to a baby in his crib; one did not learn from him.

Freud flipped this notion onto its side, showing that babies can provide the origin of fabulous speculations about all aspects of mankind. Yet still, he, and most people today, assume that the homunculus in some way exists, that the newborn baby's thoughts, feelings, and consciousness resemble, to a certain extent, our own.

In reality, as we have seen, a newborn is so little the homunculus that even his sensations barely resemble our own. During the baby's first days and months, he does indeed come to taste, to smell and to feel things something like an adult. But he hears sounds as thinner and duller than we, and nearly all that he hears is accompanied by echoes. He sees a brighter world filled with ill-defined shapes of distorted hue, lacking in detail. And his sensations intermix. He tastes his mother's voice. He smells the touch of her hand. He feels her visage.

Moreover, a newborn baby is conscious of these sensations constantly, even while he is asleep—not so conscious as an alert adult, yet conscious nonetheless, like an adult awakening from a dream.

On the other hand, an adult who is awakening from a dream understands what he is conscious of, at least to some extent. A newborn baby understands virtually nothing—not even that the world he is sensing exists. He has no mind nor emotions as we think of them, merely vague feelings of pleasure or distress. His body senses things, and he is conscious of many of these sensations, but he is unaware that his sensations represent events that occur in time and space. When he perceives something, he perceives it not through time and space, but through velocity, as sensations changing and moving quickly or slowly—quickly or slowly by his lights, which are often opposite from ours. Thus his world bears little relationship to ours. It differs not merely in quantity but also in quality.

This is no wonder; for biologically, a newborn baby is an organism that is just beginning to leave a larval state, a state that is fundamentally different from the adult. He is comparable to a tadpole that is beginning to turn into a frog. He began life, like the tadpole, as an embryo absorbing food and oxygen from the fluids surrounding it; then he went through an initial metamorphosis into a larva living a submarine existence, imbibing food and oxygen in different forms than he can use now. He took these through an organ that he lost at birth when he began to breathe, just as the tadpole loses its gills after it begins to breathe. Now the baby is breathing air, yet his body—and his mind—is still more larval than adult.

Becoming Adult

When the baby first begins to live in air, he has a very limited ability to learn. Yet slowly, he does begin to recognize some sensations. When he recognizes a sensation, he clings to it for its familiarity.

Many of the sensations he recognizes result from his movements. In these cases, holding onto the sensations means repeating his movements. By repeating them he gains experience, so that he learns.

Gradually, as he experiences more, and as his brain develops, he comes to recognize more and more of his sensations—especially those sensations reflecting parents and other people he encounters often. Some of these sensations occur so frequently that they force him to the realization that they have a cause, that things exist other than himself. These things seem ephemeral at first, appearing and disappearing like specters. But toward the middle of his first year he begins to recollect some of them after they disappear. When he is around eight months old, he comes occasionally to realize that an object that he sucked on and banged on awhile ago looks and feels like the one that he is sucking on and banging on now: he puts two and two together and realizes that the object is indeed the same one, and that it is durable. Not only do things exist other than himself, they exist permanently!

This realization is the beginning of the end of infancy. With it comes the understanding that objects exist in relation to himself—in front of him, behind him, before he ate, after he ate. He comes to understand space and time. With this understanding his consciousness comes through the looking glass into reality. The eight-month-old's world is no longer a kaleidoscope of meaningless sensations. It is a world that is fundamentally like our own.

Thus is born the baby's mind, and along with it, feelings and emotions. Now the baby begins to become the homunculus that people believe him to be at birth.

Yet his mind, newly born, is no more competent than his limbs were when his body was born. Although he understands that objects in the world *can* exist while he does not see them, he does not realize that they *do* exist unless he watches them disappear. He defines the whole world in terms of himself. When he turns to the right, the world turns to the right along with him.

On the other hand, now that his mind has emerged, the baby can absorb and assimilate into his understanding much larger pieces of information than he could before. He can learn infinitely faster— so much faster that he can begin to understand a few words of his parents' speech. This leads to understanding groups of words, then to talking on his own. By the end of his second year, he develops a fundamentally adult understanding of the world. At this time, finally, the larva is no more: the infant has become a miniature adult.

Recipes for Rearing

When we summarize the baby's metamorphosis like this, it sounds as though it occurs in a straightforward progression through time. But we have described only an outline: the details vary widely from baby to baby, and are Byzantine in their intricacy. At any given moment, a baby is always developing faster in one way than another, and he may be able to do something one day yet be unable to do it the next.

This makes it very difficult to devise a recipe for rearing children. If a study is designed and executed carefully enough, it may delineate the baby sharply under one set of circumstances, yet it is no more than a snapshot of a snowstorm. It shows where snow was blowing at the moment that it was taken, but it provides no way to tell whether at that moment the wind was coming from the prevailing direction or was an errant gust from somewhere else. A series of studies is needed to show this—but even a series can delineate only the *typical* baby, not an individual baby. All the snapshots in the world will not predict with certainty where an individual flake of snow will go.

Developmental psychology knows much more about babies now than it knew even ten years ago, but it does not know enough to provide trustworthy recipes, nor is it likely to for a very long time, if ever. The questions are just too complicated. Consider, for instance, the effect upon the baby of the mother's going back to work. In the United States, one woman in two goes back to work while her baby is less than one year old, so the question reflects a real concern.[1] Studies on the topic abound, and every new one yields a flurry of pronouncements, either dire or reassuring depending on the results. But look at some of the factors involved here. A baby may be cared for in his own home, or in somebody else's home, or in a day care center, by either a relative or a stranger. The caretaker may be trained or untrained, and may be looking after one baby or several babies. The mother may be an overbearing woman and the caretaker easygoing, or vice versa. The mother may be happy about going back to work and relaxed about giving over her baby in the morning, or she may be distressed at having to leave him with someone else: either way she may communicate her emotions to the child. At home in the evening, the mother may not have time to play with the baby because she is swamped with housework, or the babysitter or her husband may do the housework, leaving her evenings free. Her husband may be so unhappy about her returning to work that their evenings with the child become tense, or her husband may be supportive. And of course, babies differ in temperament from one to another, so they react differently to all these factors. Clearly, no one study can take all this into account.

In fact, the whole body of studies on day care has not considered these factors in much detail. And if it did, we might still be unable to draw conclusions, for we would not know how to judge the outcome. Does five-year-old Johnny play by himself because he is independent or because he is unsocial? Does six-year-old Betty boss other children around because she is a leader or because she is aggressive? Judgments of this sort reflect the observer's values at least as much as they reflect psychological truths. At this time we can say for certain that if a mother goes out to work, her baby will still become attached to her. We can also say that the baby will find it easier to leave the home for day care before he begins to develop attachments (before eight months), or after he has formed them (after eighteen months), than he will find it *while* he is forming them. But much more than this is unknown, and is likely to remain unknown for the foreseeable future.[2]

Personally, we doubt that individual details of a baby's life and environment can have lasting effects. His body is far too plastic for occasional small pressures here and there to determine immutably the rest of his life. The first two years of his life surely set a pattern for what is likely to come, but they *only* set a pattern for what is *likely* to come. They are merely preparing the site, not pouring foundations and laying bricks.

A baby must be cared for physically and receive normal

amounts of stimulation: this is what is necessary for his normal development. It may indeed be possible to advance a baby's progress by tailoring perfectly to him the stimulation you provide, but psychology can provide no specifics on how to do this. Indeed, our own predilection is that it is better not to try. Learning to talk a month earlier will not make a child into another John Stuart Mill, and constant overstimulation may make him chary of your company.

In any case, babies' needs vary from one child to another and from one minute to the next. No recipe book could possibly guide you in your interactions. You need to become attuned to your baby's needs and wants. This does not mean that you should necessarily come running the instant he whimpers. You may prefer to see if he is serious by letting him cry a bit—or you may prefer to preclude the whimpering by keeping him with you at certain times of the day. The choice is yours, but you can make it intelligently only if you have some idea of what the whimpering means. That is the reason to read books and articles about babies: not to learn how to handle babies, but to learn who and what they are. Then you will be able to decide intelligently if *your* baby is crying *now* from too much noise and light, or from too little.

As we have seen, the baby does feel details in his environment, initially as pleasantness or unpleasantness, and with some emotion later on; but traumatic experiences and monumental conflicts are beyond his capacity to feel. Little if anything can happen to a young infant that will scar his psyche for life. Rather, worrying about what to do and what not to do is likely to scar the *parents'* psyches for life, making them perpetually ask themselves in later years, "What did we do wrong?"

It may be fortunate that psychologists do not know what it is that pushes an individual child's development in one direction or another. For if we knew it, we would doubtless act upon it, and acting upon it presumes the knowledge of what sort of child is best for society. It makes an interesting digression to see where this can lead. Surely we can all agree that children should be active to keep them healthy, and that the most efficient and constructive way for adults to ensure this is to build into society a certain amount of pressure on children to take part in sports and other organized activities after school. North America and Europe have done this for years, to different extents in different places, but on the whole inefficiently. In the 1930s Germany did it very efficiently, so efficiently that boys and girls stopped having time for music lessons. Now Western Germany has a shortage of musicians to fill her orchestras, so she must import them from North America and elsewhere in Europe.[3]

We suspect that the most sensible thing parents can do with a baby is not to act according to arbitrary formulas inscribed in a book written by an author who knows nothing about them or how they live their individual lives, but to observe their baby carefully, to get to know him as well as they can, and with this knowledge, to insinuate him into their home as easily as they can. This will end up making life pleasant for themselves, and pleasant for the baby as well; for it will mean finding a way consistently to relieve his minor discomforts and to provide adequate stimulation. The baby will learn to trust and enjoy his parents as a result, and he will want to soak up the rest of the world. He will become as loving and sociable a child as his inheritance permits, as quickly as his body can.

Appendix

OBSTETRICAL KNOWLEDGE AND PRACTICE

IN THE COURSE OF writing this book, we read a large amount of obstetrical research, more reports of scientific studies than a busy obstetrician is ever likely to find the time to read. (Of course, any obstetrician will have read far more extensively on the *practice* of obstetrics: we were interested in the science underlying the practice.) Our approach was to ask certain questions—for example, what is the effect on the fetus of narcotics given the mother?—then to examine every scientific-sounding study bearing on that topic that had been published in English, plus anything that looked promising in German or French. This provided us with an unusual opportunity—indeed, it forced us—to examine how soundly obstetrics is founded upon scientific knowledge: to discover how much is really known about obstetrics and the effectiveness of its practice, as opposed to how much is merely belief that has been repeated often enough to become accepted as truth. We learned that far less is known than most people believe, and many obstetrical practices are less helpful than they seem.

To examine the scientific basis of obstetrics, let us focus on one relatively simple example, the depressing effect upon the fetus of narcotics given the mother during delivery. We said in chapter 3 that if the mother receives narcotics during childbirth, her newborn baby will act drugged for several days. This sounds so obvious it is almost a truism. It ought to be easy to confirm; and indeed, over one hundred studies purport to examine the effect of these narcotics on the newborn in a scientific fashion. (There are also innumerable articles that describe individual cases and/or treatments.) Yet of all these, only *two* support any clear, logical conclusion. From a few other cases we could infer limited conclusions, but the vast bulk of studies are so muddled by methodological errors that they cannot be interpreted.*

It is illuminating to look at the kinds of error these studies made. Many of them included no comparison group that was not exposed to drugs; they merely compared groups of babies exposed to one drug to groups of babies exposed to another. In these studies, there was no way to tell if *both* drugs caused abnormalities: if drug *A* and drug *B* were both virulent, both would be deemed benign. In many cases the authors claimed to include a comparison group whose mothers had received no drugs, yet the fine print revealed that those mothers had actually received one of the more potent potions of the pharmacopeia.

Where a real "no-drug" group did exist, often the mothers in it differed from the medicated mothers in age, social class, blood pressure, or some other way that is known to affect the fetus. This makes it impossible to tell whether the drug or something else caused an effect—or whether some other significant factor compensated for the drug, reducing its effect. Several recent studies did attempt to take these differences into account using sophisticated statistics, but they misapplied the statistics.

A large number of the studies had a serious problem with elementary statistics: they rated babies by arbitrarily applying numbers to *qualitative* descriptions (for example, $1 =$ poor, $2 =$ fair,

---

*Each of the two good studies examines the result of only *one* dose of *one* narcotic administered at *one* point during labor. This is hardly enough for a generalization. So we reasoned that if all narcotics administered to the mother depress the baby's behavior, then (1) any combination of narcotics should cause some depression, (2) adding any narcotic to that combination should increase the depression, and (3) adding a drug that vitiates one member of the combination should decrease the depression. To see if this happens, we reexamined all of the studies (often performing additional statistical analyses of their data) in which mothers received several narcotics. Most of them still proved to be uninterpretable, yet from some of them we were able to extract a reasonable amount of data dealing with a representative assortment of drugs and administrative regimes. Our "truism" stems from those.[1]

3 = good), but then they analyzed those numbers in ways that assume the numbers describe *quantities.* The fallacy of this is clear if you consider a beauty contest. Alice is the prettiest contestant, Zelda comes in last at 25, and Mary is in the middle at 13. Clearly these numbers do not let us say that Alice is twenty-five times prettier than Zelda and thirteen times prettier than Mary. Neither do they let us say that Mary is as much comelier than Zelda as she is homelier than Alice. Yet a large number of studies concluded the exact equivalent of these with different numbers and adjectives.

Many studies contain an inherent contradiction. On the one hand, the authors adjusted their data using elaborate statistical formulas purporting to take into account how several drugs interact with one another. Yet at the same time they were investigating how those drugs *act.* Since how the drugs act was not known, how they interact was clearly unknown, so the statistical allowances were guesswork. Those allowances may have hidden phenomena, or they may have created the appearance of phenomena when none existed.

Finally, many of these studies prejudiced their results in at least one of two ways. Some ignored babies with obvious problems, assuming that any obvious problem could not have been caused by the drug under study. This would make thalidomide look harmless. And many allowed examiners making subjective judgments to know both the baby's history and the purpose of the study. This last may seem innocuous, but it is insidious. Despite the best will in the world, when a person has hopes or expectations, it is impossible for these not to obtrude themselves upon his or her perceptions, even when the person is dealing with easily measured, objective events, or just punching numbers into a computer. That is the reason most of your errors balancing the checkbook are in your favor, not the bank's.

Confirmation

It is not possible to encounter fundamental errors like these in such number without feeling like the little boy who fails to see the emperor's new clothes. Yet the errors do exist, not just in studies

examining the effect of medications on the fetus but in every area
of obstetrics that we read, and apparently through all of medicine
and surgery. Here is an editorial published in the *Journal of the American Medical Association:*

> Medical authors are not apt to submit for publication manuscripts which
> contradict facts of human anatomy, or flaunt laws of physiology. Extensive
> training in the basic sciences and corrective influences of friendly experts
> caution them against perpetrating these offenses. Yet, authors of the same
> manuscripts are more likely than not to contravene "anatomy" and "physiol-
> ogy" of experimental design and statistical "dissection." In a study of 149
> articles selected at random from ten widely read and highly regarded medical
> periodicals, Schor [the American Medical Association's statistical consultant]
> and Karten . . . found that less than 28% have sufficient statistical support
> for drawn conclusions. None of the remaining 72% could pass muster in
> terms of experimental design, applicability of statistical tests, and the type
> of analysis performed.[2]

Schor and Karten found just the kinds of mistake that we
found. The difference between their 72 percent and our 98 percent
is that they looked only at papers published in the most important
journals, while we looked at papers published everywhere; they
looked at papers covering a wider variety of subjects, some of which
are easier to research; and they gave authors the benefit of the doubt
by not counting papers that were published as scientific reports but
that were really case reports in disguise.

How Can This Be?

Figures like these make some sense in light of all the medical
"breakthroughs" we hear about that do not end up breaking
through anywhere. Yet still they seem incredible. After all, how can
so many bright people of high repute publish so much—let us be
blunt about it—so much nonsense, without being challenged by
their colleagues? And if obstetrical practices are based on science so
weak as this, how can they be effective?

The answer to the first is that statistical analysis and experimental design are peripheral to medicine—indeed, they are often inimical to its practice—and hence are rarely taught in medical school nor learned afterward. To practice medicine is to act on uncertainties, not to deliberate on them. If a woman has been in labor for eight hours, there is no way to be sure whether another hour or two will see the baby through. With insufficient information, the physician must decide what to do—and having decided, he (it usually is a he) must act on his decision with certainty. He could not function if he constantly dwelt on the probability of error. Moreover, if he even appeared to be uncertain, he might lose his patient's confidence and lose some of his authority over nurses and interns; for patient, nurse, and intern all have a similar need to feel secure in knowledge that may not really exist. Thus the reduction of uncertainty becomes one of the goals in a medical life. In medical circles it is not desirable, let alone polite, to cross-examine authorities about the reliability of their information. It is preferable to accept what they say and write—not to act on it perhaps, but not to disparage it either. For this reason, medical schools discourage arguing with authorities: a student may question authorities freely to elicit information, but is likely to be squelched if his questioning is about "unnecessary" details that are required to help evaluate what the authorities say. Since medical schools discourage cross-examination, they do not teach *how* to cross-examine effectively: they all but ignore the subtleties of statistical analysis and experimental design. Under these circumstances, it is easy for a medical researcher first unwittingly to make methodological mistakes, then to publish them (usually obscured by complex jargon), without having his colleagues take notice.

The answer to the second question is more complicated, for upon close examination, modern delivery practices prove to be far less helpful than people think. They *can* be helpful, of course. They certainly save lives in some complicated pregnancies. But in uncomplicated pregnancies, they seem not to be helpful at all. Many studies have compared deliveries at home by a trained midwife with deliveries in a hospital by a physician: of those that are designed well enough to be interpreted, none finds a difference in the well-being of either mother or child when no problems were evident beforehand.[3] This does not mean there is no difference, but it does

indicate that any difference is very small indeed; that at best, overall, in uncomplicated pregnancies, physicians and hospitals help
very little.

Indeed, it indicates that in uncomplicated pregnancies, physicians and hospitals harm more or less as often as they help, through
needless surgery and needless drugs. If the studies on the topic were
much larger, a difference in safety representing some tiny percentage of women might show up in medicine's favor *or disfavor;* but at
this point we must conclude that in uncomplicated pregnancies, the
help and the harm of modern delivery practices are approximately
comparable overall.

Now we can reformulate our question more fruitfully: how can
some obstetrical interventions be effective when the science behind
them is so weak? We can see the answer by considering two pregnant women. One is and has always been healthy, and is presenting
normally; the other has impassably small hips because of rickets she
contracted in childhood. The odds that the first woman will die in
childbirth are minuscule, no matter what her obstetrician does, so
it is difficult for a physician to tell which of his practices are helpful
and which are not. With women like this, physicians can distinguish the helpful from the harmful only by careful, methodical
study of large numbers. On the other hand, if our second woman
tries to deliver naturally, she will die: with her it is easy to tell
whether an intervention works. This example is extreme and sim-
plistic, of course, yet it does demonstrate the epistemological mechanism through which, in complicated pregnancies—and *only* in
complicated pregnancies—useful interventions have evolved.

Clinical Experience

In lieu of science, a physician is left to clinical intuition, gained
through his own and others' experience. Alas, as Hippocrates says,
"Life is short; art is long [τέχνη μακρὴ]; opportunity fugitive; experience delusive; judgment difficult." Consider the clinical intuition
of a mid-nineteenth-century Austrian physician. This man is very
well educated, in another intellectual league from his American

contemporaries. He graduated from the *gymnasium,* then studied five years at the University of Vienna, one of the finest medical schools in the world. He has had twenty years of experience in general practice. This experience tells him, as does every textbook and authority, that miasmas cause fever—noxious emanations of the atmosphere that accompany noisome smells. After all, that is only sensible. For fever is most common in noisome areas, in both city and country alike; and the overwhelmingly dominant impression of a sickroom—enormously more powerful then than now—is its stench. (Remember that infections stink, and are not yet controlled with antibiotics; the privy in the backyard is far away, so a commode sits by the bed; and the patient's clothes and bedclothes are filthy, for since they must be washed by hand, they are changed infrequently.) The odds are that this man has heard of Ignaz Semmelweis, who has made himself obnoxious throughout the medical community by accusing prominent physicians of murder and calling maternity hospitals "murder-dens." Semmelweis claims that even after you scrub your hands with soap and water, invisible particles cling to them and cause fevers. This is patent nonsense. Everybody knows that miasmas cause fevers. And he claims that rinsing your hands in bleach prevents this. Sure it does, and so does eye of newt after the proper incantation. Rubbish![4]

That is the problem with clinical intuition: it *can* be accurate, but it is inextricably tied to the erroneous beliefs and prejudices of the day. When our nineteenth-century physician rises at dawn to perform an autopsy before his rounds, he does it to further his understanding of pathology—to help the patients he sees in the afternoon, not to harm them. When he goes on those rounds, he has no idea that he is distributing infection from his contact with the corpse; he *knows* that he is doing good. Similarly, when a twentieth-century physician delivers a baby in an up-to-date manner, in a hospital full of modern technicalia, he too thinks that he is helping his patients. Every authority tells him that he is; and after all, it is only common sense. It is a rare physician who sees that the authorities are ill founded and that, in an uncomplicated delivery, his sophisticated ministrations are likely to be of no value.

Notes

These notes provide bibliographic information for every citation in the text, plus additional discussion about some academic controversies. Unfortunately, want of space has forced us to pare other references mercilessly. Wherever in the text we summarize a number of studies, we cite only one exemplary reference as an entrance to the literature—a review when possible, or else either a recent study that cites earlier studies, or a study of some historical interest that may lead to current work through an index of citations. A number in brackets after an abbreviated citation refers to the complete citation earlier in the chapter.

Chapter 2

1. Holländer, H. 1979. Historical review and clinical relevance of real-time observations of fetal movement. *Contributions to Gynecology and Obstetrics* 6: 26–28.

2. Göttlicher, S., Madjarić, J., and Krone, H. A. 1981. Über die Lage des menschlichen Feten und die Wahrscheinlichkeit einer spontanen Lageänderung im Verlauf der Schwangerschaft. *Zeitschrift für Geburtshilfe und Perinatologie* 185: 288–292.

3. See, for example, Balashavo, E. 1963. Development of the vestibular apparatus. In *The Development of the Brain and Its Disturbance by Harmful Factors*, ed. B. Kosovskiv, pp. 103–116. New York: Macmillan.

4. Tymnik, von G., Donat, H., and Fischer, B. 1981. Geburtshilfliche Lageanomalien—Folge einer Vestibularisfunktionsstörung. *Zentralblatt für Gynäkologie* 103: 952–956.

5. Holländer, Historical review [1], pp. 26–27.

6. See, for example, Patrick, J., et al. 1982. Patterns of gross fetal body movements over 24-hour observation intervals during the last 10 weeks of pregnancy. *American Journal of Obstetrics and Gynecology* 142: 363–371.

7. Hooker, D. 1969. *The Prenatal Origin of Behavior.* New York: Hafner.

8. See, for example, Lind, T. 1978. The biochemistry of amniotic fluid. In *Amniotic Fluid,* ed. D. Fairweather and T. Eskes, pp. 60–81. Amsterdam: Exerpta Medica.

9. Arey, L., Tremaine, M., and Monzingo, F. 1942. The numerical and topological relations of taste buds to human circumvallate papillae throughout the life span. *Anatomical Record* 64: 9–25.

10. De Snoo, K. 1937. Das trinkende Kind im Uterus. *Monatschrift für Geburtshilfe und Gynäkologie* 105: 88–97.

11. Gitlin, D., et al. 1972. The turnover of amniotic fluid protein in the human conceptus. *American Journal of Obstetrics and Gynecology* 113: 632–645.

12. Querleu, D., Renard, X., and Crépin, G. 1981. Perception auditive et réactivité foetale aux stimulations sonares. *Journal de Gynecologie, Obstetrique et Biologie de la Reproduction* 10: 307–314; and Walker, D., Grimwade, J., and Wood, C. 1971. Intrauterine noise: A component of the fetal environment. *American Journal of Obstetrics and Gynecology* 109: 91–95. Much lower sonic pressures are reported by H. Murooka, Y. Koie, and N. Suda (1976. Analyse des sons intra-utérins et leurs effects tranquillisants sur le nouveau-né. *Journal de Gynecologie, Obstetrique et Biologie de la Reproduction* 5: 367–376), but their report lacks details and credibility. For instance, they say that their microphone had a frequency range of 3 Hz to 700 Hz, yet they present a graph of frequencies up to 3,000 Hz with no explanation.

13. Querleu, Renard, and Crépin, Perception auditive et réactivité foetale [12].

14. Walker, Grimwade, and Wood, Intrauterine noise [12].

15. Tanaka, Y., and Arayama, T. 1969. Fetal responses to acoustic stimuli. *Practica Oto-Rhino-Laryngologica* 31: 269–273. For a comprehensive albeit indiscriminate review of the many other studies of fetal hearing, see: Busnel, M-C., and Granier-Deferre, C. 1983. And what of fetal audition? In *The Behavior of Human Infants. Life-Sciences,* ed. A. Oliveiro and M. Zapula, pp. 93–126. New York: Plenum.

16. Nakai, Y. 1970. An electron microscopic study of the human fetus cochlea. *Practica Oto-Rhino-Laryngologica* 32: 257–267; and Rubel, E. 1978. Ontogeny of structure and function in the vertebrate auditory system. In *Handbook of Sensory Physiology,* vol. 9, *Development of Sensory Systems,* ed. M. Jacobson, pp. 135–238. Berlin: Springer-Verlag.

17. Salk, L. 1973. The role of the heartbeat in the relations between mother and infant. *Scientific American* 228: 24–29.

18. Tulloch, J., et al. 1964. Normal heartbeat sound and the behavior of newborn infants: A replication study. *Psychosomatic Medicine* 26: 661–670.

19. Detterman, D. 1978. The effect of heartbeat sound on neonatal crying. *Infant Behavior and Development* 1: 36–48; and Palmqvist, H. 1975. The effect of heartbeat sound stimulation on the weight development of newborn infants. *Child Development* 46: 292–295. Tulloch and associates (Normal heartbeat sound [18]) also failed to find less crying or greater weight gain in newborns exposed continuously to a 45-dB heartbeat.

20. Brackbill, Y., Adams, G., Crowell, D., and Gray, M. 1966. Arousal level in neonates and preschool children under continuous auditory stimulation. *Journal of Experimental Child Psychology* 4: 178–188.

21. Smith, C., and Steinschneider, A. 1975. Differential effects of prenatal rhythmic stimulation on neonatal arousal states. *Child Development* 46: 574–578.

22. Kendel, E. 1979. Cellular insights into behavior and learning. *The Harvey Lecture* 73: 19–92.

23. Lecanuet, J. P., et al. 1986. Fetal responses to acoustic stimulation depend on heart rate variability pattern, stimulus intensity and repetition. *Early Human Development* 13: 269–283.

24. Querleu, Renard, and Crépin, Perception auditive et réactivité foetale [12]; and Busnel and Granier-Deferre, And what of fetal audition?[15].

25. DeCasper, A. J., and Spence, M. J. 1986. Prenatal maternal speech influences newborns' perception of speech sounds. *Infant Behavior and Development* 9: 133–150.

26. DeCasper, A., and Prescott, P. 1984. Human newborns' perception of male voices: Preference, discrimination and reinforcing value. *Developmental Psychobiology* 17: 481–491.

27. Shaw, J., Wheeler, P., and Morgan, D. 1970. Mother-infant relationship and weight gain in the first month of life. *Journal of the American Academy of Child Psychiatry* 9: 428–444.

28. Because the effect is so small, it is not surprising that other studies using smaller samples failed to find a relationship between the anxiety mothers reported during pregnancy and the babies' birth weight. (See Burnstein, I., Kinch, R., and Stein, L. 1974. Anxiety, pregnancy, labor and the neonate. *American Journal of Obstetrics and Gynecology* 118: 195–199; Ottinger, D., and Simmons, J. 1964. Behavior of human neonates and prenatal maternal anxiety. *Psychological Reports* 14: 391–394; and Standley, K., Soule, B., and Copans, S. 1979. Dimensions of prenatal anxiety and their influence on pregnancy outcome. *American Journal of Obstetrics and Gynecology* 135: 22–26.) In a large sample of women who had been refused abortions and who were presumed as a result to be especially distressed, S. Blomberg (1980. Influence of maternal distress during pregnancy on fetal development. *Acta Psychiatrica Scandinavica* 62: 298–314) also failed to find an effect on birth weight. However, as he himself notes, his data are difficult to interpret because other evidence suggested that there were more miscarriages among these women, so some babies destined to be light weight may not have been born.

29. It is also difficult to interpret Sontag's frequently cited finding that the fetus becomes unusually active when the mother is stressed psychologically (Sontag, L. 1966. Implication of fetal behavior and environment for adult personalities. *Annals of the New York Academy of Sciences* 134: 782–786). Since the mothers reported both their own stress and the fetuses' movements, they may have noted more movements, not because more actually occurred, but because their stress increased their sensitivity to fetal movements or biased them to expect more. A report of pregnant Italian women terrified by an earthquake seems at first glance to avoid this difficulty, since the fetuses' unusual activity was confirmed by ultrasound (Ianniruberto, A., and Tajani, E. 1981. Ultrasonic study of fetal movements. *Seminars in Perinatology* 5: 175–181). However, the only women examined were those who had presented themselves to the hospital claiming that something was wrong. There may have been many other terrified women whose fetuses did not react.

30. Myers, R. 1977. Production of fetal asphyxia by maternal psychological stress. *Pavlovian Journal of Biological Science* 12: 51–61.

31. F. Grossman, L. Eichler, and S. A. Winickoff (1980. *Pregnancy, Birth, and Parenthood.* San Francisco: Jossey-Bass) also found that the level of anxiety and stress that first-time mothers reported during the first trimester of pregnancy predicted the level of irritability the baby would show when examined shortly after birth. There was no such effect among experienced mothers. See also Havlicek, V., Childiaeva, R., and Chernick, V. 1977. EEG frequency spectrum characteristics of sleep states in infants of alcoholic mothers. *Neuropädiatrie* 8: 360–373; Kiseleva, Z. 1963. The influence of intrauterine asphyxia on the developing brain. In *Development of the Brain,* ed. Kosovskii [3], pp. 125–136; Saco-Pollitt, C. 1981. Birth in the Peruvian Andes: Physical and behavioral consequences in the neonate. *Child Development* 52: 839–846; and Saxton, D. 1978. The behavior of infants whose mothers smoke in pregnancy. *Early Human Development* 2: 363–369.

32. Huttunen, M., and Niskanen, P. 1978. Prenatal loss of father and psychiatric disorders. *Archives of General Psychiatry* 35: 429–431.

33. Loomis, C., Tranmer, J., and Brien, J. 1982. Disposition of ethanol in human maternal blood and amniotic fluid during pregnancy. *Pharmacologist* 24: 204 [Abstract].

34. Idänpään-Heikkila, J., et al. 1972. Elimination and metabolic effects of ethanol in mother, fetus, and newborn infant. *American Journal of Obstetrics and Gynecology* 112: 387–393.

35. Lewis, P., and Boylan, P. 1979. Fetal breathing: A review. *American Journal of Obstetrics and Gynecology* 134: 587–598.

36. Lewis, P., and Boylan, P. 1979. Alcohol and fetal breathing. *Lancet* 1: 388.

37. Peden, V., Sammon, T., and Downey, D. 1973. Intravenously induced infantile intoxication with ethanol. *Journal of Pediatrics* 83: 490–493.

38. Babson, S. G. 1971. Feeding the low-birth-weight infant. *Journal of Pediatrics* 79: 694–701.

39. Pierog, S., Chandavasu, O., and Wexler, I. 1977. Withdrawal symptoms in infants with the fetal alcohol syndrome. *Journal of Pediatrics* 90: 630–633.

40. Reviewed in Finnegan, L. P. 1981. The effects of narcotics and alcohol on pregnancy and the newborn. *Annals of the New York Academy of Sciences* 362: 136–157.

41. Weiner, L., et al. 1983. Alcohol consumption by pregnant women. *Obstetrics and Gynecology* 61: 6–12.

42. Little, R. 1977. Moderate alcohol use during pregnancy and decreased infant birthweight. *American Journal of Public Health* 67: 1154–1156; Streissguth, A., Barr, H., Martin, D., and Herman, C. 1980. Effects of maternal alcohol, nicotine and caffeine use during pregnancy on infant mental and motor development at 8 months. *Alcoholism: Clinical and Experimental Research* 4: 152–164; and Streissguth, A., Barr, H., and Martin, D. 1983. Maternal alcohol use and neonatal habituation assessed with the Brazelton scale. *Child Development* 1983: 1109–1118.

43. H. L. Rosett and L. Weiner (1984. *Alcohol and the Fetus.* New York: Oxford University Press) provide a good review of other studies. The story may be more complicated among lower-class women. In a study of lower-class women with a history of alcohol abuse, C. B. Ernhart and her colleagues (1985. Alcohol related birth defects: Syndromal anomalies, intrauterine growth retardation, and neonatal behavioral assessment. *Alcoholism: Clinical and Experimental Research* 9: 447–453) found the expected relationship between maternal drinking and birth weight, but it was no longer significant when they controlled for race, sex, parental size, the adequacy of the mother's diet, and smoking. We suspect that the fetuses of bibulous lower-class mothers do not grow well primarily not because of alcohol but because their mothers live less healthful lives in general. The alcohol itself is merely one drop more in the bucket.

44. In contrast, two studies of predominantly lower-class women found no effect of the mother's drinking on the newborn's behavior, once covariates like smoking were accounted for. There was one exception: Ernhart and her colleagues (Alcohol related birth defects [43]) found a small *positive* effect of drinking on the baby's reflexes and general level of maturation. Like the studies of birth weight (see note 43), this suggests that in lower-class women, any detrimental effect may be caused by the smoking or poor diet associated with drinking, not the alcohol per se. See also Richardson, G. A., and Day, N. L. 1986. Alcohol use during pregnancy and neonatal outcome. Paper presented at the International Conference on Infant Studies, April, in Los Angeles.

45. Gusella, J. L., and Fried, P. A. 1984. Effects of maternal social drinking and smoking on offspring at 13 months. *Neurobehavioral Toxicology and Teratology* 6: 13–17; Streissguth, A. P., et al. 1984. Intrauterine alcohol and nicotine exposure: Attention and reaction time in 4-year-old children. *Developmental Psychology* 20: 533–541; and Streissguth, A. P., et al. 1986. Attention, distraction and reaction time at age 7 years and prenatal alcohol exposure. *Neurobehavioral Toxicology and Teratology* 8: 717–725.

46. See, for example, Little, R., Schultz, F., and Mandell, W. 1976. Drinking during pregnancy. *Journal of Studies on Alcohol* 37. 375–379.

47. Elton, R., and Wilson, M. 1977. Changes in ethanol consumption by pregnant pig-tailed macaques. *Journal of Studies on Alcohol* 38: 2181–2183.

48. See, for example, Ernhart et al., Alcohol related birth defects [43], and Weiner et al., Alcohol consumption by pregnant women [41].

49. A. Mukherjee and G. Hogden (1982. Maternal ethanol exposure induces transient impairment of umbilical circulation and fetal hypoxia in monkeys. *Science* 218: 700–702) have confirmed this experimentally with pregnant monkeys: shortly after alcohol was injected into the mother's blood, the umbilical cord turned white from lack of blood.

50. Rosett, H., Ouelette, E., Weiner, L., and Owens, E. 1978. Therapy of heavy drinking during pregnancy. *Obstetrics and Gynecology* 51: 41–46; Rosett, H., et al. 1979. Effects of maternal drinking on neonate state regulation. *Developmental Medicine and Child Neurology* 21: 464–473; Rosett, H., et al. 1980. Reduction of alcohol consumption during pregnancy with benefits for the newborn. *Alcoholism: Clinical and Experimental Research* 4: 178–184; and Rosett, H. L., Weiner, L., and Edelin, K. C. 1981. Strategies for prevention of fetal alcohol effect. *Obstetrics and Gynecology* 57: 1–7.

51. Included in the group of heavy drinkers who did not cut back were eight women who might well have differed from the others: they gave birth without receiving any prenatal care. Since Rosett and his co-workers did not examine the effect of prenatal care on most of the measures they report, we have ignored them. Only on growth did they analyze for the effect of prenatal care (and found none).

52. Reviewed in Abel, E. L. 1984. *Fetal Alcohol Syndrome and Fetal Alcohol Effects.* New York: Plenum.

53. Jones, K. L., Smith, D. W., Ulleland, C. N., and Streissguth, A. P. 1973. Pattern of malformation in offspring of chronic alcoholic mothers. *Lancet* 1: 1267–1271.

54. Reviewed in Abel, *Fetal Alcohol Syndrome* [52].

55. For a comprehensive (if often uncritical) summary, see Surgeon General. 1979. *Smoking and Health.* Washington, D.C.: U.S. Department of Health, Education and Welfare.

56. See, for example, Maršál, K. 1978. Fetal breathing movements: Characteristics and clinical significance. *Obstetrics and Gynecology* 52: 394–401. J. Thaler, J. Goodman, and G. Dawes (1980. Effects of maternal cigarette smoking on fetal breathing and fetal movements. *American Journal of Obstetrics and Gynecology* 138: 282–287) report that after mothers smoke, fetuses *increase* their breathing; but they used Doppler shift, which has proved an inaccurate measure of fetal breathing (see Mantell, C. 1980. The measurement of fetal breathing movements with A-scan and Doppler techniques. *Seminars in Perinatology* 4: 269–274).

57. Little, Moderate alcohol use during pregnancy [42].

58. Tennes, K., and Blackard, C. 1980. Maternal alcohol consumption, birthweight, and minor physical anomalies. *American Journal of Obstetrics and Gynecology* 138: 774–780.

59. Some of these studies are discussed by S. Garn, K. Hoff, and K. McCabe (1979. Is there nutritional mediation of the "smoking effect" on the fetus? *American Journal of Clinical Nutrition* 32: 1181–1184) and by J. Yerushalmy (1972. Infants with low birth weight born before their mothers started to smoke cigarettes. *American Journal of Obstetrics and Gynecology* 112: 277–284). For criticisms, see Goldstein, H. 1977. Smoking in pregnancy: Some notes on the statistical controversy. *British Journal of Preventive and Social Medicine* 31: 13–17; Haworth, J. C., Ellestad-Sayed, J., King, J., and Drilling, L. 1980. Fetal growth retardation in cigarette-smoking mothers is not due to decreased maternal food intake. *American Journal of Obstetrics and Gynecology* 137: 719–723; and Naeye, R. L. 1978. Effects of maternal cigarette smoking on the fetus and placenta. *British Journal of Obstetrics and Gynecology* 85: 732–737.

60. Bottoms, S., Kuhnert, B., Kuhnert, P., and Reese, A. 1982. Maternal passive smoking and fetal serum thiocyanate levels. *American Journal of Obstetrics and Gynecology* 144: 787–791.

61. Reviewed in Surgeon General, *Smoking and Health* [55].

62. See, for example, Ernhart and associates, Alcohol related birth defects [43]; Streissguth, Barr, Martin, and Herman, Effects of maternal alcohol [42]; and Tennes and Blackard, Maternal alcohol consumption [58].

Two studies that controlled for alcohol did report differences in behavior at birth. J. Chipperfield and W. O. Eaton (1986. Maternal cigarette smoking and infant activity level. Paper presented at the International Conference on Infant Studies, April, in Los Angeles) found that among the babies of smokers, those whose mothers smoked more cigarettes or who smoked longer during the pregnancy were more likely to be judged as excessively active in the first few days after birth. However, there was no difference between the babies whose mothers smoked and those whose mothers did not smoke at all; and although Chipperfield and Eaton took into account alcoholism, they ignored the more common, moderate levels of drinking.

J. Martin, D. Martin, C. Lund, and A. Streissguth (1977. Maternal alcohol ingestion and cigarette smoking and their effects on newborn conditioning. *Alcoholism: Clinical and Experimental Research* 1: 243–247) found that newborns whose mothers smoked during pregnancy were more likely to continue to show a conditional response after the response no longer yielded sugared water. They interpreted this to be a sign of poorer learning. However, the data could be interpreted in just the opposite way, and Martin and associates did not report the more relevant data on how long it took newborns to learn the conditional response.

63. Longo, L. 1977. The biological effects of carbon monoxide on the pregnant woman, fetus, and newborn infant. *American Journal of Obstetrics and Gynecology* 129: 69–103.

64. Lehtovirta, P., and Forss, M. 1978. The acute effect of smoking on intervillous blood flow of the placenta. *British Journal of Obstetrics and Gynecology* 85: 729–731.

65. Naeye, R. 1979. The duration of maternal cigarette smoking, fetal and placental disorders. *Early Human Development* 3: 229–237.

66. Socol, M., Manning, F., Murata, Y., and Druzin, M. 1982. Maternal smoking causes fetal hypoxia: Experimental evidence. *American Journal of Obstetrics and Gynecology* 15: 214–218.

67. See, for example, Heath, D., and Williams, D. 1977. *Man at High Altitude: The Pathophysiology of Acclimitization and Adaptation.* Edinburgh: Churchill Livingstone.

68. Kruger, H., and Arias-Stella, J. 1980. The placenta and infant at high altitudes. *American Journal of Obstetrics and Gynecology* 106: 586–591.

69. Saco-Pollitt, Birth in the Peruvian Andes [31].

70. Radvanyi, M. F., Monad, N., and Dreyfus-Brisac, C. 1973. Electroencéphalogramme et sommeil chez le nouveau-né en détresse respiratoire. Étude de l'influence des variations de la PaO₂ et de l'equilibre acido-basique. *Bulletin de Physio-Pathologie Respiratoire* 9: 1569–1585.

71. See, for example, Nijhuis, J., Prechtl, H., Martin, C., and Bots, R. Are there behavioural states in the human fetus? *Early Human Development* 6: 177–195.

72. Gillies, J., ed. 1965. *A Textbook of Aviation Physiology.* Oxford: Pergamon; and Towbin, A. 1970. Central nervous system damage in the human fetus and newborn infant. *American Journal of Diseases of Children* 119: 529–542.

73. Butler, N., and Goldstein, H. 1973. Smoking in pregnancy and subsequent child development. *British Medical Journal* 4: 573–575; Fogelman, K. 1980. Smoking in pregnancy and subsequent development of the child. *Child: Care, Health, and Development* 6: 233–249; and Goldstein, H. 1971. Factors influencing the height of seven-year-old children. *Human Biology* 43: 92–111.

Chapter 3

1. Lindan, O., Greenway, R., and Piazzo, J. 1965. Pressure distribution on the surface of the human body: I. Evaluation in lying and sitting positions using a "bed of springs and nails." *Archives of Physical Medicine and Rehabilitation* 46: 378–385; and Schwarcz, R., et al. 1970. Compression received by the head of the human fetus during labor. In *Physical Trauma as an Etiological Agent in Mental Retardation,* ed. C. Angle and E. Berings, pp. 133–143. Bethesda, MD: U.S. Department of Health, Education and Welfare.

2. For an excellent, readable review, see Melzack, R., and Wall, P. 1982. *The Challenge of Pain.* New York: Basic Books.

3. Many examples are given in ibid. and in Wall, P. 1979. On the relation of injury to pain. *Pain* 6: 253–264.

4. Beecher, H. 1956. Relationship of significance of wound to the pain experience. *Journal of the American Medical Association* 161: 1609–1613.

5. Wall, On the relation of injury to pain [3].

6. Parer, J. 1982. Evaluation of the fetus during labor. *Current Problems in Pediatrics* 12: 1–58.

7. Boylan, P., and Lewis, P. 1980. Fetal breathing in labor. *Obstetrics and Gynecology* 56: 35–38.

8. Rosen, M., Scibetta, J., Chik, L., and Borgstedt, A. 1973. An approach to the study of brain damage. The principles of fetal EEG. *American Journal of Obstetrics and Gynecology* 115: 37–47.

9. Noonan, J., Emory, E., and Mapp, J. 1981. Effects of Caesarean section delivery on fetal heart rate and behaviour in full-term male newborns. Paper presented at the meeting of the Society for Research in Child Development, April, in Boston.

10. Emde, R., Swedberg, J., and Suzuki, B. 1975. Human wakefulness and biological rhythms after birth. *Archives of General Psychiatry* 32: 780–783.

11. Gilman, A., L. Goodman, T. Rall, and F. Murad, eds. *Goodman and Gilman's The Pharmacological Basis of Therapeutics,* 7th ed., chap. 14, 18, 22, and 23. New York: Macmillan.

12. Brackbill, Y. 1979. Obstetrical medication and infant behavior. In *Handbook of Infant Development,* ed. J. D. Osofsky, pp. 76–125. New York: Wiley; and Brackbill, Y., McManus, K., and Woodward, L. 1985. *Medication in Maternity.* Ann Arbor: University of Michigan Press.

13. Anderson, G., and Lomas, J. 1985. Explaining variations in caesarian section rates: Patients, facilities or policies? *Canadian Medical Association Journal* 132: 235–259.

14. See, for example, Morselli, P., and Rovei, V. 1980. Placental transfer of pethidine and norpethidine and their pharmokinetics in the newborn. *European Journal of Clinical Pharmacology* 18: 25–30.

15. Reviewed in Rane, A., and Tomson, G. 1980. Prenatal and neonatal metabolism in man. *European Journal of Clinical Pharmacology* 18: 9–15.

16. The following are three of the best studies from a scientific perspective: Busacca, M., et al. 1982. Neonatal effects of the administration of meperidine and promethazine to the mother in labor. Double blind study. *Journal of Perinatal Medicine* 10: 48–53; Hodgkinson, R., Bhatti, M., Grewal, G., and Marx, G. 1978. Neonatal neurobehavior in the first 48 hours of life: Effect of the administration of meperidine with and without naloxone in the mother. *Pediatrics* 62: 294–298; and Kron, R., Stein, M., and Goddard, K. 1966. Newborn sucking behavior affected by obstetric sedation. *Pediatrics* 37: 1012–1016. See the appendix for a discussion of methodological problems in many other studies.

17. Sherman, M., and Sherman, I. 1925. Sensorimotor responses in infants. *Journal of Comparative and Physiological Psychology* 5: 53–68.

18. Alper, M. H. 1977. Anesthesia and asphyxia. In *Asphyxia and the Developing Fetal Brain,* ed. L. Gluck, pp. 225–235. Chicago: Year Book Medical Publications.

19. See, for example, Philipson, E. H., Kuhnert, B. R., and Syracuse, C. D. 1984. Maternal, fetal, and neonatal lidocaine levels following local perineal infiltration. *American Journal of Obstetrics and Gynecology* 149: 403–407.

20. Gilman et al., *Goodman and Gilman* [11], chap. 15 and 23; and Van Dyke, C., et al. 1979. Cocaine and lidocaine have similar psychological effects after intranasal application. *Life Sciences* 24: 271–274.

21. The babies delivered with 2-chloroprocaine scored more poorly on the "range of states" cluster of the Brazelton exam, which includes the variables described in the text. The results were similar for babies delivered with lidocaine, but not significant, presumably because of great variability among babies in this group. See Linn, P. L., and Kuhnert, B. R. 1985. Obstetrical medication revisted: Pharmacologic issues in the study of newborn behavior. Paper presented at the meeting of the Society for Research in Child Development, April, in Toronto.

22. Murray, A., Dolby, R., Nation, R., and Thomas, D. 1981. Effects of epidural anesthesia on newborns and their mothers. *Child Development* 52: 71–82. Some mothers in the "unmedicated" group received the local anesthetic lidocaine for repairs of an episiotomy, but only babies with insignificant amounts in the umbilical cord were included in the study. Unfortunately, there was no such control for the nine babies from the "unmedicated" group whose mothers received brief exposures to a depressant (nitrous oxide and oxygen).

Besides the differences in sleeping and crying, Murray and her colleagues report significant differences between the groups at twenty-four hours of age in motor control and physiological responses. However, methodological problems of the type discussed in the appendix make these differences difficult to interpret.

In contrast, T. K. Abboud and associates (1984. Continuous infusion epidural analgesia in parturients receiving bupivacaine, chloroprocaine, or lidocaine—maternal, fetal, and neonatal effects. *Anesthesia and Analgesia* 63: 421–428) found no differences on a test of reflexes and muscle tone at two or twenty-four hours after birth between a group exposed to various types of local anesthetic and a group whose mothers had received no medication. However, for this comparison, the authors excluded babies who were delivered by emergency cesarean section, vacuum extraction, or mid or high forceps. That excluded almost half of the group whose mothers had received bupivacaine. The authors may, therefore, have excluded the babies affected most adversely by the medication.

23. These public discussions are summarized in G. Kolata (1979. Scientists attack report that obstetrical medications endanger children. *Science* 204: 391–392). See also the replies by Y. Brackbill (1979. Obstetrical medication study [letter to the editor]. *Science* 205: 447–448) and by S. Broman (1979. Obstetrical medication study [letter to the editor]. *Science* 205: 446).

24. Ounstead, M. 1981. Pain relief during childbirth and development at 4 years [letter to the editor]. *Journal of the Royal Society of Medicine* 74: 629–630.

25. Other studies reporting adverse effects confounded depressing and stimulating medication; used complex statistical analyses not justified by the number of subjects or the character of the data; or summarized effects as significant although a careful reading of the results indicates them not to be. The well-designed studies are Murray, Dolby, Nation, and

Thomas (Effects of epidural anesthesia [22]) and Horowitz, F., et al. 1977. The effects of obstetrical medication on the behavior of Israeli newborn infants and some comparisons with Uruguayan and American infants. *Child Development* 48: 1607–1623.

26. See Semmelweis, I. [1861] 1981. *The Etiology, the Concept and the Prophylaxis of Childbed Fever,* trans. F. Murphy. Reprinted with additional materials. Birmingham, AL: The Classics of Medicine Library. To see how eighteenth-century British and Irish physicians reduced fatality rates to around 1 percent, with no useful tools or techniques save forceps, in a population rife with disease and malnourishment, see Adams, J. 1923. *Charles White of Manchester and the Arrest of Puerperal Fever.* Liverpool: University Press.

27. Atwood, R. 1976. Parturitional posture and related birth behaviour. *Acta Obstetrica Gynecologica Scandinavica Supplementum* 57: 1–25; and Flynn, A., Kelly, H., Hollins, G., and Lynch, P. 1978. Ambulation in labour. *British Medical Journal* 2: 591–593.

28. Sadovsky, E., and Polishuk, W. 1977. Fetal movements in utero. Nature, assessment, prognostic value, timing of delivery. *Obstetrics and Gynecology* 50: 49–55.

29. Dubowitz, L., Dubowitz, V., and Morante, A. 1980. Visual function in the newborn: A study of preterm and full-term infants. *Brain and Development* 2: 15–27.

30. Salapatek, P., and Banks, M. Infant sensory assessment: Vision. In *Communicative and Cognitive Abilities—Early Behavioral Assessment,* ed. F. Minifie and L. Lloyd, pp. 61–106. Baltimore, MD: University Park Press.

31. Newborns' scanning is described more thoroughly in chapter 6. See, for example, Haith, M. 1980. *Rules that Babies Look By.* Hillsdale, NJ: Lawrence Erlbaum.

32. Although any one physiological reaction cannot be transformed by expectations into *any* emotion (Leventhal, H., and Tomarken, A. J. 1986. Emotion: Today's problems. *Annual Review of Psychology* 37: 565–610), it is clear that those expectations are crucial to which of several emotions will be experienced. The following sources provide good introductions to how emotions are formed and to the influence on their formation of cognitive development: Campos, J. J., et al. 1983. Socioemotional development. In *Handbook of Child Psychology,* vol. 2, *Infancy and Developmental Psychobiology,* ed. M. M. Haith and J. J. Campos, pp. 783–915. New York: Wiley; Lewis, M., and Michalson, L. 1983. *Children's Emotions and Moods.* New York: Plenum; and Sroufe, A. 1979. Socioemotional development. In *Handbook of Infant Development,* ed. J. Osofsy, pp. 462–516. New York: Wiley.

33. This immaturity is evident in the anatomy of the newborn's brain (Conel, J. 1937. *The Postnatal Development of the Human Cerebral Cortex,* vol. 1, *The Cortex of the Newborn.* Cambridge, MA: Harvard University Press), in the electrical responses recorded over the cortex while the newborn is stimulated (Bergström, R. M. 1969. Electrical parameters of the brain during ontogeny. In *Brain and Early Behaviour: Development in the Fetus and Infant,* ed. R. J. Robinson, pp. 15–41. London: Academic Press), in the areas where his brain utilizes glucose while he is stimulated (Chugani, H. T., and Phelps, M. E. 1986. Maturational changes in cerebral function in infants determined by [18]FDG positron emission tomography. *Science* 231: 840–843), and in comparisons of newborns' behavior to that of animals in which the cortex has been removed (Bronson, G. W. 1982. Structure, status, and characteristics of the nervous system at birth. In *The Psychobiology of the Human Newborn,* ed. P. M. Stratton, pp. 99–145. New York: Wiley).

34. Bryan, E. 1930. Variations in the response of infants during first ten days of post-natal life. *Child Development* 1: 56–77.

35. Butterfield, P., Emde, R., Svejda, M., and Naiman, S. 1982. Silver nitrate and the eyes of the newborn: Effects on parental responsiveness during the initial social interaction. In *The Development of Attachment and Affiliative Systems,* ed. R. Emde and R. Harmon, pp. 95–107. New York: Plenum.

36. Von Senden, M. 1960. *Space and Sight.* London: Methuen.

37. See, for example, Smith, V. S., and Giacoia, G. P. 1986. Phototherapy in neonatal jaundice. *Postgraduate Medicine* 79 (2): 223–230.

38. Walker, D., Walker, A., and Wood, C. 1969. Temperature of human fetus. *Journal of Obstetrics and Gynecology of the British Commonwealth* 76: 503–511.

39. The classic analysis is contained in Brück, K. 1961. Temperature regulation in the newborn infant. *Biologia Neonatorum* 3: 65–119.

40. See, for example, Dahm, L., and James, L. 1972. Newborn temperature and calculated heat loss in the delivery room. *Pediatrics* 49: 504–513.

41. Mann, T., and Elliott, R. 1957. Neonatal cold injury due to accidental exposure to cold. *Lancet* 1: 229–234.

42. Oliver, T. 1977. Thermal regulation. In *Neonatal-Perinatal Medicine,* ed. R. Behrman, pp. 223–230. St. Louis: C. V. Mosby.

43. Gandy, G., et al. 1964. Thermal environmental and acid-base homeostasis in human infants during the first few hours of life. *Journal of Clinical Investigation* 43: 751–758.

44. An excellent review is Brück, K. 1978. Thermoregulation: Control mechanisms and natural processes. In *Temperature Regulation and Energy Metabolism in the Newborn,* ed. J. Sinclair, pp. 157–185. New York: Grune & Stratton.

45. Adamsons, K., Gandy, G., and James, L. S. 1965. The influence of thermal factors upon oxygen consumption of the newborn human infant. *Journal of Pediatrics* 66: 495–508.

46. Gross, K., et al. 1971. Lack of temperature control in infants with abnormalities of CNS. *Archives of Disease in Childhood* 46: 437–443; and Hardy, J. 1975. Control of body temperature. In *Neural Integration of Physiological Mechanisms and Behaviour,* ed. G. Morgenson and F. Calareser, pp. 294–307. Toronto: University of Toronto Press.

47. Leboyer, F. 1975. *Birth Without Violence.* New York: Knopf.

48. Nelson, N. 1979. A randomized clinical trial of the Leboyer method of delivery. Ph.D. diss., McMaster University, Hamilton, Ontario; and Saigel, S., Nelson, N., Bennett, K., and Enkin, M. 1981. Observations on the behavioral state of newborn infants during the first hour of life. A comparison of infants delivered by the Leboyer and conventional methods. *American Journal of Obstetrics and Gynecology* 139: 715–719. Half of the mothers insisted on having a Leboyer delivery—they refused to agree to random assignment to type of delivery—and some might argue that only they represent a "true" Leboyer group. But even in this group neither babies nor mothers appeared better off overall.

49. Budd, G., and Warhaft, N. 1966. Body temperature, shivering, blood pressure and heart rate during a standard cold stress in Australia and Antarctica. *Journal of Physiology* 186: 216–232.

50. Whitner, W., and Thompson, M. 1970. The influence of bathing on the newborn infant's body temperature. *Nursing Research* 19: 30–36.

51. Glass, L., Silverman, W., and Sinclair, J. 1960. Effect of the thermal environment on cold resistance and growth of small infants after the first week of life. *Pediatrics* 41: 1033–1046.

52. Boon, A. W., Milner, A. D., and Hopkin, I. E. 1981. Lung volumes and lung mechanics in babies born vaginally and by elective and emergency segmental caesarean section. *Journal of Pediatrics* 98: 812–815.

Chapter 4

1. Emde, R. N., Gaensbauer, T. J., and Harmon, R. J. 1976. Emotional expression in infancy. A biobehavioral study. Chap. 4: An overview of sleep and wakefulness during the first year. *Psychological Issues* 10 (Monograph 37); and Wolff, P. 1965. The development of attention in young infants. *Annals of the New York Academy of Sciences* 118: 815–830.

2. Desiraju, T., ed. 1976. *Mechanisms in Transmission of Signals for Conscious Behaviour.* Amsterdam: Elsevier, esp. chaps. 12 and 14.

3. Adults' states are reviewed in Dement, W. C. 1974. *Some Must Watch While Some Must Sleep.* San Francisco: W. H. Freeman.

4. Berger, R. 1969. Oculomotor control: A possible function of REM sleep. *Psychological Review* 76: 144–164.

5. See, for example, Parmelee, A. H., and Stern, E. 1972. Development of states in infants. In *Maturation of Brain Mechanisms Related to Sleep Behavior,* ed. C. Clemente, D. Purpura, and F. Mayer, pp. 199–228. New York: Academic Press; Prechtl, H., and O'Brien, M. 1982. Behavioural states of the full-term newborn. The emergence of a concept. In *Psychobiology of the Newborn,* ed. P. Stratton, pp. 52–73. New York: Wiley; and Thoman, E. B. 1975. Sleep and

wake behaviors in neonates: Consistencies and consequences. *Merrill-Palmer Quarterly* 21: 295–314.

6. Korner, A. 1968. REM organization in neonates. *Archives of General Psychiatry* 19: 330–340.

7. Spitz, R., and Wolf, K. 1949. Some empirical findings and hypotheses on three of its manifestations in the first year of life. *Psychoanalytic Study of the Child* 3/4: 85–120.

8. In addition to the references in note 5 earlier in this chapter, see Thoman, E. B. 1975. Early development of sleeping behaviors in infants. In *Aberrant Development in Infancy: Human and Animal Studies,* ed. N. Ellis, pp. 123–138. New York: Wiley.

9. C. Dreyfus-Brisac (1979. Neonatal electroencephalography. In *Reviews in Perinatal Medicine,* ed. E. Scarpelli and E. Cosmi, pp. 397–472. New York: Raven Press) describes the electrical activity of the cortex. We discuss its absence of control over most of the newborn's perceptions in chapters 5, 6, and 7 and its absence of control over his movements in chapters 8 and 9. See also chapter 3, note 33.

10. For more details about the electroencephalogram, see Williams, R. L., Karacan, I., and Hursch, C. J. 1974. *Electroencephalography (EEG) of Human Sleep: Clinical Applications.* New York: Wiley.

11. Good descriptions of the newborn's EEG patterns during quiet sleep are contained in Prechtl and O'Brien, Behavioural states of the full-term newborn [5], and Dreyfus-Brisac, Neonatal electroencephalography [9].

12. Akiyama, Y., Schulte, F., Schultz, M., and Parmelee, A. 1969. Acoustically evoked responses in prematures and fullterm newborn infants. *Electroencephalography and Clinical Neurophysiology* 26: 371–380; Desmedt, J., Brunko, E., and Debecker, J. 1980. Maturation and sleep correlates of the somatosensory evoked potential. In *Clinical Uses of Cerebral, Brain Stem and Spinal Somatosensory Evoked Potentials,* ed. J. E. Desmedt, pp. 146–161. Basel: Karger; and Ellingson, R. 1970. Variability of visually evoked responses in the human newborn. *Electroencephalography and Clinical Neurophysiology* 29: 10–19.

13. Dreyfus-Brisac, Neonatal electroencephalography [9].

14. See an introductory psychology textbook, such as Gleitman, H. 1986. *Psychology,* 2nd ed. New York: Norton.

15. Hoffmann, R. 1978. Developmental changes in human infant visual-evoked potentials to patterned stimuli recorded at different scalp locations. *Child Development* 49: 110–118.

16. Hoffmann judged the babies' maturity on the basis of the latency of a prominent positive wave, P2.

17. Lewkowicz, D., and Turkewitz, G. 1980. Cross-modal equivalence in early infancy: Auditory-visual intensity matching. *Developmental Psychology* 16: 597–607.

18. Bell, C. H. 1984. *Olivier Messiaen,* pp. 29–30. Boston: Twayne; Bowers, F. 1969. *Scriabin,* vol. 2, p. 205. Tokyo: Kodansha; and Yastrebtsev, V. V. 1985. *Reminiscences of Rimsky-Korsakov,* trans. F. Jonas, pp. 50–51, 72–74. New York: Columbia University Press.

19. Luria, A. R. 1969. *The Mind of a Mnemonist,* trans. L. Solotaroff. New York: Avon Books (originally published 1965).

20. Ibid., p. 23.

21. Ibid., p. 26.

22. Ibid., p. 26.

23. Ibid., p. 27.

24. T. Schneirla (1959. An evolutionary and developmental theory of biphasic process underlying approach and withdrawal. In *Nebraska Symposium on Motivation,* vol. 7, ed. M. R. Jones, pp. 1–42. Lincoln, NE: University of Nebraska Press) describes the findings that young organisms of all species extend their limbs toward stimuli of low intensity, but flex them and pull them away from strong stimuli.

25. For reviews, see Aslin, R., ed. 1985. *Advances in Neural and Behavioral Development,* vol. 1, pp. 107–129, 131–156. Norwood, NJ: Ablex.

26. Riesen, A. H. 1982. Effects of environments on development in sensory systems. In *Contributions to Sensory Physiology,* vol. 6, ed. W. D. Neff, pp. 45–75. New York: Academic Press; and Turkewitz, G., and Kenny, P. A. 1985. The role of developmental limitations of sensory

input on sensory/perceptual organization. *Journal of Developmental and Behavioral Pediatrics* 6: 302–306.

27. Lewkowicz, D., and Turkewitz, G. 1981. Intersensory interaction in newborns: Modification of visual preferences following exposure to sound. *Child Development* 52: 827–832. Similarly, newborns prefer to look at lights flashing at a fairly fast rate (8 Hz) rather than at those flashing at slower rates *unless* they were just stimulated with a high-frequency light *or* tone. Then they prefer to look at a light flashing at a slower rate (Gardner, J. M, et al. 1986. Effects of visual and auditory stimulation on subsequent visual preferences in neonates. *International Journal of Behavioral Development* 9: 251–263).

28. The preference for a light flashing at a middling rate is inferred from two findings: three-month-olds prefer 6 Hz to either slower or faster rates (Karmel, B., et al. 1977. Correlation of infants' brain and behavior response to temporal changes in visual stimulation. *Psychophysiology* 14: 134–142), while newborns—who have never been tested with rates faster than 8 Hz—prefer 8 Hz to slower rates, except when they are unswaddled before feeding, that is, when they are more stimulated in other ways (Gardner, J. M., and Karmel, B. Z. 1984. Arousal effects on visual preference in neonates. *Developmental Psychology* 20: 374–377). See also Crook, C. 1978. Taste perception in the newborn infant. *Infant Behavior and Development* 1: 52–59; Miranda, S. B., and Fantz, R. L. 1971. Distribution of visual attention by newborn infants among patterns varying in size and number of details. *Proceedings of the 79th Annual Convention of the American Psychological Association* 6: 181–182; Schneirla, An evolutionary and developmental theory [24]; and Turkewitz, G., Moreau, T., Birch, H., and Davis, L. 1971. Relationships among responses in the human newborn: The non-association and non-equivalence among different indicators of responsiveness. *Psychophysiology* 7: 233–247.

29. Aylward, G., Lazzara, A., and Meyer, J. 1978. Behavioral and neurological characteristics of a hydranencephalic infant. *Developmental Medicine and Child Neurology* 20: 211–217; and Francis, P. L., Self, P. A., and McCaffree, M. A. 1984. Behavioral assessment of a hydranencephalic neonate. *Child Development* 55: 262–266.

30. These eye movements are described on pages 45–46 of chapter 3. Similarly limited eye movements are shown by monkeys in whom the visual cortex has been ablated. See Humphrey, N. K. 1974. Vision in a monkey without striate cortex: A case study. *Perception* 3: 241–255.

31. See, for example, von Hofsten, C. 1982. Eye-hand coordination in the newborn. *Developmental Psychology* 18: 450–461.

32. Many of these effects are discussed in Wolff, P. H. 1966. The causes, controls and organization of behaviour in the neonate. *Psychological Issues* 5: 1–105.

33. See, for example, Wolff, The causes, controls and organization of behaviour in the neonate [32]; Birns, B., Blank, M., and Bridges, W. 1966. The effectiveness of various soothing techniques on human neonates. *Psychosomatic Medicine* 28: 316–322; and Brackbill, Y. 1971. Cumulative effects of continuous stimulation on arousal level in infants. *Child Development* 42: 17–26.

34. Brackbill, Y. 1975. Continuous stimulation and arousal level in infancy: Effects of stimulus intensity and stress. *Child Development* 46: 364–369; Irwin, O. 1941. Effect of strong light on the body activity of newborns. *Journal of Comparative Psychology* 32: 233–236; and Pederson, D., and Ter Vrugt, D. 1973. The influence of amplitude and frequency of vestibular stimulation on the activity of two-month-old infants. *Child Development* 44: 122–128.

35. Brackbill, Cumulative effects of continuous stimulation on arousal level [33].

36. Petre-Quadens, O. 1971. Sleep in the human newborn. In *Basic Sleep Mechanisms,* ed. O. Petre-Quadens and J. Schlag, pp. 355–380. New York: Academic Press.

37. Papoušek, H., Papoušek, M., and Koester, L. 1986. Sharing emotionality and sharing knowledge: A microanalytic approach to parent-infant communication. In *Measuring Emotions in Infants and Children,* vol. 2, ed. C. E. Izard and P. Read, pp. 93–123. Cambridge: Cambridge University Press.

38. Roffwarg, H. P., Muzio, J. N., and Dement, W. C. 1966. Ontogenetic development of the human sleep-dream cycle. *Science* 152: 604–619; and Stern, E., et al. 1969. Sleep characteristics in infants. *Pediatrics* 43: 65–70.

39. Emde, R., Swedbor, J., and Suzuki, B. 1975. Human wakefulness and biological rhythms after birth. *Archives of General Psychiatry* 32: 780–783.

40. Anders, T. F., and Roffwarg, H. P. 1973. The relationship between maternal and neonatal sleep. *Neuropädiatrie* 4: 151–161.

41. The exception is that eliciting a handful of reflexes (including the Babkin and the Babinski) will usually disturb the newborn's quiet sleep. See Anders, T. F., and Roffwarg, H. P. 1973. The effects of selective interruption and deprivation of sleep in the human newborn. *Developmental Psychobiology* 6: 79–91; and Prechtl, H. 1972. Patterns of reflex behavior related to sleep in the human infant. In *Sleep and the Maturing Nervous System,* ed. D. P. Purpura and F. E. Mayer, pp. 287–316. New York: Academic Press.

42. Thoman, E. B., et al. 1981. State organization in neonates: Developmental inconsistency indicates risk for developmental dysfunction. *Neuropediatrics* 12: 45–54.

43. Dinges, D., Davis, M., and Glass, P. 1980. Fetal exposure to narcotics: Neonatal sleep as a measure of nervous system imbalance. *Science* 209: 619–621; and Havlicek, V., Childiaeva, R., and Chernick, V. 1977. EEG frequency characteristics of sleep states in infants of alcoholic mothers. *Neuropädiatrie* 8: 360–373.

44. Reviewed in Hoppenbrouwers, T., and Hodgman, J. E. 1982. Sudden infant death syndrome (SIDS): An integration of ontogenetic, pathologic, physiologic and epidemiologic factors. *Neuropediatrics* 13 (supple.): 36–51; and Kelly, D., and Sannon, D. 1982. Sudden infant death syndrome and near sudden infant death syndrome: A review of the literature 1964 to 1982. *Pediatric Clinics of North America* 29: 1241–1261.

45. Ashton, R. 1973. The influence of state and prandial condition upon the reactivity of the newborn to auditory stimulation. *Journal of Experimental Child Psychology* 15: 315–327.

46. Ashton looked at two responses for habituation to two tones. While the babies were asleep, they showed habituation to both tones with both reflexes, but while they were awake they showed it only to the more intense tone with one reflex (quickening of the pulse).

47. Lewis, M., Dodd, C., and Harwitz, M. 1969. Cardiac responsivity to tactile stimulation in waking and sleeping infants. *Perceptual Motor Skills* 29: 259–269.

48. Campos, J., and Brackbill, Y. 1973. Infant state: Relationship to heartrate, behavioral response, and response decrement. *Developmental Psychobiology* 6: 9–19; and Martinius, J., and Papoušek, H. 1970. Responses to optic and extroceptive stimuli in relation to state in the human newborn: Habituation to the blink reflex. *Neuropädiatrie* 1: 452–460.

49. Sander, L., Julia, H., Stechler, G., and Burns, P. 1972. Continuous 24-hour interactional monitoring in infants reared in two caretaking environments. *Psychosomatic Medicine* 34: 270–282.

50. Coons, S., and Guilleminault, C. 1984. Development of consolidated sleep and wakeful periods in relation to the day/night cycle in infancy. *Developmental Medicine and Child Neurology* 26: 169–176.

51. Parmelee and Stern, Development of states in infants [5].

52. Despite this progress, neither quiet sleep nor wakefulness are completely adult: EEG patterns and the cycles of sleep and wakefulness change gradually through adolescence. Reviewed in Ellingson, R. 1975. Ontogenesis of sleep in the human. In *Experimental Study of Human Sleep,* ed. G. Lairy and P. Salzarulo, pp. 129–146. Amsterdam: Elsevier.

53. Such changes are reviewed in Turkewitz, G., Lewkowicz, D., and Gardner, J. 1983. Determinants of infant perception. In *Advances in the Study of Behavior,* vol. 13, ed. J. Rosenblatt, R. Hinde, C. Beer, and M. Busnel, pp. 39–62. New York: Academic Press.

54. Ellingson, R., Lathrop, G., Danahy, T., and Nelson, R. 1973. Variability of visual evoked potentials in human infants and adults. *Electroencephalography and Clinical Neurophysiology* 34: 113–124.

55. Ibid., and Ellingson, Ontogenesis of sleep in the human [52].

56. Anders, T. 1978. Home recorded sleep in 2 and 9 month old infants. *Journal of the American Academy of Child Psychiatry* 17: 421–431.

57. Emde, Gaensbauer, and Harmon, Emotional expression in infancy [1].

58. Kohlberg, L. 1969. Stage and sequence: The cognitive-developmental approach to socialization. In *Handbook of Socialization Theory and Research,* ed. D. A. Goslin, pp. 347–480. Chicago: Rand-McNally.

Chapter 5

1. Bowen-Jones, A., Thompson, C., and Drewett, R. F. 1982. Milk flow and sucking rates during breast-feeding. *Developmental Medicine and Child Neurology* 24: 626–633.

2. Weber, F., Woolridge, M. W., and Baum, J. D. 1986. An ultrasonographic study of the organisation of sucking and swallowing by newborn infants. *Developmental Medicine and Child Neurology* 28: 19–24.

3. Hytten, F. E. 1954. Clinical and chemical studies in human lactation. *British Medical Journal* 1: 175–182.

4. Ibid.

5. Drewett, R. F. 1982. Returning to the suckled breast: A further test of Hall's hypothesis. *Early Human Development* 6: 161–163.

6. Kaye, H. 1967. Infant sucking behavior and its modification. In *Advances in Child Development and Behavior,* vol. 3, ed. L. Lipsitt and C. Spiker, pp. 2–52. New York: Academic Press.

7. Howie, P. S., et al. 1981. How long should a breastfeed last? *Early Human Development* 5: 71–77.

8. Woolridge, M. W., Baum, J., and Drewett, R. 1980. Changing the composition of human milk: Its effect on sucking patterns and milk intake. *Lancet* 2: 1292–1294.

9. For a comprehensive and readable review, see Steiner, J. 1979. Human facial expressions in response to taste and smell stimulation. In *Advances in Child Development and Behavior,* vol. 13, ed. H. Reese and L. P. Lipsitt, pp. 257–295. New York: Academic Press.

10. This study is reviewed in ibid. D. Rosenstein and H. Oster (1981. Facial expression as a method for exploring infants' taste response. Paper presented at the Society for Research in Child Development, April, in Boston) studied two-hour-old North American babies and found similar reactions to sugar and to quinine, but not to sour salt, perhaps because they placed less of the substances on the babies' tongues than Steiner had.

11. Ganchrow, J., Steiner, J., and Daher, M. 1983. Neonatal facial expressions in response to different qualities and intensities of gustatory stimuli. *Infant Behavior and Development* 6: 189–200.

12. Crook, C. 1978. Taste perception in the newborn infant. *Infant Behavior and Development* 1: 52–59.

13. Described in Steiner, Human facial expressions [9].

14. Finberg, L., Kiley, J., and Luttrell, C. 1963. Mass accidental salt poisoning in infancy. *Journal of the American Medical Association* 184: 187–190.

15. For a good review, see Moncrieff, R. W. 1967. *The Chemical Senses.* London: Leonard Hill.

16. Cain, W. S. 1974. Contribution of the trigeminal nerve to perceived odor magnitude. *Annals of the New York Academy of Sciences* 237: 28–34.

17. Bartoshuk, L. 1978. Gustatory systems. In *Handbook of Behavioral Neurobiology,* vol. 1, *Sensory Integration,* ed. R. B. Masterton, pp. 503–567. New York: Plenum.

18. Research on the trigeminal system is reviewed in Engen, T. 1982. *The Perception of Odors.* New York: Academic Press.

19. Engen, T., Cain, W., and Rovee, C. 1968. Direct scaling of olfaction in the newborn and the adult human observer. In *Theories of Odor and Odor Measurement,* ed. N. Tanyolac, pp. 271–296. Istanbul: Robert College Research Center; and Rovee, C. 1969. Psychophysical scaling of olfactory response to the aliphatic alcohols in human neonates. *Journal of Experimental Child Psychology* 7: 245–254.

20. Engen, Cain, and Rovee (Direct scaling of olfaction [19]) found that newborns' perceptions resemble adults' in another way: adults report that, as the concentration of an alcohol is increased, its strength seems to increase, but much more so for short-chained alcohols than for long-chained ones (the long-chained alcohols seem strong even at weak concentrations). Similarly, newborns' reactions increased as the concentration of alcohol increased, but more so for short-chained alcohols than for long-chained ones.

21. Reviewed in Steiner, Human facial expressions [9].

22. Forty years earlier Dorothy Disher (1934. The reactions of newborn infants to chemical stimuli administered nasally. In *Studies in Infant Behavior*, ed. F. C. Dockeray, pp. 1–52. Athens: Ohio State University Press) found that babies were more likely to move when presented with a number of odorants rather than pure air, especially when the odorants were more saturated. The odors they sensed included violet, asafoetida, sassafras, citronella, turpentine, pyridine, and lemon. J. Rieser, A. Yonas, and K. Wikner (1976. Radial localization of odors by human newborns. *Child Development* 47: 856–859) provide additional evidence that infants and adults smell odors similarly: two-thirds of the newborns turned away from the smell of ammonia.

23. Steiner, Human facial expressions [9].

24. Macfarlane, A. 1975. Olfaction in the development of social preferences in the human neonate. In *Parent-Infant Interaction*, ed. R. Porter and M. O'Connor, pp. 103–117. Ciba Foundation Symposium 33. Amsterdam: Elsevier/Excerpta Medica/North-Holland.

25. Brown, R. 1979. Mammalian social odors: A critical review. *Advances in the Study of Behavior* 10: 103–162; and Schaal, B., et al. 1980. Les stimulations olfactives dans les relations entre l'enfant et la mère. *Reproduction, Nutrition, Development* 20: 843–858.

26. Some portion of the increase in sensitivity in the days after birth could also result from a decrease in the depressing effects of obstetric medication, to which we assume many of the babies had been exposed. See Lipsitt, L. P., Engen, T., and Kaye, H. 1963. Developmental changes in the olfactory threshold of the neonate. *Child Development* 34: 371–376.

27. Cernoch, J. M., and Porter, R. H. 1985. Recognition of maternal axillary odors by infants. *Child Development* 56: 1593–1598.

28. Lind, T. 1978. The biochemistry of amniotic fluid. In *Amniotic Fluid: Research and Clinical Application*, ed. D. Fairweather and T. Eskes, pp. 60–81. Amsterdam: Excerpta Medica.

29. Johnson, P., and Salisbury, D. M. 1975. Breathing and sucking during feeding in the newborn. In *Parent-Infant Interaction*, ed. Porter and O'Connor [24], pp. 119–135.

30. Ben-Aryeh, H., et al. 1984. Composition of whole unstimulated saliva of human infants. *Archives of Oral Biology* 29: 357–362.

31. These changes are reviewed in Bartoshuk, Gustatory systems [17].

32. A good introductory review is Keverne, E. B. 1982. Chemical senses: Taste. In *The Senses*, ed. H. B. Barlow and J. D. Mollon, pp. 428–447. Cambridge: Cambridge University Press.

33. Desor, J. A., Maller, O., and Andrews, K. 1975. Ingestive responses of newborns to salty, sour and bitter stimuli. *Journal of Comparative and Physiological Psychology* 89: 966–970.

34. Moskowitz, H. 1971. The sweetness and pleasantness of sugars. *American Journal of Psychology* 84: 387–405.

35. Desor, J., Maller, O., and Turner, R. 1973. Taste in acceptance of sugars by human infants. *Journal of Comparative and Physiological Psychology* 84: 496–501.

36. Reviewed in Crook, C. 1987. Taste and smell. In *Handbook of Infant Perception*, vol. 1, *From Sensation to Perception*, ed. P. Salapatek and L. Cohen, pp. 237–260. New York: Academic Press.

37. Crook, Taste perception in the newborn infant [12].

38. Crook (ibid.) found an increase in the effectiveness of the sugar solution with increasing concentrations up to 40 percent, then an insignificant drop at the highest concentration (60 percent). G. Beauchamp (1981. The development of taste in infancy. In *Infant and Child Feeding*, ed. J. Bond, et al., pp. 413–426. New York: Academic Press) found an increase with increasing concentrations up to 30 percent, and then a leveling off at the next highest concentration (60 percent). Both results suggest that to infants, as to adults, sucrose solutions more concentrated than 50 percent do not taste increasingly sweet.

39. See Milstein, R. 1980. Responsiveness in newborn infants of overweight and normal weight parents. *Appetite* 1:65–74. Although several other studies have confirmed this, D. H. Ashmead, B. M. Reilly, and L. P. Lipsitt (1980. Neonates' heart rate, sucking rhythm, and sucking amplitude as a function of the sweet taste. *Journal of Experimental Child Psychology* 29: 264–281) found the opposite.

40. J. A. Grinker (1981. Behavioral and metabolic factors in childhood obesity. In *The Uncommon Child*, ed. M. Lewis and L. A. Rosenblum, pp. 115–150. New York: Plenum) dis-

cusses the possible role that this and other differences between "normal" and fat babies play in the development of obesity.

41. Desor, Maller, and Andrews, Ingestive responses of newborns [33].

42. Weingarten, H. P. 1985. Stimulus control of eating: Implications for a two-factor theory of hunger. *Appetite* 6: 387–401.

43. Taylor, R. 1917. Hunger in the infant. *American Journal of Diseases of Children* 14: 233–257.

44. Kaye (Infant sucking behavior [6]) summarizes the observations of indiscriminate sucking. It is *possible* for newborns' sucking to be conditioned, but apparently only if a stimulus signals that a pacifier or sugar water is going to be placed on the baby's tongue immediately and invariably. Then newborns will start to suck in anticipation, and later cry when the signal occurs without the reinforcement (Blass, E., Ganchrow, J., and Steiner, J. 1984. Classical conditioning in newborn humans 2–48 hours of age. *Infant Behavior and Development* 7: 223–236). When, as in real life, the reinforcement is delayed or intermittent, newborns do not learn the connection.

45. The effect of anticipation upon digestion has been studied most thoroughly in rats: although rats do not vomit, they do not digest food well when their stomach is not prepared for it. See, for example, Molina, F., Thiel, T., Deutsch, J. A., and Puerto, A. 1977. Comparison between some digestive processes after eating and gastric loading in rats. *Pharmacology Biochemistry and Behavior* 7: 347–350.

46. Gaensbauer, T., and Emde, R. 1973. Wakefulness and feeding in human newborns. *Archives of General Psychiatry* 28: 894–897; Howie et al., How long should a breastfeed last? [7]; and Marquis, D. 1941. Learning in the neonate: The modification of behavior under three feeding schedules. *Psychological Bulletin* 29: 263–282.

47. Marquis, D. A. 1943. A study of frustration in newborn infants. *Journal of Experimental Psychology* 32: 123–138.

48. Wasz-Höckert, O., et al. 1968. The infant cry. A spectographic and auditory analysis. *Clinics in Developmental Medicine* 29. Lavenham, Suffolk: Spastics International Medical Publications.

49. Gesell, A., and Ilg, F. 1937. *Feeding Behavior of Infants. A Pediatric Approach to the Mental Hygiene of Early Life.* Philadelphia: J. B. Lippincott.

50. Wasz-Höckert et al., The infant cry [48], p. 5.

51. Irwin, O. C. 1930. The amount and nature of activities of newborn infants under constant external stimulating conditions during the first ten days of life. *Genetic Psychology Monographs* 8: 1–92.

52. Crook, C. 1979. The organization and control of infant sucking. *Advances in Child Development and Behavior* vol. 14, ed. H. W. Reese and L. P. Lipsitt, pp. 209–252. New York: Academic Press.

53. Jonas, A. 1980. Human milk at different stages of lactation. In *Human Milk. Its Biological and Social Value,* ed. S. Freier and A. Eideman, pp. 51–55. Amsterdam: Excerpta Medica.

54. Reviewed in Booth, D. 1981. How should questions about satiation be asked? *Appetite* 2: 237–244.

55. Drewett, R., and Woolridge, M. 1979. Sucking patterns of human babies on the breast. *Early Human Development* 3: 315–320; and Lucas, A., Lucas, P., and Baum, J. 1979. Pattern of milk flow in breast-fed infants. *Lancet* 2: 57–58.

56. Dubignon, J., and Campbell, D. 1969. Sucking in the newborn period during a feed. *Journal of Experimental Child Psychology* 7: 282–298.

57. Gesell and Ilg, *Feeding Behavior of Infants* [49].

58. Fomon, S., et al. 1975. Influence of formula concentration on caloric intake and growth of normal infants. *Acta Pædiatrica Scandinavica* 64: 172–181.

59. Lucas, A., Lucas, P., and Baum, J. D. 1981. Differences in the pattern of milk intake between breast and bottle fed infants. *Early Human Development* 5: 195–199.

60. Ibid.

61. In addition to Kaye (Infant sucking behavior, [6]), see Wolff, P. H. 1968. The serial organization of sucking in the young infant. *Pediatrics* 42:943–956.

62. Davis, H., Sears, R., and Brodbeck, A. 1948. Effects of cup, bottle, and breast-feeding on oral activities of newborn infants. *Pediatrics* 2: 549–558.

63. In the work by B. Birns, M. Blank, and W. Bridger (1968. The effectiveness of various soothing techniques on human neonates. *Psychosomatic Medicine* 28: 316–322) the pacifier was sweetened, so it is possible the newborns were soothed by the sweet taste and not by sucking per se. In any case, it demonstrates soothing from stimulation of the mouth. See also Gunnar, M., Fisch, R., and Malone, S. 1984. The effects of a pacifying stimulus on behavioral and adrenocortical responses to circumcision in the newborn. *Journal of the Academy of Child Psychiatry* 23: 34–38.

64. Ali, Z., and Lowry, M. 1981. Early maternal-child contact: Effects on later behaviour. *Developmental Medicine and Child Neurology* 23: 337–345.

65. Although early nursing is not *necessary* to breast-feed successfully, several studies suggest that it may facilitate breast-feeding (see, for example, Salariya, E., Easton, P., and Cater, J. 1978. Duration of breast-feeding after early initiation and frequent feeding. *Lancet* 2: 1141–1143; but see also Woolridge, M. W., Greasley, V., and Silpisornkosol, S. 1985. The initiation of lactation: The effect of early versus delayed contact for suckling on milk intake in the first week post-partum. A study in Chiang Mai, Northern Thailand. *Early Human Development* 12: 269–278). It is not possible to draw a more definite conclusion, for often mothers who nursed early were treated differently from the control group in other respects as well—allowed more frequent contact with the baby, given more encouragement, and so on. See also Anderson, G. C., et al. 1982. Development of sucking in term infants from birth to four hours postbirth. *Research in Nursing and Health* 5:21–27.

66. For a critical review, see Svejda, M. J., Pannabecker, B. J., and Emde, R. N. 1981. Parent-to-infant attachment. A critique of the early "bonding" model. In *The Development of Attachment and Affiliative Systems,* ed. R. N. Emde and R. J. Harmon, pp. 83–93. New York: Plenum. See also Kennell, J., Trause, M., and Klaus, M. 1975. Evidence for a sensitive period in the human mother. In *Parent-infant Interaction,* ed. Porter and O'Connor [24], pp. 87–101.

67. Sackett, W. W., Jr. 1953. Results of three years experience with a new concept of baby feeding. *Southern Medical Journal* 46: 358–363. Reprinted in: 1976. *Infant Nutrition,* ed. D. H. Merritt. Stroudsburg, PA: Dowden, Hutchinson & Ross; and Sackett, W. W. 1956. Use of solid foods early in infancy. *G.P.* 14: 98–102.

68. Gesell and Ilg, *Feeding Behavior of Infants* [49].

69. Anders, T. 1975. Maturation of sleep patterns in the newborn infant. In *Advances in Sleep Research,* vol. 2, ed. E. D. Weitzman, pp. 43–66. New York: Spectrum; and Morath, M. 1974. The four-hour feeding rhythm of the baby as a free running endogenously regulated rhythm. *International Journal of Chronobiology* 2: 39–45.

70. Although all one-month-olds will adjust their intake if fed consistently with a richer formula (Fomon, et al., Influence of formula concentration [58]), only heavier babies do so during a single feeding (Chan, S., Pollitt, E., and Leibel, R. 1979. Effects of nutrient cues on formula intake in 5-week-old infants. *Infant Behavior and Development* 2: 201–208).

71. Gesell and Ilg, *Feeding Behavior of Infants* [49].

72. Davis, C. 1928. Self-selection of diet by newly weaned infants. *American Journal of Diseases of Children* 36: 651–679, © 1928 American Medical Association; and Davis, C. 1939. Results of self-selection of diets by young children. *Canadian Medical Association Journal* 41 (September): 257–261.

73. Davis, Self-selection of diet by newly weaned infants [72], p. 660.

74. Ibid., p. 662.

75. Ibid., p. 668.

76. Davis, Results of self-selection of diets by young children [72], pp. 260–261.

77. Davis, Self-selection of diet by newly weaned infants [72], pp. 669–670.

78. Ibid., p. 671.

79. Davis, Results of self-selection of diets by young children [72], p. 258.

80. Ibid., p. 260.

81. Cowart, B. J., and Beauchamp, G. K. 1986. Factors affecting acceptance of salt by human infants and children. In *Interaction of the Chemical Senses with Nutrition,* ed. M. R. Kare and J. G. Brand, pp. 25–44. New York: Academic Press.

82. Sinclair, D. 1978. *Human Growth after Birth,* 3rd ed. London: Oxford University Press.

Chapter 6

1. Examples are described in Haith, M. 1980. *Rules that Babies Look By.* Hillsdale, NJ: Lawrence Erlbaum; and Lewis, T., and Maurer, D. 1980. Central vision in the newborn. *Journal of Experimental Child Psychology* 29: 475–480.

2. Documented in Slater, A., Morison, V., Town, C., and Rose, D. 1985. Movement perception and identity constancy in the new-born baby. *British Journal of Developmental Psychology* 3: 211–220.

3. van Hof-van Duin, J., and Mohn, G. 1986. The development of visual acuity in normal fullterm and preterm infants. *Vision Research* 26: 909–916.

4. Lewis, T. L., and Maurer, D. 1986. Preferential looking as a measure of visual resolution in infants and toddlers: A comparison of psychophysical methods. *Child Development* 57: 1062–1075.

5. Atkinson, J., Braddick, O., and French, J. 1979. Contrast sensitivity of the human neonate measured by the visual evoked potential. *Investigative Ophthalmology and Visual Science* 18: 210–213. See also V. Porciatti (1984. Temporal and spatial properties of the pattern-reversal VEPs in infants below 2 months of age. *Human Neurobiology* 3: 97–102) confirmed these results in two newborns who were tested with checkerboards flashing at a theoretically better rate. Later results diverge: visually evoked responses indicate that acuity becomes nearly adult by six months of age, but preferential looking indicates that this takes many years. It could be that young children can see fine stripes but do not "prefer" them to a plain gray, yet this seems unlikely because older children are rewarded for looking at or pointing toward the stripes. It seems more likely that the visually evoked response overestimates acuity because some signals reach the visual cortex of the young child without entering conscious perception. Possible reasons for the different results are discussed in M. S. Banks and J. L. Dannemiller (1987. Infant visual psychophysics. In *Handbook of Infant Perception,* vol. 1, *From Sensation to Perception,* ed. P. Salapatek and L. B. Cohen, pp. 115–176. New York: Academic Press).

6. A good description with useful illustrations is contained in chap. 10 of Hurvich, L. 1981. *Color Vision.* Sunderland, MA: Sinauer.

7. Yuodelis, C., and Hendrickson, A. 1986. A qualitative and quantitative analysis of the human fovea during development. *Vision Research* 26: 847–856.

8. M. K. Powers and V. Dobson (1982. Effect of focus on visual acuity of human infants. *Vision Research* 22: 521–528) found that blurring the image with the wrong spectacle lens reduces the acuity of six-week-olds only minimally, although it markedly degrades the acuity of adults. The minor effect of misfocusing on infants' acuity can also be inferred from the fact that adults' sensitivity to wide stripes is affected only minimally by optical blur (Green, D. G., and Campbell, F. W. 1965. Effect of focus on the visual response to a sinusoidally modulated spatial stimulus. *Journal of the Optical Society of America* 55: 1154–1157).

9. A good introduction is Barlow, H. B., and Mollon, J. D., eds. 1982. *The Senses.* Cambridge: Cambridge University Press.

10. Powers, M. K., Schneck, M., and Teller, D. Y. 1981. Spectral sensitivity of human infants at absolute visual threshold. *Vision Research* 21: 1005–1016.

11. See, for example, Adams, R. J., and Maurer, D. 1984. Detection of contrast by the newborn and 2-month-old infant. *Infant Behavior and Development* 7: 415–422.

12. Reviewed in Banks, M. 1982/83. The development of spatial and temporal contrast sensitivity. *Current Eye Research* 2: 191–198.

13. For a good description of adults' accommodation, see *The Senses,* ed. Barlow and Mollon [9], chap. 3.

14. Braddick, O., Atkinson, J., French, J., and Howland, H. 1979. A photorefractive study of infant accommodation. *Vision Research* 19: 1319–1330.

15. Note that this poor focusing does not cause his poor acuity. See Banks, M., with Salapatek, P. 1983. Infant visual perception. In *Handbook of Child Psychology,* vol. 2, *Infancy and Developmental Psychobiology,* ed. M. Haith and J. Campos, pp. 435–571. New York: Wiley.

16. In adults, convergence—how far inward the eyes are turned—and accommodation are linked. When an object changes its distance, the eyes turn in or out to maintain fixation on it, and they change their focus. Changing either convergence or accommodation will change the other. See Aslin, R. N., and Jackson, R. W. 1979. Accommodative-convergence in young infants: Development of a synergistic sensory-motor system. *Canadian Journal of Psychology* 33: 222–231.

17. Green, D. G., Powers, M. K., and Banks, M. S. 1980. Depth of focus, eye size and visual acuity. *Vision Research* 20: 827–835.

18. Banks, M. S. 1980. The development of visual accommodation during early infancy. *Child Development* 51: 646–666.

19. McKenzie, B. E., and Day, R. H. 1972. Object distance as a determinant of visual fixation in early infancy. *Science* 178: 1108–1110.

20. K. E. Brookman's results (1980. Ocular accommodation in human infants. Ph.D. diss., Indiana University, Bloomington) suggest that babies may initially get worse at accommodating, as they establish a link between accommodation and convergence (see note 16 this chapter). See also Banks (The development of visual accommodation [18]).

21. Maurer, D. 1974. The development of binocular convergence in infants. Ph.D. diss., University of Minnesota.

22. Fonarev, A. M. 1959. [Coordination in the eyeball movements of newborn children and problems of space perception. Communication I.] *Doklady Akademu Pedagogicheskikh Nauk RSFSR* 4: 85–88.

23. Wickelgren, L. 1969. The ocular response of human newborns to intermittent visual movement. *Journal of Experimental Child Psychology* 8: 469–482.

24. Lewis, T., Maurer, D., and Blackburn, K. 1985. The development of young infants' ability to detect stimuli in the nasal visual field. *Vision Research* 25: 943–950.

25. Maurer, D., Clarke, A. L., and Lewis, T. L. 1986. The development of peripheral detection during infancy. *Investigative Ophthalmology and Visual Science* 27 (supple.): 264 [Abstract].

26. Lewis, T. L., Maurer, D., and Soleas, C. 1987. Peripheral detection in 1-month-olds: Influence of stimulus' size. Paper presented at the Society for Research in Child Development, April, in Baltimore; and Mohn, G., and van Hof-van Duin, J. 1986. Development of the binocular and monocular visual fields of human infants during the first year of life. *Clinical Vision Sciences* 1: 51–64.

27. Both reactions occur in adults when one eye suddenly turns in. S. Shimojo, J. Bauer, K. M. O'Connell, and R. Held (1986. Pre-stereoptic binocular vision in infants. *Vision Research* 26: 501–510) present indirect evidence that young babies see double.

28. For a good introduction, see Sekuler, R., and Blake, R. 1985. *Perception.* New York: Knopf.

29. Younger babies show no evidence of stereopsis even when they are tested in such a way that it does not matter if they are fixating the same point with both eyes (Birch, E. E., Gwiazda, J., and Held, R. 1983. The development of vergence does not account for the onset of stereopsis. *Perception* 12: 331–336).

30. For a good description with helpful illustrations, see Sekuler and Blake, *Perception* [28].

31. Reviewed in Yonas, A., Arterberry, M. E., and Granrud, C. E. 1987. Space perception in infancy. In *Annals of Child Development,* vol. 4, ed. R. Vasta, pp. 1–34. Greenwich, CN: JAI Press.

32. Yonas, A., Cleaves, W., and Pettersen, L. 1978. Development of sensitivity to pictorial depth. *Science* 200: 77–79.

33. Slater, A., Rose, D., and Morison, V. 1984. Newborn infants' perception of similarity and differences between two- and three-dimensional stimuli. *British Journal of Developmental Psychology* 2: 287–294. Although five-month-olds appear insensitive to depth defined *only* by pictorial cues (see note 31 this chapter), such cues might add to the perception of depth

defined by other cues. So it is possible the babies used both motion parallax and pictorial cues to distinguish the objects from their photographs, or in the case of Yonas et al.'s experiment (ibid.), to perceive which side of the window frame was nearer.

34. Robert, A. 1976. The newborn's response to looming stimuli. Ph.D. diss., Queens University, Kingston, Ontario.

35. The findings of B. R. Stephens and M. S. Banks (1985. The development of contrast constancy. *Journal of Experimental Child Psychology* 40: 528–547) suggest another possibility. As an object moves closer or farther away, adults perceive the contrast between its features as unchanging—that is, they show *contrast constancy.* So do twelve-week-olds, but apparently not six-week-olds. This implies that young infants will see the features and texture of an approaching object as increasing in contrast.

36. Conel, J. 1939. *The Postnatal Development of the Human Cerebral Cortex,* vol. 1, *The Cortex of the Newborn.* Cambridge, MA: Harvard University Press, 1939.

37. Aslin, R. N. 1981. Development of smooth pursuit in human infants. In *Eye Movements: Cognition and Visual Perception,* ed. D. F. Fisher, R. A. Monty, and J. W. Senders, pp. 31–51. Hilldsdale, NJ: Lawrence Erlbaum.

38. For a discussion of suppression during saccades, see a textbook on perception such as Sekuler and Blake (*Perception* [28]). Note that when adults follow a target they do not use these jerky eye movements but follow smoothly. During smooth pursuit, the image of the target does not blank out.

39. Bloch, H. 1983. La poursuite visuelle chez le nouveau-né à terme et chez le prématuré. *Enfance* 1: 19–29.

40. Aslin, Development of smooth pursuit [37].

41. Humphrey, N. K. 1974. Vision in a monkey without striate cortex: A case study. *Perception* 3: 324–337.

42. See, for example, Aslin, R. N. 1985. Oculomotor measures of visual development. In *Measurement of Audition and Vision during the First Year of Life: A Methodological Overview,* ed. G. Gottlieb and N. Krasnegor, pp. 391–417. Norwood, NJ: Ablex; and Maurer, D. 1983. The scanning of compound figures by young infants. *Journal of Experimental Child Psychology* 35: 437–448.

43. See, for example, Bushnell, I.W.R., Gerry, G., and Burt, K. 1983. The externality effect in neonates. *Infant Behavior and Development* 6: 151–156.

44. Maurer, D., and Barrera, M. 1981. Infants' perception of natural and distorted arrangements of a schematic face. *Child Development* 52: 196–202.

45. Unlike newborns, one-month-olds can discern changes in the internal elements of a figure, but only when those elements are oscillating or flashing inside a static frame or are salient and of high contrast. In contrast, three- to four-month-olds can do so even when the internal elements are stationary and not especially salient. E. S. Klitsch and D. S. Woodruff (1985. Compound pattern perception in early infancy. *Child Study Journal* 15: 1–12) reported this ability in infants at all ages between one and four months, but they studied very few babies at each age and did not test whether babies at every age showed the discriminations. For a review of much of this literature, see Maurer, D. 1985. Infants' perception of facedness. In *Social Perception in Infants,* ed. T. Field and N. Fox, pp. 73–100. Norwood, NJ: Ablex.

46. Maurer, D., and Lewis, T. 1979. A physiological explanation of infants' early visual development. *Canadian Journal of Psychology* 33: 232–252.

47. For a good discussion of this phenomenon and its methodological implications, see Jacobs, G. H. 1981. *Comparative Color Vision.* New York: Academic Press.

48. For a good discussion of this problem and the strengths and weaknesses of various ways of overcoming it, see Teller, D. Y., and Bornstein, M. 1987. Infant color vision and color perception. In *Handbook of Infant Perception,* vol. 1, ed. Salapatek and Cohen [5], pp. 185–232.

49. Moscowitz-Cook, A. 1979. The development of photopic spectral sensitivity in human infants. *Vision Research* 19: 1133–1142.

50. Werner, J. 1982. Development of scotopic sensitivity and the absorption spectrum of the human ocular media. *Journal of the Optical Society of America* 72: 247–258.

51. The results for yellow, red, green, and blue are from a collaborative study with Russell Adams and are reported in Adams, R. J., Maurer, D., and Cashin, H. 1985. Effect of

stimulus' size on newborns' detection of hue. *Investigative Ophthalmology and Visual Science* 26 (supple.): 136 [Abstract]; and Adams, R. J., Maurer, D., and Davis, M. 1986. Newborns' discrimination of chromatic from achromatic stimuli. *Journal of Experimental Child Psychology* 41: 267–281. The results for chartreuse are reported in Adams, R. 1987. Evidence for a deficiency in human newborns' B/Y opponent channel. *Investigative Ophthalmology and Visual Science* 28 (supple.): 216 [Abstract]. The results for orange, turquoise, and purple were obtained by Adams by the same method and are as yet unpublished.

52. Adams, R. J. 1986. Chromatic discrimination in the human newborn. Paper presented at the International Conference on Infant Studies, April, in Los Angeles.

53. In the most typical forms of adult color-blindness—protanopia and deuteranopia—the adult can distinguish virtually all colors from gray, but sees the world exclusively in shades of yellow and blue. So the fact that the newborn distinguishes some colors from gray does not mean that he necessarily sees any of them as a normal adult does. For an introduction to color blindness, see Hurvich, *Color Vision* [6].

54. The data for blue are reported in D. Maurer and R. J. Adams, 1987. Emergence of the ability to discriminate a blue from grey at one month of age. *Journal of Experimental Child Psychology* 44: 147–156. The other data are from unpublished studies by Maurer and by Adams.

55. Teller and Bornstein, Infant color vision and color perception [48].

56. Reviewed in Bornstein, M. H. 1985. Infant into adult: Unity to diversity in the development of visual categorization. In *Neonate Cognition: Beyond the Blooming Buzzing Confusion,* ed. J. Mehler and R. Fox, pp. 115–138. Hillsdale, NJ: Lawrence Erlbaum.

57. Ibid.

58. Granrud, C. E. 1986. Binocular vision and spatial perception in 4- and 5-month-old infants. *Journal of Experimental Psychology: Human Perception and Performance* 12: 36–49.

59. Newborns may be able to discriminate between faces that they can both see and smell (Field, T., Cohen, D., Garcia, R., and Greenberg, R. 1984. Mother-stranger discrimination by the newborn. *Infant Behavior and Development* 7: 19–26). But when babies can only see the faces, even one-month-olds do not differentiate them if they match in brightness (D. Maurer, unpublished observations; and Melhuish, E. C. 1982. Visual attention to mother's and stranger's faces and facial contrast in 1-month-old infants. *Developmental Psychology* 18: 229–231).

60. Cohen, L. B., and Younger, B. A. 1984. Infant perception of angular relations. *Infant Behavior and Development* 7: 37–47.

61. For a good introduction to Fourier analysis and its application to infants' vision, see Banks, M. S., and Salapatek, P. 1981. Infant pattern vision: A new approach based on the contrast sensitivity function. *Journal of Experimental Child Psychology* 31: 1–45.

62. Banks, M. S., and Ginsburg, A. P. 1985. Infant visual preferences: A review and new theoretical treatment. *Advances in Child Development and Behavior,* vol. 19, ed. H. W. R. Reese, pp. 207–245. New York: Academic Press.

63. Although authors disagree on what limits newborns' vision, all agree that by two or three months of age, the visual cortex is controlling what they see. In addition to Maurer and Lewis (A physiological explanation of infants' early visual development [46]), see Braddick, O., and Atkinson, J. In press. Sensory selectivity, attentional control, and cross-channel integration in early visual development. In *Minnesota Symposia on Child Psychology,* vol. 1., ed. A. Yonas. Hillsdale, NJ: Lawrence Erlbaum; and Bronson, G. 1972. The postnatal growth of visual capacity. *Child Development* 45: 873–890.

64. Some of these studies are reviewed in P. C. Dodwell, G. K. Humphrey, and D. W. Muir (1987. Shape and pattern perception. In *Handbook of Infant Perception,* vol. 2, *From Perception to Cognition,* ed. Salapatek and Cohen [5], pp. 1–66).

65. Reviewed in Maurer, Infants' perception of facedness [45].

66. Dannemiller, J., and Stephens, B. In press. A critical test of infant pattern preference models. *Child Development.*

67. Reviewed in Zucker, K. J. 1985. The infant's construction of his parents in the first six months of life. In *Social Perception in Infants,* ed. Field and Fox [45], pp. 127–156.

68. Reviewed in Nelson, C. 1985. The perception and recognition of facial expression in infancy. In *Social Perception in Infants,* ed. Field and Fox [45], pp. 101–125.

69. Bertenthal, B. I., Campos, J. J., and Haith, M. M. 1980. Development of visual organization: The perception of subjective contours. *Child Development* 51: 1072–1080.

70. Aslin, R. N. 1987. Motor aspects of visual development in infancy. In *Handbook of Infant Perception*, vol. 1, ed. Salapatek and Cohen [5], pp. 43–107.

71. Reviewed in von Noorden, G. K. 1985. Amblyopia: A multi-disciplinary approach. *Investigative Ophthalmology and Visual Science* 26: 1704–1716.

72. Aslin, R. N. 1981. Experiential influences and sensitive periods in perceptual development: A unified model. In *Development of Perception*, vol. 2, *The Visual System*, ed. R. N. Aslin, J. R. Alberts, and M. R. Petersen, pp. 45–93. New York: Academic Press.

73. von Noorden, Amblyopia [71].

74. Reviewed in Maurer, D., Lewis, T. L., and Brent, H. P. In press. The effects of deprivation on human visual development: Studies of children treated for cataracts. In *Applied Developmental Psychology*, vol. 3, ed. F. J. Morrison, C. E. Lord, and D. P. Keating. New York: Academic Press.

Chapter 7

1. Gardner, M. 1968. Historical background of the Haas and/or precedence effect. *Journal of the Acoustical Society of America* 43: 1243–1248; and Whitfield, J. 1982. Coding in the auditory cortex. In *Contributions to Sensory Physiology*, vol. 6, ed. W. D. Neff, pp. 159–178. New York: Academic Press.

2. J. Conel (1939. *The Postnatal Development of the Human Cerebral Cortex*, vol. 1, *The Cortex of the Newborn*. Cambridge, MA: Harvard University Press) describes the auditory cortex of the newborn as less mature anatomically than the visual cortex, yet H. T. Chugani and M. E. Phelps (1986. Maturational changes in cerebral function in infants determined by [18]FDG positron emission tomography. *Science* 231: 840–843) found that the auditory cortex is more active after the baby is stimulated than is the visual cortex. Like our later discussion of speech and music, this suggests that in some ways the auditory cortex is precocious despite its immature anatomy.

3. The original observations are described in R. Clifton, B. Morrongiello, J. Kulig, and J. Dowd (1981. Newborns' orientation toward sound: Possible implications for cortical development. *Child Development* 52: 833–838). Clifton's later chapter discusses subsequent work and its implications: Clifton, R. 1985. The precedence effect: Its implications for developmental questions. In *Auditory Development in Infancy*, ed. S. Trehub and B. Schneider, pp. 85–99. New York: Plenum.

4. Clifton, R., Morrongiello, B., Kulig, J., and Dowd, J. 1981. Developmental changes in auditory localization in infancy. In *Development of Perception. Psychobiological Perspectives*, vol. 1, *Audition, Somatic Perception, and the Chemical Senses*, ed. R. Aslin, J. Alberts, and M. Petersen, pp. 141–160. New York: Academic Press.

5. A subsequent study confirmed these findings with both shorter and longer delays between the first and second sounds: Morrongiello, B., Clifton, R., and Kulig, J. 1982. Newborn cardiac and behavioral orienting responses to sound under varying precedence-effect conditions. *Infant Behavior and Development* 5: 249–259.

6. Muir, D. 1982. The development of human auditory localization in infancy. In *Localization of Sound: Theory and Applications*, ed. R. W. Gatehouse, pp. 220–243. Groton, CN: Amphora Press.

7. Clarkson, M. G., Morrongiello, B. A., and Clifton, R. K. 1982. Stimulus-presentation probability influences newborns' head orientation to sound. *Perceptual and Motor Skills* 55: 1239–1246.

8. For a more detailed introduction to sound, see Benade, A. 1976. *Fundamentals of Musical Acoustics*. New York: Oxford University Press.

9. For a comprehensive review, see Mills, W. 1972. Auditory localization. In *Foundations of Modern Auditory Theory*, vol. 2, ed. J. V. Tobias, pp. 301–345. New York: Academic Press.

10. Morrongiello, B., and Clifton, R. 1984. Effects of sound frequency on behavioral and cardiac orienting in newborn and five-month-old infants. *Journal of Experimental Child Psychology* 38: 429–446.

11. At first blush R. Bundy's work (1980. Discrimination of sound localization cues in young infants. *Child Development* 51: 292–294) appears to contradict this, since his eight-week-olds seemed not to distinguish when the louder version of a sound came into the left ear from when it came into the right. However, although Bundy's method involved boring the babies with the louder sound coming from one side, then switching sides to see if they perked up—yet according to his own published data, the eight-week-olds never got bored. In addition, we would not expect eight-week-olds to locate sounds; for at eight weeks, but not at birth, the cortex is inhibiting the midbrain's processing of directionality (see note 12 this chapter).

12. Reviewed in Muir, D. W. 1985. The development of infants' auditory spatial sensitivity. In *Auditory Development in Infancy,* ed. Trehub and Schneider [3], pp. 51–83.

13. Clifton, R., Morrongiello, B., and Dowd, J. 1984. A developmental look at an auditory illusion: The precedence effect. *Developmental Psychobiology* 17: 519–536.

14. Morrongiello, B., and Rocca, P. 1986. Infants' localization of sounds in the horizontal plane. Paper presented at the International Conference on Infant Studies, April, in Los Angeles; and Muir, D., and Clifton, R. K. 1985. Infants' orientation to the location of sound sources. In *Measurement of Audition and Vision during the First Year of Postnatal Life: A Methodological Overview,* ed. G. Gottlieb and N. Krasnegor, pp. 167–194. Norwood, NJ: Ablex.

15. Morrongiello and Clifton, Effects of sound frequency on behavioral and cardiac orienting [10].

16. For a more detailed discussion with helpful illustrations, see Aslin, R. N., Pisoni, D. B., and Jusczyk, P. W. 1983. Auditory development and speech perception in infancy. In *Handbook of Child Psychology,* vol. 2, *Infancy and Developmental Psychobiology,* ed. M. H. Haith and J. J. Campos, pp. 573–687. New York: Wiley.

17. Van Bergeik, W., Pierce, J., and David, E. 1961. *Waves and the Ear,* pp. 124–125. London: Heineman..

18. Vernix is described in M. McLellan and C. Webb (1961. Ear studies in the newborn infant II. *Journal of Pediatrics* 58: 523–527). A good review of the other anatomical properties is contained in Aslin, Pisoni, and Jusczyk (Auditory development and speech perception [16]). Benade (*Fundamentals of Musical Acoustics* [8]) discusses the effects of damping on different frequencies.

19. Hecox, K. 1975. Electrophysiological correlates of human auditory development. In *Infant Perception: From Sensation to Cognition,* vol. 2, *Perception of Space, Speech, and Sounds,* ed. L. Cohen and P. Salapatek, pp. 152–192. New York: Academic Press. For a comprehensive review of other studies, see Aslin, Pisoni, and Jusczyk (Auditory development and speech perception [16]); but see also note 21 this chapter.

20. The difference between the quietest clicks that evoked responses in newborns and in adults was 17 dB. Adults hear a 17 dB difference between two tones as approximately a fourfold difference in loudness. Although Hecox's repeated clicks were not tones, from the discussion by S. Stevens and H. Davis (1938. *Hearing: Its Psychology and Physiology,* pp. 154–159, New York: Wiley), we expect this estimate would also apply, at least as a first approximation.

Hecox showed elsewhere that in newborns, frequencies below 500 Hz do not evoke responses of the sort he measured. Given this, if newborns were relatively more sensitive to low frequencies than adults, their overall hearing might be better than Hecox's results indicate. But this is unlikely since studies using other measures and/or testing lower-frequency sounds have not found that newborns can hear any better than Hecox found. Any error is more likely to be in the other direction, because Hecox compared responses of the brain stem, yet for comparable hearing the newborn's immature cortex could require stronger signals from the brain stem than the adult's cortex. If the newborn's cortex does require stronger signals, then newborns would hear less well than Hecox's figure indicates.

21. Note that in their review of this work, B. Schneider, S. Trehub, and D. Bull (1979. The development of basic auditory processes in infants. *Canadian Journal of Psychology* 33: 306–319) summarize it as we do but reach a contrary conclusion: that newborns hear highs

better than lows. They base this on work of their own which showed that a high-frequency sound can be quieter (to an adult) than a low-frequency sound yet still cause a baby to turn toward it. We think their results are different because (1) they tested babies from six to twenty-four months old, babies in whom the ear probably no longer damps high frequencies; and (2) they required babies not only to hear the sound but to locate and turn toward it, although Morrongiello and Clifton (Effects of sound frequency on behavioral and cardiac orienting [10]) showed that five-month-olds turn more often toward high- than low-frequency sounds even when they hear both. K. M. Berg and M. C. Smith (1983. Behavioral thresholds for tones during infancy. *Journal of Experimental Child Psychology* 35: 409–425) found that, as expected, when six-month-olds are required to indicate only *when* they hear a sound, not to turn toward *where* it came from, they are slightly less adult in their sensitivity to high frequencies than in their sensitivity to lower frequencies. That is also the pattern in the evoked responses recorded from the auditory brainstem (Teas, D. C., Klein, A. J., and Kramer, S. J. 1982. An analysis of auditory brainstem responses in infants. *Hearing Research* 7: 19–54).

22. For a more detailed discussion of hearing the missing fundamental, see Benade, *Fundamentals of Musical Acoustics* [8].

23. I. C. Whitfield (1980. Auditory cortex and the pitch of complex tones. *Journal of the Acoustical Society of America* 67: 644–647) discusses the role of the auditory cortex in mediating this ability in the cat.

24. Bundy, R., Colombo, J., and Singer, J. 1982. Pitch perception in young infants. *Developmental Psychology* 18: 10–14.

25. Clarkson, M., and Clifton, R. K. 1985. Infant pitch perception: Evidence for responding to pitch categories and the missing fundamental. *Journal of the Acoustical Society of America* 77: 1521–1528.

26. In addition to Schneider, Trehub, and Bull (The development of basic auditory processes in infants [21]) and Berg and Smith (Behavioral thresholds for tones during infancy [21]), see J. Sinnott, D. Pisoni, and R. Aslin (1983. A comparison of pure tone auditory thresholds in human infants and adults. *Infant Behavior and Development* 6: 3–17). (But see also note 21 this chapter on the difficulty of interpreting tests based on auditory localization.)

27. Schneider, B. A. 1986. The development of basic auditory abilities. Paper presented at the International Conference on Infant Studies, April, in Los Angeles.

28. This precocity is suggested by the high level of activity in the auditory cortex after the baby is stimulated (see note 2 this chapter), and by the specialization of the two cortical hemispheres (see notes 33 and 34 this chapter).

29. Condon, W., and Sander, L. 1974. Synchrony demonstrated between movements of the neonate and adult speech. *Child Development* 45: 456–462. A. Austin and J. C. Perry (1983. Analysis of adult-neonate synchrony during speech and nonspeech. *Perceptual and Motor Skills* 57: 455–459) later reported similar observations.

30. Kato, T., et al. 1983. A computer analysis of infant movements synchronized with adult speech. *Pediatric Research* 17: 625–628. In slightly older babies, J. M. Dowd and E. Z. Tronick (1986. Temporal coordination of arm movements in early infancy: Do infants move in synchrony with adult speech? *Child Development* 57: 762–776) were unable to find a relationship between fast movements of a baby's wrist and changes in the vowels he was hearing. However, they might have found a relationship had they, like the other researchers, included in their analyses all of the baby's movements and all of the speech that the baby was hearing. It is also likely that as the baby becomes less synesthetic (see chapter 4), energy from speech and movement become less likely to intermix.

31. Reviewed in Segalowitz, S. 1983. *Language Functions and Brain Organization*. New York: Academic Press.

32. Reviewed in Dennis, M., and Whitaker, H. A. 1977. Hemispheric equipotentiality and language acquisition. In *Language Development and Neurological Theory*, ed. S. J. Segalowitz and F. A. Gruber, pp. 93–106. New York: Academic Press.

33. See, for example, Witelson, S. F. 1983. The bumps on the brain: Right-left asymmetry in brain anatomy and function. In *Language Functions and Brain Organization*, ed. S. J. Segalowitz, pp. 117–144. New York: Academic Press.

34. This work is reviewed in D. W. Shucard, J. L. Shucard, and D. G. Thomas (1984. The development of cerebral specialization in infants. In *Continuities and Discontinuities in Development*,

ed. R. Emde and R. Harmon, pp. 293–314. New York: Plenum) and in A. W. Young (1982. Asymmetry of cerebral hemispheric function during development. In *Brain and Behavioural Development,* ed. J. W. T. Dickerson and H. McGurk, pp. 168–202. Glasgow: Surrey University Press). In some studies specialization has not been apparent in babies two to three months old (see Best, C. T., Hoffman, H., and Glanville, B. B. 1982. Development of infant ear asymmetries for speech and music. *Perception and Psychophysics* 31: 75–85; Shucard, J. L., Shucard, D. W., Cummins, K. R., and Campos, J. J. 1981. Auditory evoked potentials and sex related differences in brain development. *Brain and Language* 13: 91–102; and Vargha-Khadem, F., and Corballis, M. C. 1979. Cerebral asymmetry in infants. *Brain and Language* 8: 1–9). The different results could be caused by methodological differences between studies, by individual differences among babies in the degree of specialization, or by a disruption of cortical processing at two to three months of age like that which explains the deterioration of auditory localization at this age (see note 12 this chapter). See also Mehler, J. 1985. Language related dispositions in early infancy. In *Neonate Cognition: Beyond the Blooming Buzzing Confusion,* ed. J. Mehler and R. Fox, pp. 7–28. Hillsdale, NJ: Lawrence Erlbaum.

35. MacKain, K., Studdert-Kennedy, M., Spieker, S., and Stern, D. 1983. Infant intermodal speech perception is a left-hemisphere function. *Science* 219: 1347–1349.

36. Aslin, Pisoni, and Jusczyk (Auditory development and speech perception) provide a good introduction with helpful illustrations [16].

37. Eimas, P., Siqueland, E., Jusczyk, P., and Vigorito, J. 1971. Speech perception in infants. *Science* 171: 303–306.

38. J. Conel (1941. *The Postnatal Development of the Human Cerebral Cortex,* vol. 2, *The Cortex of the One-month Infant.* Cambridge, MA: Harvard University Press) summarizes the anatomical evidence. There are also a number of demonstrations that newborns can distinguish between other phonemes, for example, *a* from *i, ba* from *ga,* and *da* from *ba.* See, for example, Molfese, D., and Molfese, V. 1985. Electrophysiological indices of auditory discrimination in newborn infants: The bases for predicting later language development? *Infant Behavior and Development* 8: 197–211.

39. Mehler, J. 1978. La perception du langage chez la nourrison. *La Recherche* 9: 324–330.

40. Streeter, L. 1976. Language perception of two-month-old infants shows effects of both innate mechanisms and experience. *Nature* 259: 39–41.

41. In addition to ibid., see Kuhl, P., and Miller, J. 1975. Speech perception by the chinchilla: Voiced-voiceless distinction in alveolar plosive consonants. *Science* 190: 6972; and Kuhl, P. K., and Padden, D. M. 1982. Enhanced discriminability at the phonetic boundaries for the voicing feature in macaques. *Perception and Psychophysics* 32: 542–550.

42. Early studies suggested one exception: babies learning English appeared to have difficulty hearing the difference between fricatives like *fa* and *tha* or *sa* and *za* (for example, Eilers, R., Wilson, W., and Moore, J. 1977. Developmental changes in speech discrimination in infants. *Journal of Speech and Hearing Research* 20: 766–780). But more recent studies (summarized in Jusczyk, P. 1981. Infant speech perception: A critical appraisal. In *Perspectives on the Study of Speech,* ed. P. D. Eimas and J. L. Miller, pp. 113–164. Hillsdale, NJ: Lawrence Erlbaum) have shown that they can hear such distinctions. For a comprehensive (albeit opinionated) review of babies' ability to distinguish speech sounds, see Eimas, P. D., Miller, J. L., and Jusczyk, P. M. 1987. On infant speech perception and the acquisition of language. In *Categorical Perception,* ed. S. Harnad, pp. 161–195. New York: Cambridge University Press.

43. Werker, J. 1986. The development of cross-language speech perception. Paper presented at the meeting of the Acoustical Society of America, May, in Cleveland, Ohio.

44. The anecdote is a personal communication; the data are reported in Trehub, S. 1976. The discrimination of foreign speech contrasts by infants and adults. *Child Development* 47: 466–472.

45. Colombo, J. 1985. Spectral complexity and infant attention. *Journal of Genetic Psychology* 146: 519–526.

46. Aslin, Pisoni, and Jusczyk (Auditory development and speech perception [16]) provide a good review. Note that newborns and even seven- to nine-month-olds react when the intensity of a sound is turned up, but show no evidence of noticing when its intensity is turned down (Kisilevsky, B. 1986. Habituation and dishabituation of the startle reflex to auditory stimulation as a function of intensity in newborn infants. Paper presented at the

International Conference on Infant Studies, April, in Los Angeles; and Sinnott, J., and Aslin, R. 1985. Frequency and intensity discrimination in human infants and adults. *Journal of the Acoustical Society of America* 78: 1986–1992). Thus they might notice when mom raises her voice or stresses a word, but not when she lowers her voice.

47. Stubbs, E. 1934. The effects of the factors of duration, intensity, and pitch of sound stimuli on the responses of newborn infants. *University of Iowa Studies on Child Welfare* 9 (4): 75–135.

48. Studies on this topic contain a hidden pitfall: as the frequency of a tone changes, adults hear not only a change of pitch, we hear a change of loudness. For example, a 500-Hz tone sounds much louder than a 150-Hz tone of the same physical intensity. When newborns distinguished between "frequencies" in these studies, they may have heard merely differences in loudness, not differences in pitch. See Aslin, Pisoni, and Jusczyk (Auditory development and speech perception in infancy [16]) for a review. See also Bench, J. 1969. Some effects of audio-frequency stimulation on the crying baby. *Journal of Auditory Research* 9: 122–128.

49. Hutt, S., et al. 1968. Auditory responsivity in the human neonate. *Nature* 218: 888–890.

50. Reviewed in Trehub, S. E. 1985. Auditory pattern perception in infancy. In *Auditory Development in Infancy*, ed. Trehub and Schneider [3], pp. 183–195.

51. Kessen, W., Levine, J., and Wendrick, K. 1979. The imitation of pitch in infants. *Infant Behavior and Development* 2: 93–99.

52. Culp, R., and Boyd, E. 1975. Visual fixation and the effect of voice quality and content differences in two-month-old infants. In Visual attention, auditory stimulation and language discrimination in young infants, ed. F. Horowitz, *Monographs of the Society for Research in Child Development* 39 (5-6, series 158): 78–91; and Morse, P. A. 1972. The discrimination of speech and nonspeech stimuli in early infancy. *Journal of Experimental Child Psychology* 14: 477–492.

53. DeCasper, A., and Fifer, W. 1980. Of human bonding: Newborns prefer their mothers' voices. *Science* 208: 1174–1176.

54. DeCasper, A., and Prescott, P. 1984. Human newborns' perception of male voices: Preference, discrimination, and reinforcing value. *Developmental Psychobiology* 17: 481–491.

55. Simner, M. 1971. Newborn's response to the cry of another infant. *Developmental Psychology* 5: 136–150.

56. Although most studies have found that newborns react differently to their own cry, the cry of another newborn, other cries, and normal hospital noise, some studies have not found that babies cry most when they hear their own cry. The different results may have been caused by differences among babies in how much they cry, by differences in how typical were the cries presented, or by different scoring criteria. In any case the results show that at birth newborns differentiate their own cry from a variety of other crylike sounds. See Martin, G. B., and Clark, R. D. 1982. Distress crying in neonates: Species and peer specificity. *Developmental Psychology* 18: 3–9; Riccillo, S. C., and Watterson, T. 1984. The suppression of crying in the human neonate: Response to human vocal tract stimuli. *Brain and Language* 23: 34–42; and Sagi, A., and Hoffman, M. L. 1976. Empathic distress in the newborn. *Developmental Psychology* 12: 175–176.

57. Cullen, J., Fargo, N., Chase, R., and Baker, P. 1968. The development of auditory feedback monitoring: I. Delayed auditory feedback studies on infant cry. *Journal of Speech and Hearing Research* 11: 85–93.

58. Werker, The development of cross-language speech perception [43].

59. Reviewed in Papoušek, M., Papoušek, H., and Bornstein, M. H. 1985. The naturalistic vocal environment of young infants: On the significance of homogeneity and variability in parental speech. In *Social Perception in Infants*, ed. T. M. Field and N. Fox, pp. 269–297. Norwood, NJ: Ablex.

60. Fernald, A. 1985. Four-month-old infants prefer to listen to motherese. *Infant Behavior and Development* 8: 181–196.

61. Karzon, R. G. 1985. Discrimination of polysyllabic sequences in one to four month old infants. *Journal of Experimental Child Psychology* 39: 326–342. Another reason may be that the slower speech keeps later sounds from masking the trace of earlier sounds (Cowan, N., Suomi, K., and Morse, P. A. 1982. Echoic storage in infant perception. *Child Development* 53: 984–990).

Chapter 8

1. McGraw, M. B. 1939. Swimming behavior in the human infant. *Journal of Pediatrics* 15: 485–490; and Zelazo, P. 1983. The development of walking: New findings and old assumptions. *Journal of Motor Behavior* 15: 99–137.

2. Mackintosh, N. J. 1974. *The Psychology of Animal Learning.* London: Academic Press.

3. Papoušek, H. 1967. Experimental studies of appetitional behavior in human newborns and infants. In *Early Behavior: Comparative and Developmental Approaches,* ed. H. W. Stevenson, E. H. Hess, and H. L. Rheingold, pp. 249–278. New York: Wiley. This experiment does not fit the academic prescription for classical conditioning, because the babies were rewarded for making the appropriate response. Yet it illustrates clearly the difficulty in teaching newborns that a signal predicts what will happen next. E. Blass, J. Ganchrow, and J. Steiner (1984. Classical conditioning in newborn humans 2–48 hours of age. *Infant Behavior and Development* 7: 223–236) did succeed in teaching newborns an association between stroking of the forehead and sweetened water. However, the newborns learned this association only when the stroking *always* occurred *immediately* before the water. With any of the variation or delay that occurs outside the laboratory, learning did not occur.

4. Lipsitt, L. P. 1963. Learning in the first year of life. In *Advances in Child Development and Behavior,* vol. 1, ed. L. P. Lipsitt and C. C. Spiker, pp. 147–195. New York: Academic Press.

5. von Hofsten, C. 1982. Eye-hand coordination in the newborn. *Developmental Psychology* 18: 450–461.

6. Peiper, A. 1963. *Cerebral Function in Infancy and Childhood.* New York: Consultants Bureau.

7. For an introduction to these systems, see a textbook of kinesiology, or Benson, A. J. 1982. The vestibular sensory system. In *The Senses,* ed. H. B. Barlow and J. D. Mollon, pp. 333–368. Cambridge: Cambridge University Press; Iggo, A. 1982. Cutaneous sensory mechanisms. In *The Senses,* ed. Barlow and Mollon, pp. 369–408; McCloskey, D. I. 1980. Knowledge about muscular contractions. *Trends in Neurosciences* 3: 311–314; and Vierck, C. 1978. Somatosensory system. In *Handbook of Behavioral Neurobiology,* vol. 1, ed. R. Masterton, pp. 249–307. New York: Plenum.

8. Reviewed in Iggo, Cutaneous sensory mechanisms [7].

9. Holbrook, K. A. 1982. A histological comparison of infant and adult skin. In *Neonatal Skin: Structure and Function,* ed. H. Maibach and E. K. Boisits, pp. 3–31. New York: Marcel Dekker.

10. Cauna, N. 1965. The effects of aging on the receptor organs of the human dermis. In *Advances in the Biology of the Skin,* vol. 6, *Aging,* ed. W. Montagna, pp. 63–95. New York: Pergamon.

11. The greater maturity of the somatosensory cortex is indicated by anatomical studies (Conel, J. 1939. *The Postnatal Development of the Human Cerebral Cortex,* vol. 1, *The Cortex of the Newborn.* Cambridge, MA: Harvard University Press), by comparison of the cortical responses evoked by stimulation of different senses (Hrbek, A., Karlberg, P., and Olsson, T. 1973. Development of visual and somatosensory evoked potentials in preterm newborn infants. *Electroencephalography and Clinical Neurophysiology* 34: 225–232), and by the amount of glucose utilized by different cortical areas after the young baby is stimulated (Chugani, H. T., and Phelps, M. E. 1986. Maturational changes in cerebral function in infants determined by [18]FDG positron emission tomography. *Science* 231: 840–843). From their study of somatosensorarily evoked responses, J. Desmedt, E. Brunko, and J. Debecker (1976. Maturation of the somatosensory evoked potentials in normal infants and children, with special reference to the early N_1 component. *Electroencephalography and Clinical Neurophysiology* 40: 43–58) concluded that the somatic system is very immature at birth. However, this conclusion was based solely on their calculation that signals are transmitted more slowly in newborns than in adults. Like other researchers, they found that the form of the response recorded from the cortex was already adultlike at birth, in contrast to those evoked by stimulating other senses.

12. Reviewed in Turkewitz, G. 1977. The development of lateral differences in the human infant. In *Lateralization in the Nervous System,* ed. S. Harnad, et al., pp. 251–259. New York: Academic Press.

13. Ellis, R. R., and Ellingson, R. J. 1973. Response to electrical stimulation of the median nerve in the human newborn. *Developmental Psychobiology* 6: 235–244.

14. See Bell, R., and Costello, N. 1964. Three tests for sex differences in tactile sensitivity in the newborn. *Biologia Neonatorum* 7: 335–347; and Lipsitt, L., and Levy, N. 1959. Electrotactual threshold in the neonate. *Child Development* 30: 547–554. However, girls are not more sensitive to poking from a thin straw (Jacklin, C. N., Snow, M. E., and Maccoby, E. E. 1981. Tactile sensitivity and muscle strength in newborn boys and girls. *Infant Behavior and Development* 4: 261–268) and are not always more sensitive to a puff of air against the belly (Yang, R., and Douthitt, T. C. 1974. Newborn responses to threshold tactile stimulation. *Child Development* 45: 237–242). These studies may have obtained different results because individual differences in sensitivity *within* each sex are larger than any difference *between* the sexes, so that a small sample may not be representative of the sex. In addition, Yang and Douthitt excluded about 40 percent of the babies because they did not respond at all to the puff of air, but do not report whether one sex was excluded more often than the other.

15. Note, however, that J. F. Rosenblith and L. A. De Lucia (1963. Tactile sensitivity and muscular strength in the neonate. *Biologia Neonatorium* 5: 266–282) found no difference in the overall score that newborns of each sex received on tests of motor maturity and tactile sensitivity. In addition to Jacklin, Snow, and Maccoby (Tactile sensitivity and muscle strength in newborn boys and girls [14]), see Bell, R., and Darling, J. 1965. The prone head reaction in the human neonate: Relation with sex and tactile sensitivity. *Child Development* 36: 943–949.

16. Wolff, P., et al. 1974. The effect of white noise on the somatosensory evoked responses in sleeping newborn infants. *Electroencephalography and Clinical Neurophysiology* 37: 269–274.

17. For a good introduction, see McCloskey, Knowledge about muscular contractions [7].

18. The maturity of proprioception at birth is also indicated by the adultlike form of evoked responses (for example, Hrbek, A., et al. 1968. Proprioceptive evoked potentials in newborn infants and adults. *Developmental Medicine and Child Neurology* 10: 164–167), by the baby's ability to synchronize his movements with the speech he hears (see chapter 7), and by the ease with which proprioceptive reflexes can be elicited (for example, Lenard, H., von Bernuth, H., and Prechtl, H. 1968. Reflexes and their relationship to behavioural state in the newborn. *Acta Paediatrica Scandinavica* 57: 177–185). G. Butterworth (1986. Hand to mouth activity in the newborn baby: Evidence for innate intentionality? Paper presented at the International Conference on Infant Studies, April, in Los Angeles) describes newborns' attempts to get their hands to their mouths.

19. For a detailed introduction see Benson, The vestibular sensory system [7].

20. Balashavo, E. 1963. Development of the vestibular apparatus. In *The Development of the Brain and Its Disturbance by Harmful Factors,* ed. B. Klosovskii, pp. 106–121. New York: Macmillan.

21. Lawrence, M., and Feind, C. 1953. Vestibular responses to rotation in the newborn infant. *Pediatrics* 12: 300–305.

22. Ornitz, E. 1983. Normal and pathological maturation of vestibular function in the human child. In *Development of Auditory and Vestibular Systems,* ed. R. Romand, pp. 479–536. New York: Academic Press.

23. Hainline, L., Lemerise, E., Abramov, I., and Turkel, J. 1984. Orientational asymmetries in small-field optokinetic nystagmus in human infants. *Behavioural Brain Research* 13: 217–230.

24. Jouen, F. 1982. Le rôle des informations visuelles dans l'élaboration du comportement postural anti-gravitaire chez le nourrisson. *Cahiers de Psychologie Cognitive* 7: 341–356; Jouen, F. 1983. Les réactions au mouvement visuel chez le nourrisson. *Enfance,* 1–2: 129–137; and Jouen, F. 1984. Visual-vestibular interactions in infancy. *Infant Behavior and Development* 7: 135–145.

25. Wenzel, D. 1978. The development of the parachute reaction: A visuo-vestibular response. *Neuropädiatrie* 9: 351–359.

26. Described in Bertenthal, B. I., Campos, J. J., and Barrett, K. C. 1984. Self-produced locomotion: An organizer of emotional, cognitive, and social development in infancy. In *Continuities and Discontinuities in Development,* ed. R. N. Emde and R. J. Harmon, pp. 175–210. New York: Plenum.

27. Campos, J. 1986. Contemporary issues in the study of infant emotion. Paper presented at the International Conference on Infant Studies, April, in Los Angeles.

28. Reviewed in Campos, J. J., Svejda, M. J., Campos, R. G., and Bertenthal, B. 1982. The emergence of self-produced locomotion: Its importance for psychological development in infancy. In *Intervention with At-risk and Handicapped Infants,* ed. D. Brinker, pp. 195–216. Baltimore, MD: University Park Press.

29. A comparison of the work of Campos, Svejda, Campos, and Bertenthal (The emergence of self-produced locomotion [28]) and of N. Rader, M. Bausano, and J. Richards (1980. On the nature of the visual-cliff avoidance response in human infants. *Child Development* 51: 61–68) suggests that a baby's locomotory experience affects his reaction to the visual cliff for only a short time after he learns to crawl. When Rader and her colleagues tested a group of infants, all of whom had had experience with a "walker" and most of whom had been crawling for some months, they found no effect of how long each baby had been crawling.

30. Bertenthal, Campos, and Barrett (Self-produced locomotion [26]) describe an experimental version of this procedure.

31. The benefits of salient landmarks and of letting the baby move himself are described in L. Acredolo and D. Evans (1980. Developmental changes in the effects of landmarks on infants' spatial behavior. *Developmental Psychology* 16: 312–318) and in J. B. Benson (1984. A longitudinal study of the role of self-initiated movement in spatial knowledge. Paper presented at the International Conference on Infant Studies, April, in New York), respectively. In fact, in the absence of distinctive landmarks, babies perform no better after eight weeks of crawling than after just two weeks of crawling (McComas, J., and Field, J. 1984. Does early crawling experience affect infants' emerging spatial orientation abilities? *New Zealand Journal of Psychology* 13: 63–68). Extensive experience with locomotion also helps to eliminate the baby's bias to look for an object where he found it before, rather than where he just saw it hidden (Horobin, K., and Acredelo, L. 1986. The role of attentiveness, mobility history, and separation of hiding sites on Stage IV search behavior. *Journal of Experimental Child Psychology* 41: 114–127).

32. Reviewed in Hunt, J. M. 1979. Psychological development: Early experience. *Annual Review of Psychology* 30: 103–143.

33. Dennis, W. 1960. Causes of retardation among institutional children: Iran. *Journal of Genetic Psychology* 96: 47–59.

34. Reviewed in Schanberg, S. M., and Field, T. M. In press. Maternal deprivation and supplemental stimulation. In *Stress and Coping across Development,* ed. T. Field, P. McCabe, and N. Schneiderman. Hillsdale, NJ: Lawrence Erlbaum.

35. Schanberg, S. M., Evoniuk, G., and Kuhn, C. M. 1984. Tactile and nutritional aspects of maternal care: Specific regulator of neuroendocrine function and cellular development. *Proceedings of the Society for Experimental Biology and Medicine* 175: 135–146.

36. Bril, B., and Sabatier, C. 1986. The cultural context of motor development: Postural manipulations in the daily life of Bambara babies (Mali). *International Journal of Behavioral Development* 9: 439–453; and Hopkins, B. 1976. Culturally determined patterns of handling the human infant. *Journal of Human Movement Studies* 2: 1–27.

37. Kilbride, J. E., Robbins, M. C., and Kilbride, P. L. 1979. The comparative motor development of Baganda, American white and American black infants. *American Anthropologist* 72: 1422–1428.

38. Dixon, S. T., Tronick, E., Keefer, C., and Brazelton, T. B. 1982. Perinatal circumstances and newborn outcome among the Gusii of Kenya: Assessment of risk. *Infant Behavior and Development* 5: 11–32.

39. This conclusion is also supported by the findings that stroking and massaging promote not only the physical growth of premature babies, but also their motor and mental development (see, for example, Rice, R. D. 1977. Neurophysiological development in premature infants following stimulation. *Developmental Psychology* 13: 69–76). Furthermore, the motor development of normal full-term babies is accelerated after they have experienced sixteen half-hour sessions of sudden and rapid spinning (Clark, D. L., Kreutzberg, J. R., and Chee, F.K.W. 1977. Vestibular stimulation influence on motor development in infants. *Science* 196: 1228–1229).

Chapter 9

1. Einstein, A. 1905. Zur Elektrodynamik bewegter Körper. *Annalen der Physik* 17: 891–921.

2. For an interesting elaboration on the roles of space and time in relativity written near the end of his life, see Einstein, A. 1954. *Relativity: The Special and the General Theory*, 15th ed., Appendix 5, Relativity and the problem of space, trans. R. Lawson. London: Methuen.

3. Weast, R., Astle, M., and Beyer, W., eds. 1984. *Handbook of Chemistry and Physics*, 65th ed., pp. F-92 and F-100. Boca Raton, FL: CRC Press.

4. As would be expected, the baby is more likely to fall asleep, the more energy floods into his system—that is, the more quickly the rocking occurs or the greater distance it covers (see, for example, Pederson, D. R., and Ter Vrugt, D. 1973. The influence of amplitude and frequency of vestibular stimulation on the activity of two-month-old infants. *Child Development* 44: 122–128) and if it is continuous rather than intermittent (see Byrne, J. M., and Horowitz, F. D. 1981. Rocking as a soothing intervention: The influence of direction and type of movement. *Infant Behavior and Development* 4: 207–218).

5. Brackbill, Y. 1973. Continuous stimulation reduces arousal level: Stability of the effect over time. *Child Development* 44: 43–46.

6. Maurer, D., and Lewis, T. 1979. A physiological explanation of infants' early visual development. *Canadian Journal of Psychology* 33: 232–252.

7. Reviewed in Parmelee, A. H., and Sigman, M. D. 1983. Perinatal brain development and behavior. In *Handbook of Child Psychology*, vol. 2, *Infancy and Developmental Psychobiology*, ed. M. H. Haith and J. J. Campos, pp. 95–155. New York: Wiley.

8. Regal, D. M. 1981. Development of critical flicker frequency in human infants. *Vision Research* 21: 549–555.

9. These clocks mark periods in seconds (Parmelee, A. H., Akiyama, Y., Stern, E., and Harris, M. A. 1969. A periodic cerebral rhythm in newborn infants. *Experimental Neurology* 25: 575–584), minutes (Robertson, S. 1985. Cyclic motor activity in the human fetus after midgestation. *Developmental Psychobiology* 18: 411–419), hours (Campbell, K. 1980. Ultradian rhythms in the human fetus during the last 10 weeks of gestation: A review. *Seminars in Perinatology* 4: 301–310), and days (Patrick, J., et al. 1982. Patterns of gross fetal body movements over 24-hour observation intervals during the last 10 weeks of pregnancy. *American Journal of Obstetrics and Gynecology* 142: 363–371).

10. Young babies look longer at closer objects and at moving objects (see chapter 6), especially when the objects are off to the side (de Schonen, S., McKenzie, B., Maury, L., and Bresson, F. 1978. Central and peripheral object distances as determinants of the effective visual field in early infancy. *Perception* 7: 499–506; and Tronick, E. 1972. Stimulus control and the growth of the infant's effective visual field. *Perception and Psychophysics* 11: 373–375). In fact, if an object is far away, they will often look at it *only* if it is moving (McKenzie, B., and Day, R. 1976. Infants' attention to stationary and moving objects at different distances. *Australian Journal of Psychology* 28: 45–51).

11. Bertenthal, B. I., Proffitt, D. R., and Cutting, J. E. 1984. Infant sensitivity to figural coherence in biomechanical motions. *Journal of Experimental Child Psychology* 37: 213–230; Kaufmann-Hayoz, R., Kaufmann, F., and Stucki, M. 1986. Recognition of moving dot paths in infancy. Paper presented at the International Conference on Infant Studies, April, in Los Angeles; Kellman, P., and Spelke, E. 1983. Perception of partly occluded objects in infancy. *Cognitive Psychology* 15: 483–524; Kellman, P. J., Spelke, E. S., and Short, K. R. 1986. Infant perception of object unity from translatory motion in depth and vertical translation. *Child Development* 57: 72–86; and Spelke, E. 1985. Preferential-looking methods as tools for the study of cognition in infancy. In *Measurement of Audition and Vision in the First Year of Postnatal Life: A Methodological Overview*, ed. G. Gottlieb and N. Krasnegor, pp. 323–363. Norwood, NJ: Ablex.

12. McKenzie and Day, Infants' attention to stationary and moving objects [10].

13. He rocks, shakes his head, kicks his legs, waves an arm, flexes a finger, and so on, all with rhythmic repetition. Such stereotyped behaviors are typical during the middle of the first year, but can be seen in the baby's kicking even during the first month of life. They are especially common if the baby is rarely rocked, jiggled, or bounced. See Ornitz, E. 1983. Normal and pathological maturation of vestibular function in the human child. In *Development of Auditory and Vestibular Systems*, ed. R. Roman, pp. 479–536. New York: Academic Press;

Thelen, E. 1981. Rhythmical behavior in infancy: An ethological perspective. *Developmental Psychology* 17: 237–257; and Thelen, E., and Fisher, D. M. 1983. The organization of spontaneous leg movements in newborn infants. *Journal of Motor Behavior* 15: 353–377.

14. Hack, M., Estabrook, M. M., and Robertson, S. S. 1985. Development of sucking rhythm in preterm infants. *Early Human Development* 11: 133–140.

Chapter 10

1. The newborn habituates to repeated sounds (chapters 2 and 7), odors (chapter 5), sweet substances (chapter 2), squares (chapter 6), and a variety of other stimuli including tickling and pinpricks. Much of this research is reviewed in Kessen, W., Haith, M. H., and Salapatek, P. H. 1970. Infancy. In *Carmichael's Manual of Child Psychology*, vol. 1, ed. P. H. Mussen, pp. 287–445. New York: Wiley.

2. Such operant conditioning is reviewed in Sameroff, A. J., and Cavanaugh, P. J. 1979. Learning in infancy: A developmental perspective. In *Handbook of Infant Development*, ed. J. Osofsky, pp. 344–392. New York: Wiley.

3. It takes many weeks for him to learn to recognize his father's voice (see chapter 7) or even to recognize his own name (see Ungerer, J., Brody, L., and Zelazo, P. 1978. Long-term memory for speech in 2- to 4-week-old infants. *Infant Behavior and Development* 1: 127–140). The fragility of memory during early infancy is reviewed in Werner, J. S., and Perlmutter, M. 1979. Development of visual memory in infants. In *Advances in Child Development and Behavior*, vol. 14, ed. H. W. Reese and L. P. Lipsitt, pp. 1–56. New York: Academic Press.

4. See, for example, Sameroff, A. 1968. The components of sucking in the human newborn. *Journal of Experimental Child Psychology* 6: 607–623.

5. For a review, see L. Lipsitt (1970. Developmental psychology. In *Contemporary Scientific Psychology*, ed. A. Gilgen, pp. 147–182. New York: Academic Press). R. Panneton and J. DeCasper (1984. Newborns prefer intrauterine heartbeat sounds to male voices. Paper presented at the International Conference on Infant Studies, April, in New York) seem to contradict this: they used the turning on and off of a tone to signal the availability of two different reinforcers (heartbeat or a man reading a nursery rhyme), and found that babies increased their sucking to hear the heartbeat. However, there is no way to tell from this study whether the babies sucked more because the beating heart induced them to begin sucking, or merely because *after* they had begun, the beating heart reinforced them for sucking.

6. Reviewed in Sameroff and Cavanaugh, Learning in infancy [2].

7. Ungerer, Brody, and Zelazo, Long-term memory for speech in 2- to 4-week-old infants [3].

8. The development of object permanence is described by Jean Piaget (1952. *The Origins of Intelligence*, trans. M. Cook. New York: Norton [Originally published 1936]). A good summary is presented by H. Ginsburg and S. Opper (1979. *Piaget's Theory of Intellectual Development*. Englewood Cliffs, NJ: Prentice-Hall). Although babies' knowledge of object permanence increases with age, how well they perform at any age depends on the task. (See, for example, Baillargeon, R., Spelke, E. S., and Wasserman, S. 1985. Object permanence in five-month-old infants. *Cognition* 20: 191–208.)

9. Dunst, C., Brooks, P., and Doxsey, P. 1982. Characteristics of hiding places and the transition to Stage IV performance in object permanence tasks. *Developmental Psychology* 18: 671–681.

10. The baby's difficulty in understanding interiority is also suggested by G. Pieraut-Le Bonniec's (1985. From visual-motor anticipation to conceptualization: Reaction to solid and hollow objects and knowledge of the function of containment. *Infant Behavior and Development* 8: 413–424; and 1985. Hand-eye coordination and infants' construction of convexity and concavity. *British Journal of Development Psychology* 3: 272–280) observation that not until nine or ten months of age does he adjust his hand appropriately when reaching for convex versus concave objects or appear surprised when he cannot reach into a hollow object.

11. Brody, L. 1981. Visual short-term cued recall memory in infancy. *Child Development* 52: 242–250.

12. This is the typical stage four *"A* not *B"* error, first described by Piaget in *The Origins of Intelligence* [8] and since verified by many other investigators. For a review see Bremner, J. 1982. Object localization in infancy. In *Spatial Abilities: Development and Physiological Foundations,* ed. M. Potegal, pp. 79–106. New York: Academic Press. See also Butterworth, G., Jarrett, N., and Hicks, L. 1982. Spatiotemporal identity in infancy: Perceptual competence or conceptual deficit? *Developmental Psychology* 18: 435–449; Gratch, G., et al. 1975. Piaget's Stage IV object concept error: Evidence of forgetting or object conception? *Child Development* 45: 71–77; and Landers, W. 1971. Effects of differential experience on infants' performance in a Piagetian Stage IV object-concept task. *Developmental Psychology* 5: 48–54.

13. Squire, R. R., and Butters, N., eds. 1984. *Neuropsychology of Memory.* New York: Guilford Press.

14. Graham, F., Leavitt, L., Strock, B., and Brown, J. 1978. Precocious cardiac orienting in a human anencephalic infant. *Science* 199: 322–324.

15. Reviewed in Graham, F., Anthony, B., and Zeigler, B. 1983. The orienting response and developmental processes. In *Orienting and Habituation: Perspectives in Human Research,* ed. D. Siddle, pp. 371–430. Chichester, England: Wiley.

16. The study by A. N. Meltzoff and R. Borton (1979. Intermodal matching by human neonates. *Nature* 282: 403–404) is controversial, both because of its surprising findings and because older babies have sometimes failed to show cross-modal matching (for example, Lewkowicz, D. 1986. Developmental changes in infants' bi-sensory response to synchronous durations. *Infant Behavior and Development* 9: 335–353). However, older babies have never been tested in the same way as newborns: the tests given to older babies may have been more difficult. Moreover, as babies become less synesthetic in the months after birth, we would expect them to have more difficulty recognizing the similarity of information presented to different modalities. Three other studies from independent laboratories have found that very young babies treat information received from different modalities as equivalent: they treat intensity similarly when they listen to sounds and when they look at lights (see chapter 4); they make a similar distinction between a hard, rigid object and a soft, deforming one when they mouth it and when they look at it (Walker-Andrew, A. S., and Gibson, E. G. 1985. What develops in bi-modal perception. In *Advances in Infancy Research,* vol. 4, ed. L. P. Lipsitt and C. Rovee-Collier, pp. 171–181. Norwood, NJ: Ablex); and at least under some circumstances, they look at the one of two films that matches the sound they are hearing (Born, W., Spelke, E., and Prather, P. 1982. Detection of auditory-visual relationships by newborn infants. Paper presented at the International Conference on Infant Studies, March, in Austin).

The nature of the early cross-modal confusion may explain why K. W. Brown and A. W. Gottfried (1985. Cross-modal transfer of shape in early infancy: Is there reliable evidence? In *Advances in Infancy Research,* vol. 4, ed. Lipsitt and Rovee-Collier, pp. 163–170) failed to find any cross-modal effect in one-month-olds. They gave each baby four different pairs of shapes to differentiate: the smooth and knobby pacifier that Meltzoff and Borton used, a cylinder and a solid triangle or cross, and a cylinder with one side cut out and a square. After sucking or manipulating one of these objects, babies looked equally long at it and the other member of the pair. That is not surprising, since the results were collapsed over all four pairs: a baby might see the knobby and smooth pacifier after previous exposure to several other objects, so his reaction would result from the combination of the sensations caused by all of those objects.

17. Vinter, A. 1986. The role of movement in eliciting early imitations. *Child Development* 57: 66–71; and Jacobson, S. W. 1979. Matching behavior in the young infant. *Child Development* 50: 425–430. Neonatal imitation was first reported by A. Meltzoff and M. Moore (reviewed in Meltzoff, A. 1985. The roots of social and cognitive development: Models of man's original nature. In *Social Perception in Infants,* ed. T. Field and N. Fox, pp. 1–30. Norwood, NJ: Ablex), who found that three-week-old infants will apparently imitate someone sticking out his tongue, opening and closing his mouth, pouting, or moving his fingers. They later reported that even newborns will apparently imitate a number of gestures. Meltzoff and Moore's reports are controversial because (1) facial imitation appears to be learned gradually during the second half of the first year (see note 25 this chapter), (2) their first experiment may have been influenced by their biases, and (3) some other investigators have been unable to find the phenomenon (Hayes, L., and Watson, J. 1981. Neonatal imitation: Fact or artifact? *Developmental Psychology* 17: 655–660; Koepke, J., Hamm, M., Legerstee, M., and Russell, M. 1983. Neonatal imitation: two failures to replicate. *Infant Behavior and Development* 6: 97–102; and

McKenzie, B., and Over, R. 1983. Young infants fail to imitate facial and manual gestures. *Infant Behavior and Development* 6: 97–102). However, the careful work of Vinter and of Jacobson make clear that young babies do sometimes *appear* to imitate facial gestures.

18. Piaget (*The Origins of Intelligence* [8]) describes the development of such primary circular reactions.

19. Piaget described this repetition, as have all observers of developing children. H. Papoušek and M. Papoušek (1986. Sharing emotionality and sharing knowledge: A microanalytic approach to parent-infant communication. In *Measuring Emotions in Infants and Children*, vol. 2, ed. C. E. Izard and P. Read, pp. 93–123. Cambridge: Cambridge University Press) describe the joy the baby expresses while he repeats a successful action.

20. Reviewed in Rovee-Collier, C. 1984. The ontogeny of learning and memory in human infants. In *Comparative Perspectives on the Development of Memory*, ed. R. Kail and N. Spear, pp. 103–134. Hillsdale, NJ: Lawrence Erlbaum.

21. Piaget (*The Origins of Intelligence* [8]) called this kind of learning the development of secondary circular reactions. His observations characterize infants' development so well that they have been translated into widely-used scales for assessing a baby's development: Uzgiris, I. C., and Hunt, J. McV. 1975. *Assessment in Infants: Ordinal Scales of Psychological Development.* Urbana, IL: University of Illinois Press.

22. See chapter 8 and: Acredelo, L. 1978. Development of spatial orientation in infancy. *Developmental Psychology* 14: 224–234.

23. Such coordination of secondary circular reactions is described in Piaget's *The Origins of Intelligence* [8] and confirmed by Uzgiris and Hunt, *Assessment in Infants* [21].

24. For the decline of released imitation as the baby becomes less synesthetic, see E. Abravanel and A. D. Sigafoos (1984. Exploring the presence of imitation during early infancy. *Child Development* 55: 381–392) and T. Field, S. Goldstein, N. Vega-Lahr, and K. Porter (1986. Changes in imitative behavior during early infancy. *Infant Behavior and Development* 9: 415–421). J. Piaget (1962. *Play, Dreams, and Imitation,* trans. C. Gattegno and F. M. Hodgson. New York: Norton [Originally published 1945]) described the gradual emergence of true imitation during the second half of the first year. These observations have been confirmed by numerous others, including I. C. Uzgiris (1972. Patterns of vocal and gestural imitation in infants. In *Determinants of Behavioral Development,* ed. F. J. Monks, W. W. Hartup, and J. deWitt, pp. 467–471. New York: Academic Press).

25. In addition to Piaget, *Play, Dreams, and Imitation* [24], see Kaye, K., and Marcus, J. 1981. Infant imitation: The sensory-motor agenda. *Developmental Psychology* 17: 258–265.

26. Sroufe, L., and Waters, E. 1977. Attachment as an organizational construct. *Child Development* 48: 1184–1199.

27. This was originally described by Piaget in *The Origins of Intelligence* [8]. For a review of more recent research, see M. Sexton (1983. The development of the understanding of causality in infancy. *Infant Behavior and Development* 6: 201–210). As with the development of an understanding of objects' permanence, younger babies show rudimentary understanding in a few circumstances (for example, Leslie, A. 1982. The perception of causality in infants. *Perception* 11: 173–186).

28. See Piaget, *The Origins of Intelligence* [8], and chapter 11.

29. Beginning at about eight or nine months, babies anticipate that an object or event will reappear in the same place in a room in relation to conspicuous landmarks, even when they have changed their own location in the room. Unless those landmarks are unusually salient, younger babies expect it to reappear in the same place in relation to their own bodies. Not until about eighteen months of age do babies perform correctly even when there are no landmarks. For a review, see Keating, M. B., McKenzie, B., and Day, R. 1986. Spatial localization in infancy: Position constancy in a square and circular room with and without a landmark. *Child Development* 57: 115–124.

30. This development was described by Piaget, *The Origins of Intelligence* [8], and has been confirmed by many others, including Uzgiris and Hunt, *Assessment in Infants* [21].

31. C. Harding and R. Golinkoff (1979. The origins of intentional vocalizations in prelinguistic infants. *Child Development* 50: 33–40) confirmed a relationship between the first attempts to communicate with speech and the development of understanding that other people exist and can be causal agents. For a more general discussion of the relationship between cognitive

development and the beginnings of language, see Anisfeld, M. 1984. *Language Development from Birth to Three.* Hillsdale, NJ: Lawrence Erlbaum.

32. For a review, see Anisfeld, *Language Development from Birth to Three* [31].

33. McCune-Nicolich, L. 1981. The cognitive bases of relational words in the single word period. *Journal of Child Language* 8: 15–34.

34. In addition to Piaget, *Plays, Dreams, and Imitation* [24], see Kagan, J. 1981. *The Second Year: The Emergence of Self-Awareness.* Cambridge: Harvard University Press.

35. Reviewed in Bloom, L., and Lahey, M. 1978. *Language Development and Language Disorders.* New York: Wiley.

36. Many of these studies are reviewed in Younger, B., and Cohen, L. 1985. How infants form categories. In *The Psychology of Learning and Motivation. Advances in Research and Theory,* vol. 19, ed. G. H. Brown, pp. 211–247. New York: Academic Press.

37. One study (Antell, S., and Keating, D. 1983. Perception of numerical invariance in neonates. *Child Development* 54: 695–701) suggests that this ability may be present at birth, but it did not include sufficient controls to rule out the possibility that the babies attended to area, not number. Studies with appropriate controls indicate that the ability is present by seven to ten months of age, and possibly as early as five months. See Strauss, M. S., and Curtis, L. E. 1984. Development of numerical concepts in infancy. In *The Origins of Cognitive Skills,* ed. C. Sophian, pp. 131–155. Hillsdale, NJ: Lawrence Erlbaum; and van Loosbroek, E., and Smitsman, A. W. 1986. The visual perception of number invariance in infants. Paper presented at the International Conference on Infant Studies, April, in Los Angeles.

38. See, for example, Bayley, N. 1970. Development of mental abilities. In *Carmichael's Manual of Child Psychology,* 3rd ed., ed. P. Mussen, pp. 1163–1209. New York: Wiley.

39. Reviewed in Bornstein, M., and Sigman, M. 1986. Continuity in mental development from infancy. *Child Development* 57: 251–274.

40. M. H. Bornstein (1985. How infant and mother jointly contribute to developing cognitive competence in the child. *Proceedings of the National Academy of Science of the United States of America* 82: 7470–7473) shows that later vocabulary and IQ are predicted best by the combination of the baby's rate of habituation and the extent to which his mother encourages him to pay attention to objects and their properties. For a review of the interaction of the baby's potential with his environment, see Brownell, C., and Strauss, M. 1985. Infant stimulation and development: Conceptual and empirical considerations. *Journal of Children in Contemporary Society* 17: 109–130.

41. Piaget, *The Origins of Intelligence* [8].

42. For a review, see Bornstein and Sigman, Continuity in mental development from infancy [39].

43. Bayley, Development of mental abilities [38]; and Bornstein and Sigman, Continuity in mental development from infancy [39].

Chapter 11

1. Emde, R. N., and Koenig, K. L. 1969. Neonatal smiling and rapid eye movement states. *Journal of the American Academy of Child Psychiatry* 8: 57–67.

2. Emde, R. N., and Koenig, K. L. 1969. Neonatal smiling, frowning, and rapid eye movement states. II. Sleep cycle study. *Journal of the American Academy of Psychiatry* 8: 637–656.

3. Emde, R. N., McCartney, R. D., and Harmon, R. J. 1971. Neonatal smiling in REM states. IV: Premature study. *Child Development* 42: 1657–1661.

4. P. H. Wolff (1963. Observations on the early development of smiling. In *Determinants of Infant Behavior,* vol. 2, ed. B. M. Foss, pp. 113–134. London: Methuen) also observed that these smiles occur in bursts when the baby is not discharging energy in other ways (through mouthing, startles, etc.). For a good review, see chap. 6 of Emde, R. N., Gaensbauer, T. J., and Harmon, R. J. 1976. Emotional expression in infancy. A biobehavioral study. *Psychological Issues* 10 (Monograph 37).

5. Newborn boys may make more limb movements because they are usually heavier and longer at birth (Feldman, J., Brody, N., and Miller, S. 1980. Sex differences in non-elicited neonatal behaviors. *Merrill-Palmer Quarterly* 26: 63–73). When physical size and maturity are controlled, sex differences may disappear (Deganhardt, A. 1982. Die Interpretation von Geshlechtsunterschieden im Spontanverhalten Neugeborener. *Zeitschrift für Entwicklungspsychologie und Pädagogische Psychologie* 14: 161–172). That affects how one conceptualizes the cause of the sex differences, but it does not change the fact that parents of baby girls and of baby boys are usually presented with babies who behave differently.

6. The observations of middle-class white mothers are from E. B. Thoman, P. H. Leiderman, and J. P. Olson (1972. Neonate-mother interaction during breast-feeding. *Developmental Psychology* 6: 110–118); those of lower-class black mothers are from J. Brown and associates (1975. Interactions of black inner-city mothers with their new infants. *Child Development* 46: 677–686). B. Caesar and I. Weber (1979. Geschlectstypische Entwicklungs- und Sozialisationsbedingungen bei Neugeborenen: Ein Literaturüberblick. *Zeitschrift für Entwicklungspsychologie und Pädagogische Psychologie* 4: 275–299) provide a critical review of the many studies showing that adults' behavior toward infants depends on the sex of the baby, with the direction of the effect dependent on culture, parity, social class, and so on.

7. Wolff, Observations on the early development of smiling [4].

8. Emde, R. N., and Harmon, R. J. 1972. Endogenous and exogenous smiling systems in early infancy. *Journal of the American Academy of Child Psychiatry* 11: 177–200.

9. For a good review and theoretical integration, see Sroufe, L. A., and Waters, E. 1976. The ontogenesis of smiling and laughter: A perspective on the organization of development in infancy. *Psychological Review* 83: 173–189.

10. Emde and Harmon, Endogenous and exogenous smiling systems [8]; and Wolff, Observations on the early development of smiling [4].

11. Reviewed in Campos, J. J., et al. 1983. Socioemotional development. In *Handbook of Child Psychology*, vol. 2, *Infancy and Developmental Psychobiology*, ed. M. M. Haith and J. J. Campos, pp. 783–915. New York: Wiley; Cicchetti, D., and Hesse, P. 1983. Affect and intellect: Piaget's contributions to the study of infant emotional development. In *Emotion: Theory, Research, and Experience*, vol. 2, *Emotions in Early Development*, ed. R. Plutchik and H. Kellerman, pp. 115–170. New York: Academic Press; and Sroufe, A. 1979. Socioemotional development. In *Handbook of Infant Development*, ed. J. Osofsky, pp. 462–516. New York: Wiley.

12. The baby's reaction to circumcision is described in M. Gunnar, S. Malone, G. Vance, and R. O. Fisch (1985. Coping with aversive stimulation in the neonatal period: Quiet sleep and plasma cortisol levels during recovery from circumcision. *Child Development* 56: 824–834). The other stimuli are discussed in previous chapters.

13. Reviewed in Schwartz, G. E. 1982. Psychophysiological patterning and emotion revisited: A systems perspective. In *Measuring Emotions in Infants and Children*, ed. C. E. Izard, pp. 67–93. Cambridge: Cambridge University Press.

14. For a comprehensive introduction, see Lewis, M., Brooks, J., and Haviland, J. 1978. Hearts and faces: A study in the measurement of emotion. In *The Development of Affect*, ed. M. Lewis and L. A. Rosenblum, pp. 77–123. New York: Plenum; and Sroufe, L., and Waters, E. 1977. Heart rate as a convergent measure in clinical and developmental research. *Merrill-Palmer Quarterly* 23: 3–27.

15. These examples are based on laboratory experiments showing that when newborns are quiet and awake, their heart slows in a positive orienting reaction to the turning on of a simple tone or a homogeneous colored light (Adkinson, C. D., and Berg, W. K. 1976. Cardiac deceleration in newborns: Habituation, dishabituation, and offset responses. *Journal of Experimental Child Psychology* 21: 46–60; and Berg, W. K. 1986. Influence of transient and sustained aspects of auditory stimuli on neonate attention. Paper presented at the International Conference on Infant Studies, April, in Los Angeles), but accelerates when they are rocked or stroked (Pomerleau-Malcuit, A., and Clifton, R. K. 1973. Neonatal heart-rate response to tactile, auditory, and vestibular stimulation in different states. *Child Development* 44: 485–496). An excellent summary of this literature is Graham, F., Anthony, B., and Zeigler, B. 1983. The orienting response and developmental processes. In *Orienting and Habituation: Perspectives in Human Research*, ed. D. Siddle, pp. 371–430. Chichester, England: Wiley.

16. Reviewed in Graham, Anthony, and Zeigler (The orienting response and developmental processes [15]).

17. In addition to ibid., see Campos, J., Emde, R., Gaensbauer, T., and Henderson, C. 1975. Cardiac and behavioral interrelationships in the reactions of infants to strangers. *Developmental Psychology* 11: 589–601; Hruska, K., and Yonas, A. 1971. Developmental changes in cardiac responses to the optical stimulus of impending collision. Paper presented at the meeting of the Society for Psychophysiological Research, October, in St. Louis; and Schwartz, A., Campos, J., and Baisel, E. 1973. The visual cliff: Cardiac and behavioral correlates on the deep and shallow sides at five and nine months of age. *Journal of Experimental Child Psychology* 15: 85–99.

18. Although C. Goren, M. Sarty, and P. Wu (1975. Visual following and pattern discrimination of face-like stimuli by newborn infants. *Pediatrics* 56: 544–549) claim that newborns recognize a face, our subsequent work showed that the ability emerges at two months of age (reviewed in Maurer, D. 1985. Infants' perception of facedness. In *Social Perception in Infants*, ed. T. Field and N. Fox, pp. 73–100. Norwood, NJ: Ablex).

19. Described in Wolff (Observations on the early development of smiling [4]) and in Emde and Harmon (Endogenous and exogenous smiling systems[8]).

20. Extensive tests are described in Wolff (Observations on the early development of smiling [4]) and in Ahrens, R. 1954. Beitrag zur Entwicklung des Physiognomie- und Mimikerkennens. *Zeitschrift für experimentelle und angewandte Psychologie* 2: 599–633; and Spitz, R. A., and Wolf, K. M. 1946. The smiling response: A contribution to the ontogenesis of social relations. *Genetic Psychology Monographs* 34: 57–125.

21. Sroufe, L. A., and Wunsch, J. P. 1972. The development of laughter in the first year of life. *Child Development* 43: 1326–1344.

22. Campos, Emde, Gaensbauer, and Henderson (Cardiac and behavioral interrelationships [17]) and Schwartz, Campos, and Baisel (The visual cliff [17]) provide specific examples. Sroufe (Socioemotional development [11]) summarizes the evidence.

23. Emde, Gaensbauer, and Harmon (Emotional expression in infancy [4]) and Sroufe (Socioemotional development [11]) review the evidence on the development of fear.

24. Reviewed in Ekman, P., ed. 1973. *Darwin and Facial Expression*. New York: Academic Press, esp. chap. 4; and Lewis, M., and Rosenblum, L. A., eds. 1978. *The Development of Affect*. New York: Plenum, chaps. 4 and 16.

25. See chapter 10. For a comprehensive discussion of the relationship between these cognitive changes and changes in emotions, see Cicchetti and Hesse (Affect and intellect [11]), Sroufe (Socioemotional development [11]), or Lewis and Rosenblum (*The Development of Affect* [24], esp. chaps. 6 and 7).

26. See Sroufe and Wunsch (The development of laughter [21]), Emde, Gaensbauer, and Harmon (Emotional expression in infancy [4]), and S. Scarr and P. Salapatek (1970. Patterns of fear development during infancy. *Merrill-Palmer Quarterly of Behavior and Development* 16: 53–90).

27. Lester, B. M., and Boukydis, C. F. 1985. *Infant Crying: Theoretical and Research Perspectives*. New York: Plenum, esp. chaps. 4, 8, and 9; and Porter, F. L., Miller, R. H., and Marshall, R. E. 1986. Neonatal pain cries: Effect of circumcision on acoustic features and perceived urgency. *Child Development* 57: 790–802.

28. In addition to chap. 1 of Lester and Boukydis (*Infant Crying* [27]), see Wolff, P. 1969. The natural history of crying and other vocalizations in early infancy. In *Determinants of Infant Behavior*, vol. 4, ed. B. M. Foss, pp. 81–109. London: Methuen.

29. Reviewed in Campos et al. (Socioemotional development [11]) and Sroufe (Socioemotional development [11]).

30. Reviewed in Campos et al. (Socioemotional development [11]). See also Stenberg, C. R., Campos, J. J., and Emde, R. N. 1983. The facial expression of anger in seven-month-old infants. *Child Development* 54: 178–184.

31. Reviewed in Sroufe (Socioemotional development [11]).

32. Reviewed in ibid.

33. Clyman, R. B., Emde, R. N., Kempe, J. E., and Harmon, R. J. 1986. Social referencing and social looking among twelve-month-old infants. In *Affective Development in Infancy*, ed. T.

Brazelton and M. W. Yogman, pp. 75–94. Norwood, NJ: Ablex; and Klinnert, M. D., et al. 1983. Emotions as behavior regulators: Social referencing in infancy. In *Emotion: Theory, Research, and Experience,* vol. 2, *Emotions in Early Development,* ed. R. Plutchik and H. Kellerman, pp. 57–86. New York: Academic Press.

34. Reviewed in Sroufe (Socioemotional development [11]) and in Kagan, J. 1981. *The Second Year: The Emergence of Self-Awareness.* Cambridge, MA: Harvard University Press.

35. Reviewed in Radke-Yarrow, M. 1986. Affective development in young children. In *Affective Development in Infancy,* ed. Brazelton and Yogman [33], pp. 145–152.

36. Reviewed in Ainsworth, M. 1973. The development of infant-mother attachment. In *Review of Child Development Research,* vol. 3, ed. B. M. Caldwell and H. N. Ricciuti, pp. 1–94. Chicago: University of Chicago Press.

37. Good descriptions of this attunement are contained in Schaffer, H. R., ed. 1977. *Studies in Mother-Infant Interaction.* London: Academic Press, esp. chaps. 5, 6, 7, 8, and 17; and Stern, D. 1985. *The Interpersonal World of the Infant.* New York: Basic.

38. Parke, R. D. 1979. Perspectives on father-infant interaction. In *Handbook of Infant Development,* ed. Osofsky [11], pp. 549–590.

39. Jackson, E., Campos, J. J., and Fischer, K. W. 1978. The question of decalage between object permanence and person permanence. *Developmental Psychology* 14: 1–10; and Schaffer, H. R. 1971. Cognitive structure and early social behavior. In *The Origins of Human Social Relations,* ed. H. R. Schaffer, pp. 247–267. London: Academic Press.

40. Lester, B. M., et al. 1974. Separation protest in Guatemalan infants: Cross-cultural and cognitive findings. *Developmental Psychology* 10: 79–85.

41. In addition to Ainsworth (The development of infant-mother attachment [36]), see Bowlby, J. 1969. *Attachment and Loss,* vol. 1, *Attachment.* New York: Basic; and Sroufe, L. A., and Fleeson, J. 1986. Attachment and the construction of relationships. In *Relationships and Development,* ed. W. Hartup and Z. Rubin, pp. 51–71. Hillsdale, NJ: Lawrence Erlbaum.

42. Ainsworth, M.D.S., and Wittig, B. A. 1969. Attachment and the exploratory behavior of one-year-olds in a strange situation. In *Determinants of Infant Behavior,* vol. 4, ed. Foss [28], pp. 111–136; and Ainsworth, M.D.S., Blehar, M. C., Waters, E., and Wall, S. 1978. *Patterns of Attachment: A Psychological Study of the Strange Situation.* Hillsdale, NJ: Lawrence Erlbaum.

43. See, for example, Fox, N. 1977. Attachment of kibbutz infants to mother and metapelet. *Child Development* 48: 1228–1239; Rubenstein, J. L. 1985. The effects of maternal employment on young children. In *Applied Developmental Psychology,* vol. 2, ed. F. J. Morrison, C. Lord, and D. Keating, pp. 98–128. Orlando, FL: Academic Press; and Schaffer, H. R., and Emerson, P. E. 1964. The development of social attachments in infancy. *Monographs of the Society for Research in Child Development* 29 (3, serial no. 94): 5–77.

44. Ainsworth, Blehar, Waters, and Wall, *Patterns of Attachment* [42]; and Stayton, D. J., and Ainsworth, M. D. S. 1973. Individual differences in infant responses to brief, everyday separations as related to other infant and maternal behaviors. *Developmental Psychology* 9: 226–235.

45. In addition to Ainsworth, Blehar, Waters, and Wall (*Patterns of Attachment* [42]), see Donovan, W. L., and Leavitt, L. A. 1985. Cardiac responses of mothers and infants in Ainsworth's Strange Situation. In *The Psychobiology of Attachment and Separation,* ed. M. Reite and T. Field, pp. 369–387. Orlando, FL: Academic Press; Parkes, C. M., and Stevenson-Hinde, J., eds. 1982. *The Place of Attachment in Human Behavior.* London: Tavistock, chaps. 1 and 2; and Waters, E., and Deane, K. E. 1982. Infant-mother attachment: Theories, models, recent data, and some tasks for comparative developmental analysis. In *Parenting: Its Causes and Consequences,* ed. L. W. Hoffman and R. J. Gandelman, pp. 19–54. Hillsdale, NJ: Lawrence Erlbaum.

46. For examples, see the references in note 45 this chapter.

47. Reviewed in Gardner, W., Lamb, M., Thompson, R., and Sagi, A. 1986. On individual differences in strange situation behavior: Categorical and continuous measurement systems in a cross-cultural data set. *Infant Behavior and Development* 9: 355–375; and Grossmann, K. E., Grossmann, K., and Schwan, A. 1986. Capturing the wider view of attachment: A reanalysis of Ainsworth's Strange Situation. In *Measuring Emotions in Infants and Children,* vol. 2, ed. E. E. Izard and P. Read, pp. 124–171. Cambridge: Cambridge University Press.

48. See, for example, Kagan, J. 1982. *Psychological Research on the Human Infant: An Evaluative Summary.* New York: W. T. Grant Foundation; and Lewis, M. and Rosenblum, L. A., eds. *The Effect of the Infant on Its Caregiver.* New York: Wiley, esp. chaps. 1, 2, 3, 5, and 9.

49. Freedman, D. G. 1974. *Human Infancy: An Evolutionary Perspective.* Hillsdale, NJ: Lawrence Erlbaum. Quotation from p. 150.

50. Parmelee, A. 1985. Presidential address. Paper presented at the Society for Research in Child Development, April, in Toronto.

51. Korner, A. F., et al. 1985. The relation between neonatal and later activity and temperament. *Child Development* 56: 38–42. The initial differences among babies might have been caused by differences in exposure to obstetric medication, but their persistence suggests this is unlikely. Whatever the cause, parents were presented with different raw material. The differences at school age presumably reflect the combined effect of any original differences in temperament and the parents' reaction.

52. Bornstein, M., Gaughran, J., and Homel, P. 1986. Infant temperament: theory, tradition, critique, and new assessments. In *Measuring Emotions in Infants and Children,* vol. 2, ed. Izard and Read [47], pp. 172–199; and Thomas, A., and Chess, S. 1977. *Temperament and Development.* New York: Brunner/Mazel.

53. Egeland, B., and Farber, E. A. 1984. Infant-mother attachment: Factors related to its development and changes over time. *Child Development* 55: 753–771.

54. Belsky, J., Rovine, M., and Taylor, D. G. 1984. The Pennsylvania Infant and Family Development Project, III: The origins of individual differences in infant-mother attachment. *Child Development* 55: 718–728.

55. Lamb, M. E., Hwang, C-P., Frodi, A. M., and Frodi, M. 1982. Security of mother- and father-infant attachment and its relation to sociability with strangers in traditional and nontraditional Swedish families. *Infant Behavior and Development* 5: 355–367.

56. Schaffer and Emerson, The development of social attachments in infancy [43].

57. All studies agree that in every culture, securely attached babies have mothers who, earlier during the first year, responded consistently and quickly to the babies' distress and were sensitive to the level of stimulation the babies desired. Although the studies also agree that mothers of insecurely attached babies are less responsive and sensitive, they disagree on the characterization of mothers of unsocial and anxious babies. Mothers of unsocial babies may be unresponsive, rejecting, and/or overstimulating; mothers of anxious babies may be unresponsive, intrusive, and/or ignoring. In any case, their behavior is not tuned to the baby. In addition to Ainsworth, Blehar, Waters, and Wall (*Patterns of Attachment* [42]), Egeland and Farber (Infant-mother attachment [53]), and Belsky, Rovine, and Taylor (Pennsylvania Infant and Family Development Project [54]), see Crockenberg, S. 1981. Infant irritability, mother responsiveness, and social support influences on the security of infant-mother attachment. *Child Development* 52: 857–865; and Thompson, R. S., and Lamb, M. E. Individual differences in dimensions of socioemotional development in infancy. In *Emotion,* vol. 2, ed. Putchick and Kellerman [11], pp. 87–114.

58. All this varies with sex, the mother's style of interaction, and on the type of preschool the child enters. L. A. Sroufe (1983. Infant-caregiver attachment and patterns of adaptation in preschool: The roots of maladaptation and competence. In *Minnesota Symposia on Child Psychology,* vol. 16, ed. M. Perlmutter, pp. 41–83. Hillsdale, NJ: Lawrence Erlbaum) provides a good summary of the early research. See also Erickson, M. F., Sroufe, L. A., and Egeland, B. 1985. The relationship between quality of attachment and behavior problems in preschool in a high-risk sample. *Monographs of the Society for Research in Child Development* 50 (1–2, serial no. 209): 147–166; and Main, M., Kaplan, N., and Cassidy, J. 1985. Security in infancy, childhood, and adulthood: A move to the level of representation. *Monographs of the Society for Research in Child Development* 50 (1–2, serial no. 209): 66–106.

Chapter 12

1. Hayghe, H. 1986. Rise in Mothers' Labor Force Activity Includes Those with Infants. *Monthly Labor Review* 109: 43–45.

2. Note that because the evidence is so limited, the following reviewers reached contrary conclusions from the same data: Belsky, J. 1986. Infant day care: A cause for concern? *Zero*

to Three 6: 1–7; Gamble, T., and Zigler, E. 1986. Effects of infant day care: Another look at the evidence. *American Journal of Orthopsychiatry* 56: 26–42; and Rubenstein, J. L. 1985. The effects of maternal employment on young children. In *Applied Developmental Psychology*, vol. 2, ed. F. J. Morrison, C. Lord, and D. Keating, pp. 99–128. Orlando, FL: Academic Press.

3. For an introduction to the Hitler Youth, see Grunberger, R. 1971. *A Social History of the Third Reich.* Harmondsworth, Eng.: Penguin, esp. chap. 18 and pp. 525–527. Between 1950 and 1970—and mostly before 1960—the number of musicians in West Germany dropped approximately 40 percent while the opportunities for work remained constant (Fohrbeck, K., and Wiesand, A. J. 1974. Zum Berufsbild der Kulturberufe. Teilergebnisse der Künstler-Enquete. *Kölner Zeitschrift für Soziologie und Sozialpsychologie*, Sonderheft 17, *Künstler und Gesellschaft*: 309–325). As we write this in 1987, the *Hofer Symphoniker*, a provincial Bavarian orchestra, is advertising six positions for which the final auditions will be held in New York.

Appendix

1. The two best studies (from a scientific perspective) are Busacca, M., et al. 1982. Neonatal effects of the administration of meperidine and promethazine to the mother in labor. Double blind study. *Journal of Perinatal Medicine* 10: 48–53; and Kron, R., Stein, M., and Goddard, K. 1966. Newborn sucking behavior affected by obstetric sedation. *Pediatrics* 37: 1012–1016. Methodological problems common in other studies are reviewed in Kuhnert, B. R., Linn, P. L., and Kuhnert, P. M. 1985. Obstetric medication and neonatal behavior. Current controversies. *Clinics in Perinatology* 12: 423–440.

2. Although this editorial (March 28, 1966. *Journal of the American Medical Association* 195: 167; © 1966 American Medical Association) appeared more than 20 years ago, the situation has not improved. See, for example, Misser, F., and Andersen, B. 1986. Ordinal scale and statistics in medical research. *British Medical Journal* 292: 537–538; and Sheps, S. B., and Schecter, M. T. 1984. The assessment of diagnostic tests. A survey of current medical research. *Journal of the American Medical Association* 252: 2418–2422.

3. Reviewed in Kitzinger, S., and Davis, J. A., eds. 1978. *The Place of Birth.* Oxford: Oxford University Press.

4. See chapter 3, note 26.

Index